Understanding | Combining · Typefaces

PHILIPP STAMM

Understanding Typefaces
Combining Typefaces

TYPEFACE COMBINATION
AS TYPOGRAPHIC STIMULUS

Birkhäuser
Basel

Contents

Introduction 7

1
Historical considerations 11
Interplay 12

2
A typology of type 39
Writing 40
Writing system 40
Typeface category 41
Typeface genre 44
Type form 45
Typeface 45
Type family 47
Font style 48
Typeface series 49
Type appearance 49
Typeface character 53

3
Basic shapes | Measurements 55
Basic shapes 57
Em quad 65
Body width 66
Kerning 67
Tracking 68
Measurement systems 69
Point size 70
Font size 72
Type size 74
Design size 75
Opticals 78
Pixel 78
Type format 80

4
Typeface classification 83
Typeface classification systems 84
Pro typeface classification 93
Type form | Class 95
Attribute 95
Stroke contrast 96
Type style 96
Classification groups 97
I   Glyphic 98
II   Script 100
III Blackletter 102
IV   Antiqua 104
V   Egyptian 110
VI   Grotesque 112
VII Latin 114
Tables of the groups I–VII 116

5
Typeface concepts 131
Type family: dyad 132
Type family: triad 133
Extended type family 134
The designer effect 135
Superfamily 137
Multiple master 141
Variable fonts 145

6
Typeface combination | Criteria 149
Analogy 154
Contrast 155
Varieties of contrast *Table* 156
Design features *Tables* 160
1 Type form 166
2 Curve form – Letter O 167
3 Heights 167
4 Type style 172
4.1 Stress axis | Counter 173
4.2 Curve direction | Counter 174
4.3 Instroke | Outstroke 175
4.4 Rhythm | Proportions 176
4.5 Offset | Center position 177
5 Weight – Typographic color 178
5.1 Stroke weight 179
5.2 Stroke contrast 180
6 Width 182
7 Slant 184
8 Ductus 186
8.1 Connection 186
8.2 Movement 186
9 Shaping 187
9.1 Stroke and curve 187
9.2 Stroke and curve terminals 189
9.3 Bracket 191
9.4 Juncture 191
10 Letter design 192
11 Effect | Decoration 193
11.1 Fill 193
11.2 Outline 194
12 Setting length – Words | Texts 195
13 Type size 195
14 Color 196

7
Typeface combination | Instructions 199
Configuring a matrix 202
Using in the layout 206

8
Typeface combination | Examples 209

▼
Appendix 335
Notes 336
Index of names 343
Index of typefaces 345
Bibliography 348
Illustrations 354
Postscript 357
Author | Thanks 358

Introduction

Typeface combination as typographic stimulus, the subtitle of this specialist book, includes a term deliberately chosen for its ambiguity. On the one hand, stimulus suggests something appealing, alluring. On the other hand, we also sense the opposite in the term, the sting in contrast to the caress, the possibility of our eyes, or rather our point of view, being overtaxed. The combination of two or more different type designs stimulates – due to difference, to the unfamiliar or even the unorthodox.

During my research in the field of typeface combination, this ambivalence repeatedly asserted itself. In specialist articles in various Swiss and German magazines from the nineteenth and twentieth centuries and in diverse specialist books, this 'for and against' as well as 'yes, but' is constantly expressed. The different, often opposing views have endured over time, locked in a permanent to-and-fro. The question of typeface combination has divided the typographic community into supporters and opponents – a dispute that has quite often assumed an ideological character.

And inevitably, still another impression emerges: that the use of typeface combinations represents a peak discipline within typography. Either the practice is emphatically advised against (at least for beginners) or it is pointed out that it requires a good feeling for typefaces, that is, one developed over years. Although one repeatedly encounters passages on the topic prescribing shorter or longer sets of rules, the authors often find it difficult to make precise statements. Consulting several texts often reveals much that is contradictory when it comes to *what fits* and *what does not fit together*.

That combining typefaces presupposes a sophisticated level of knowledge and skill is possibly indicated by the fact that, as far as I know, there has hitherto been no comprehensive treatment of the topic. This does not mean that there have been no significant contributions to this field of inquiry. Indeed, there is already a somewhat longer, informative German-language contribution available, a five-page newspaper article furnished with several examples and written, not surprisingly, by JAN TSCHICHOLD. The text was published in 1935 under the title "Schriftmischungen" (Typeface combinations) in the Swiss typographic magazine *Typographische Monatsblätter*.[1] Unfortunately, this interesting and important article has been all but forgotten even though the text was printed in the first volume of the two-volume book *Jan Tschichold: Schriften* (Jan Tschichold: Writings), which appeared in 1991.[2]

The view that the development of a good feeling for typefaces is a necessary prerequisite for good typeface combination is one I support. In this context a profound knowledge of typeface classification (see chapter 4) is useful.* It is also my view that a good feeling for typefaces can be cultivated by detailed engagement, most effectively by practicing calligraphy and hand lettering and by creating many typeface combinations and observing and naming them in relation to one another. Step by step, the desired formal sensibility develops. The understanding of the typefaces and their forms is developing and their different qualities become apparent through the making.

It is not possible to forge complete agreement among specialists when it comes to combining typefaces. And this will undoubtedly be the case in relation to a number of examples presented in this book. That is as it should be. What is shown here can of course be challenged; it is not expected that everything will please everybody. Some of the examples feature typefaces that I myself would probably never use because, although they combine well with another type, they are unsatisfactory in both aesthetic and practical terms. Nevertheless, such typefaces can be suited to very particular uses, if only to support a visual statement in this book.

This publication combines an overview of typefaces, analysis and instruction with a collection of examples. It aims to promote an awareness of typefaces and critical engagement with them. It also aims to acknowledge the unbelievable wealth of good and/or interesting typefaces available. If the exploration of the theme presented here contributes to a sensitization and a more conscious approach to typefaces and typography, then it will already have achieved something. However, this book can possibly achieve more, because the possibilities and qualities of typeface combinations seem to me to be too little recognized or at least too little practiced. The combination of two (or more) typefaces has an enormous power and expressive quality. As JAN TSCHICHOLD writes soberly yet almost euphorically,[3] "A lively, yet carefully chosen contrast has a refreshing effect."[4]

But are we concerned here with homogeneity versus heterogeneity? Isn't it contrast *and* analogy that are interesting when it comes to the combination of typefaces? And if this is the case, how do two typefaces relate to one another in terms of the relationship between these two poles? These are the questions this book seeks to answer. And we anticipate that it will prove easier to pose these questions than to answer them.

---

* Compared to the German edition published six months ago, the text for this edition has been refined in a number of places and few typeface examples have been changed. The improvements concerned relate for the most part to the Pro typeface classification system, which is still being developed and extended.

At one of the two poles, the situation is simple. Analogy alone is not an option when combining two typefaces. If homogeneity is the goal, then it makes no sense to combine two typefaces. It suffices to work with one font style – very simple and by no means the worst possibility. The situation is much more difficult at the other pole. Although contrast alone can be an option, it is anything but simple to generate such typeface combinations that unite tension and harmony in equal measure – at least when two adjacent typefaces are supposed to be perceived as of equal size. A good typeface combination is based on mutual support between typefaces, or, better, mutual enhancement. If one type is so dominant that it suppresses the others, the typeface combination will be spoiled.

When combining typefaces, we usually operate within a field of tension between the two poles. Mixing typefaces requires engagement with contrast *and* analogy. In each case it is important to get a sense of how much heterogeneity and how much homogeneity will benefit the typeface combination, such that harmony and tension are able to unfold and radiate their power to its full extent. And for those who find this too overwrought – even though I maintain that this is all pertinent to the development of a *feeling* for typefaces – I particularly recommend the comprehensive analyses in chapter 6, *Typeface combination | Criteria*.

Chapter 8 contains many and diverse typeface combinations. These include examples that are suited to integrated emphasis in a body text; others are suited to active accentuations of titles and headlines; while still others offer possibilities for advertisement and the development of word marks, logotypes, brands, and visual identities.

A good typeface combination, and good typography in general, requires enjoyment of the métier and sensitivity, along with knowledge and a sufficient degree of engagement and endurance. Or, as the saying goes: with doing comes experience, and with experience comes ability. And all of a sudden this feeling for typefaces is manifested, if only for a moment. Yet the reward for intense engagement with typefaces is worth it: the experience of typography beginning to sing.

Historical considerations

Interplay

A look back into antiquity illustrates the long history of three basic approaches to type: singular, paucal, and plural, that is, the maintenance of unity, the combination of a few typefaces, and the decision for multiplicity. It also becomes clear that over certain periods of time there has been an interplay between supporters and opponents of the practice of combining different typefaces.

There is no question that typeface combination is seldom mandatory, because good typography can also function without it. As FRIEDRICH BAUER wrote in 1931, "When it comes to written communications presenting a longer chain of thought whose elements are equivalent or regarded as such, then it has always been the case and remains the norm to string together characters of the same size and design in each line and to distribute the lines in an equal flow over the surface. The need to set off certain parts of the normal content was only rarely felt in earlier times because only what seemed worth the effort was recorded in writing. One thing was as important as the other and superficial elements were abstained from. This original and natural conception of the symbolic value of lettering is expressed in memorial inscriptions just as generally as it is in handwriting and printed works, and it has not lost its significance in the present."[1]

The search for purity and simplicity, the concentration on and reduction to the essential, is a search for high quality – not only with regard to type and typography, but in this field in particular. Good typesetting requires a lot of careful preparation. This consists of the selection of appropriate – that is to say, reader-friendly and pleasing – typefaces, the definition of coherent technical parameters relating to point size, letterspacing (tracking), word spacing, and line spacing (leading), as well as a proportionate type area (grid) in keeping with the type, coordination of point size and line length (measure), suitable margins, and a harmonious format.

Limitation to one font style – in the extreme case even to a single size – allows for the generation of calm, static, as well as active, dynamic, and even playful, experimental typography. This is solely dependent on the approach to alignment – its emphasis or avoidance – and to white space – its uniformity or the deliberately chosen difference between distances and directions, for example horizontal, vertical, diagonal, ascending or descending.

There is not the space here for a comprehensive discussion of the possibilities of typographic design with *one* typeface. The focus of this book is above

Combination of three writing systems:
Rosetta Stone, Egypt,
196 BCE
01 ▶

all on the opposite. However, the aspect of homogeneity is indispensable for the historical positioning of typeface combination.

There are many reasons for combining typefaces: to place emphasis within a body text, to structure different contents, to create a textual hierarchy and highlight headings, to increase conciseness, to differentiate and individualize expression. Multilingual texts that include different writing systems can also make a combination of different typefaces necessary. Here, several examples are cited as representative of many others.

The *Rosetta Stone* |01| is regarded as one of the most important archaeological finds in the field of writing. Discovered in 1799 during Napoleon Bonaparte's Egyptian campaign near Alexandria,[2] the stone fell into the hands of the English following the French surrender and since 1802 has been on display in the British Museum in London. The inscription pays homage to the pharaoh Ptolemy V and dates back to 196 BCE. What makes the text on the stone so special is that it is carved in three languages. The uppermost text is carved in hieroglyphics, the middle version in Demotic, and the lower version in Ancient Greek. It is thanks to the Rosetta Stone (or a transcript of it) as well as other sources that Jean-François Champollion was able to decipher the Demotic text and decode the hieroglyphs in 1822.[3] The combination of almost identical texts in three writing systems, including Ancient Greek, was decisive for this achievement.

In the second example, the reason for the combination of letterings probably has to do with textual differentiation and the amount of information involved. While the stonemason chiseled the lines of a dedicatory inscription into the marble using *Capitalis quadrata,* he resorted to the narrower, more spatially economical *Capitalis rustica* in the five columns used to alphabetically list the names of the people concerned |02|.[4] The fact that in Roman inscriptions the spatial planning was not always precise is evident on the right edge of this tablet from the second century.

The next example is from the *Grandval Bible* |03|, a Carolingian illuminated manuscript produced at the monastery in Tours, France, around the year 840 as a codex, that is, a bound book.[5] According to Donald Jackson, the Carolingian age, which lasted from the eighth to the tenth century, and particularly the reign of Charlemagne (Charles the Great), saw a revival of antiquity. A renewed interest in ancient Roman inscriptions emerged,

Capitalis quadrata and Capitalis rustica: Latin dedicatory inscription, early 2nd century
02

and a hierarchical order of letterings developed (in part following their chronological development). According to Jackson, at the top of the hierarchy were the capital letters used in Roman inscriptions, which were based on the square and semi-square. These were followed by the rounded *Roman uncial* used for chapter headings. Lower down was *Capitalis rustica* and finally came *Carolingian minuscule*, which Jackson characterizes as bringing a degree of calm and spatiality to the text.[6] The oldest documented example of a *Carolingian minuscule*, also known as *Carolina*, originates from the scriptorium of Corbie and dates to around 765.[7]

The combination of *Capitalis quadrata*, *Uncial*, and *Carolingian minuscule* remained in use over several centuries, albeit not necessarily subject to the hierarchy outlined above, as witnessed by the book page showing the beginning of the Gospel of John from the twelfth century. Here it seems that a purely aesthetic approach was taken when writing the chapter headings and colored initial capitals. The scribe sometimes chooses the angular form of the *Capitalis quadrata* E and H, sometimes the rounded form of *Uncial* – and does so within the same line and when using the same words, such as ERAT and ET |04|.

Since JOHANNES GUTENBERG based his *Blackletter* typefaces on the handwritings of his time, it is hardly surprising that around 1450, when setting papal indulgences, he used a combination of typefaces, combining *Textura* for highlighting with *Bastarda* for the body text |05|. The *Textura* was the B42-Type, the typeface used for the body text of his 42-line Bible (→p. 62 |16|).[8] *Bastarda* is a Blackletter hybrid, best described as a combination of a carefully written book hand and a rapidly written cursive.[9]

Blackletter typefaces do not include any emphasis forms such as an italic cut. Where emphasis was required, the typesetter used either a larger point size of the same type or combined the more recent style of typeface with the older one. In German-language printing, for example, *Fraktur* as a text typeface was combined with *Schwabacher* as an emphasis typeface. It was the critique of this typeface combination by the German type founder JOHANN FRIEDRICH UNGER in 1793 that ultimately led to the widespread use of letterspacing to provide emphasis. However, increasing the space between letters did not produce better results.[10] On the contrary, it resulted in word spacing that was too large and this in turn led to gaps in the text block, the effect of which is still in part evident today.

The situation was different in the case of *Antiqua*, serif typefaces that were derived from *Gotico-Antiqua* in Italy in the second half of the fifteenth century. Soon after an upright roman cut was produced, an italic version was developed to provide an appropriately slanted version. Both types were used separately in proximity to one another as well as in different combinations with one another. In some cases the roman cut is the main typeface and the italic version the additional one |06|, in others – at least in parts of one book edition – vice versa |07|.

While in the Romance-language countries *Antiqua* very quickly became popular, north of the Alps different *Blackletter* typefaces persisted. As a result we repeatedly find combinations of the two types. Such a combination is illustrated by the example from England dating back to 1568. The main text, set in *Textura*, contains an ornamented and framed *Antiqua* versal (decorative initial block). At the beginning and end of the broadside proclamation there are also lines in a roman and an italic cut |08|.

INCIPIT LIBER EXODVS

HAEC SVNT Cap. I.
NOMINA
FILIORV̄
ISRAHEL
QVI INGRES
SI SVNT IN
AEGYPTV̄
CVM IACOB
SINGVLI
CVM DOMI
BVS SVIS
INTROIE
RVNT

Ruben. symeon. leui. Iuda. issachar. zabulon et beniamin. dan et nepthalim. gad et aser. Erant igitur omnes animae eorum quae egressae sunt de femore iacob. septuaginta quinque. Ioseph autem. in aegypto erat. Quo mortuo et uniuersis fratrib; eius omniq; cognatione sua. filii isr't creuerunt. et quasi germinantes multiplicati sunt. ac robore nimis impleuer̄ terrā. Surrexit interea rex nouus super aegyptum qui ignorabat ioseph. et ait ad populum suum. Ecce populus filiorum isr't multus et fortior nobis ē. uenite sapienter opprimamus eum. ne forte multiplicetur. Et si ingruerit contra nos bellum. addatur inimicis nr̄is. Expugnauitq; nobis. egrediatur e terra. Praeposuit itaq; eis magistros operum. ut affligerent eos oneribus. Aedificaueruntq; urbes tabernaculorum pharaoni. phiton et ramesses. Quantoq; opprime bantur. tanto magis multiplicabantur et crescebant. Oderantq; filios isr't aegyptii et affligebant illudentes eis. atq; ad amaritudinem perducebant uitam eorum operib; duris luti et

pueros seruaretis. Quae responderunt non sunt hebraeae sicut aegyptiae mulieres. Ipse enim obstetricandi habent scientiam. Priusquam ueniamus ad eas. pariunt. Bene ergo fecit d̄s obstetricib; et creuit populus Confortatusq; ē nimis. Et quia timuerant obstetrices d̄m. aedificauit illis domos. Praecepit ergo pharao. omni populo suo dicens. Quicquid masculini sexus natum fuerit. in flumine proicite. Quicquid feminei. reseruate.

Egressus ē post haec uir de domo leui. accepta uxore stirpis suae. quae concepit et peperit filium. Et uidens eum elegantem. abscondit trib; mensib; Cumq; iam celare non posset. sumpsit fiscellam scirpeam. et liniuit eam bitumine ac pice. posuitq; intus infantulum et exposuit eum in carecto ripae fluminis stante procul sorore eius. et considerante euentum rei. Ecce autem descendebat filia pharaonis. ut lauaretur in flumine. et puellae eius gradiebantur per crepidinem aluei. Quae cum uidisset fiscellam in papyrione. misit unam e famulis suis. Et allatam aperiens. cernensq; in ea paruulum uagientem. miserta eius. ait. De infantab; hebraeorum. ē hic. Cui soror pueri. Vis in quit ut uadam et uocem tibi hebraeam mulierem quae nutrire possit infantulum? Respondit Vade. Perrexit puella. et uocauit matrem eius. Ad quam locuta filia pharaonis. Accipe ait puerum istum et nutri michi. ego tibi dabo mercedem tuam. Suscepit mulier. et nutriuit puerum Adultumq; tradidit filiae pharaonis. Quem illa adoptauit in locum filii. Vocauitq; nomen eius moysi. dicens. quia de aqua tuli eum.

In diebus illis postquam creuerat moyses. egressus ad fratres suos. uidit afflictionem eorum. et uirum aegyptum percutientem quendam de hebraeis fratrib; suis. Cumq; circumspexisset huc atq; illuc. et nullum adesse uidisset. percussum aegyptum abscondit sabulo. Et egressus die altero. conspexit duos hebraeos rixantes. Dixitq; ei qui

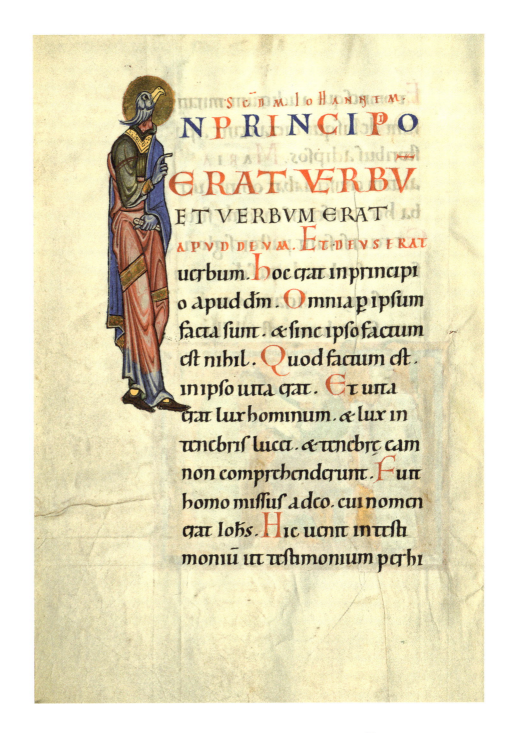

03 Capitalis quadrata, Uncial, Carolina: handwritten codex, Tours, 9th century

04 Letters E/H: Capitalis (angular), Uncial (round); text in a late form of Carolina, 12th century

Vniuersis Cristifidelibus prntes lras inspecturis Paulinus Chappe Cōsiliarius Ambasiator & pcurator generalis Serenissimi Regis Cypri in hac parte Salm in dno Cu Sactissimo i xpo pr & dns nr dns Nicolaus diuia prudetia pp quitus Afflicti Regni Cypri misericorditer cōpaties cōtra pfidissios crucis xpi hostes Theucros & Saracenos gratis cōcessit omib; xpifidelibz vbilibet cōstitutis ipos p aspsione sanguis dni nri ihu xpi pie exhortādo qui infra triennu a prima die May Anni dni Mccccli incipiendu p defesione catholice fidei & regni pdicti de facultatibz suis magis uel minus put ipor videbitur conscientijs pcutoribus uel nūcijs substitutis pie eroguauerint ut confessores ydonei seculares uel regulares p ipos eligēdi confessionibus eor auditis p cōmissis etiā sedi aplice reseruatis excessibus criminibz atqz delictis quātūcūqz grauibus p vna vice tātu debita absolutione impedere & penitētia salutarem iniungere Recno si d humiliter petierit ipos a quibuscūqz excōicationum suspensionu & interdicti alijsqz sentencijs cesuris & penis ecclesiasticis a iure uel ab hōie promulgatis quibz forsan innodati existunt absoluere. Iniucta p modo culpe penitētia salutari uel alijs q de iure fuerit iniungēdo ac eis vere penitētibz & confessis uel si forsan propter amissionem loqle cōfiteri nō poterit signa contricōnis ostēdēdo plenissimā oīm pctor suor de quibz ore confessi & corde contriti fuerint Indulgentia ac plenaria remissionē semel in vita & semel in mortis articulo ipius auctate aplica cōcedere valeāt. Satisfactione p eos facta si supuixerint aut p eor heredes si tūc transierit Sic tamē qp post indultu cōcessum p vnū annū singulis sextis ferijs uel quada alia die ieiunet. legittimo impedimēto ecclesie precepto regulari obseruatia pnīa iniucta voto uel alias nō obstan. Et ipis impeditis in dicto āno uel eius parte anno sequēti uel alias quam primū poterint ieiunabūt Et si in aliquo annor uel eor parte dictū ieiuniū cōmode adimplere nequiuerit Confessor ad id electus in alia comutare poterit caritatis opa q ipi facere etiā teneātur Dūmodo tn ex cōfidentia remissionis huōi quod absit pctare nō prsumāt Alioqui dicta cōcessio quo ad plenaria remissionē in mortis articulo et remissio quo ad pcta ex cōfidentia ut prmittitur cōmissa nullius sint roboris uel momenti Et quia deuoti _in cristo dord quanter Et thompe vxor eius su catholicalis legitim et Tileke monder_ iuxta dictum indultu de facultatibus suis pie erogaurint merito huiusmodi indulgentijs gaudere debet. In veritatis testimoniū sigillū ad hoc ordinatū prntibz lris testimonialibz est appensum Datū _in Criminsinck_ Anno dni Mccccelquito die vero _vicesim quita_ mensis _Aprilis_

Forma plenissime absolutionis et remissionis in vita

Misereatur tui zc Dns noster ihesus xps p suā sanctissimā et pijssimā miam te absoluat Et aucte ipius beatorūqz petri & pauli aplor eius ac aucte aplica michi cōmissa & tibi cōcessa Ego te absoluo ab omibz pctis tuis contritis confessis & oblitis Etiā ab omibz casibz excessibus criminibus atqz delictis quātūcūqz grauibz sedi aplice reseruatis Recno a quibuscūqz excōicationum suspensionū & interdicti alijsqz sentencijs censuris & penis ecclesiasticis a iure uel ab hōie promulgatis si quas incurristi dando tibi plenissima oīm pctor tuor indulgentia & remissionē Inquātū claues sancte matris ecclie in hac parte se extendūt. In noie patris & filij & spiritus sancti Amen.

Forma plenarie remissionis in mortis articulo

Misereatur tui zc Dns noster ut supra Ego te absoluo ab omibus pctis tuis cōtritis cōfessis et oblitis restituendo te vnitati fidelium & sacramentis ecclesie Remittendo tibi penas purgatorij quas propter culpas & offensas incurristi dando tibi plenaria oīm pctor tuor remissionē. Inquantū claues sancte matris ecclie in hac parte se extendūt. In noie patris & filij & spiritus sancti Amen.

From today's perspective the combination of *Blackletter* and *Antiqua* in scholarly German-language publications from the sixteenth to the eighteenth century seems somewhat curious. As Friedrich Bauer writes, "It is odd that for almost three centuries German letterpress printers regarded Antiqua roman together with italic as appropriate for typesetting in Latin. Textura, Rotunda and Schwabacher were unhesitatingly used for typesetting in German and Latin. However, with a few exceptions in the initial period, Fraktur was the typeface used for the German language. Even in this case, printers could not decide to set Latin words and sentences within German wordings completely in Fraktur. This went so far that words with a Latin primary form and a German ending were set partly in Antiqua and partly in Fraktur. Since these two fundamentally different typefaces seldom fitted together in terms of size and baseline […] the result was a confused text appearance […]."[11] | 09 |

A new era of typeface combination began around the middle of the eighteenth century. Here, copperplate engraving – and subsequently lithography – played a fundamental role. Until then it had been common practice to combine two or three – in exceptional cases four – typefaces, insofar as they were combined at all; now a whole range of typefaces were employed. As we shall see, this was later to trigger a fierce debate.

After the emphasis on the vertical in the Gothic period – seen both in architecture and in book typography, with its use of a two-column grid and *Textura* type – Renaissance typographers showed a preference for longer horizontal lines and a sense of calm in the text block. Baroque did not change anything fundamental in this respect. However, from 1710 onwards, under the influence of the late Baroque and Rococo styles featuring ornaments, opulence, and playfulness, an obvious change is evident. In writing and typography, ornamentation was no longer limited to versals and the borders of books. Typefaces were themselves decorated, so that title lines were now furnished with ornamentation. Many decorated typefaces were produced in the foundries, and these were prominently presented. In the second half of the eighteenth century at the latest, we find in the work of Pierre-Simon Fournier in France | 10 | and in the Netherlands | 11 | printing featuring a different typeface in practically every line of titling.[12] At this time, stylistic innovations in type design came for the most part from these two countries.

Text in Bastarda, emphases in Textura: papal indulgence, Mainz, 1454

De dissectione partium corporis humani, Liber secundus.

Proœmium.

Væ partes in humano corpore solidiores & exteriores erant,quæ'q; ipſam machinam potiſſimum conſtituebant,ſatis iam explicatæ nobis videntur libro ſuperiore. Sequitur, vt internas percurramus quæ maximè pertinent ad vitam, & ad earum facultatum quibus incolumes viuimus conſeruationem. In quo (quemadmodū inſtituimus) ſubſtantia, ſitus, forma, numerus, cōnexio, earum partium de quibus ſermo futurus eſt, breuiter exponenda. Ad quod munus ſtatim aggrediemur, ſi pauca prius de inſtituto ac de iudicio noſtro ſubiunxerimus. Quanq̃ enim hic noſter in ſcribendo ac diſſecando labor, complures non modo in anatomes cognitione, ſed etiam in Galeni ſententiæ interpretatione iuuare poterit: tamen interdū veremur, ne quibuſdam nomen hoc anatomicum ſit inuiſum : mirentúrq; in ea diſſectione tantum nos operæ & temporis ponere: cum alioqui ab ijs qui nummorum potius quàm artis aucupio dant operam facile negligatur. Atq; ita nobis occurritur, dum quærunt: ſatiſne conſtanter facere videamur, qui cum corporis humani partiū longiori indagationi ſtudemus , quæ magis ſunt vtilia, imprimiſq; neceſſaria prætermittimus: ſatius eſſe affirmantes, eius rei cognitionem ſicco (vt aiūt) pede percurrere, in qua alia certa, alia incerta eſſe dicunt: alia probabilia, alia minus probabilia inueniri. Quod certe dictum (ſi qui tamen inueniantur qui hoc dicant) hominum mihi videtur parū conſyderate loquentium: atq; in maximis rebus errantium. Quibus vellem ſatis cognita eſſet noſtra ſententia. Non enim (vt inquit quidā) ſumus ij quorum vagetur animus errore : & incertis rebus demus operam, neque habeamus vnq̃ quod ſequamur . Quid enim eſt, per deos, abſoluta anatomes cognitione optabilius? quid præſtantius? quid Medico vtilius? quid Chirurgo dignius? quā qui expetunt & adſequuntur, tundemū Medici ac Chirurgi dicendi ſunt: nec quicq̃ eſt aliud, quod Medicum aut Chirurgum magis commendet, quàm ipſa anatome. Cuius ſtudium qui vituperat, haud ſanè intelligo quidnam ſit quod laudādum in huiuſmodi viris aut artibus putet. Nam ſiue oblectatio quæritur animi: quid æquè delectat, aut ingenuos animos afficit, atq; conditoris noſtri, in hoc microcoſmo procreando, diligenter perſcrutatum artificium? ſiue perfectio, & abſoluta quædam ars petitur : certe abſq; anatome, Medicina aut ars nō erit, aut nulla omnino. Itaque neceſſe eſt, qui hæc omnia in quibus tantopere inſudamus, neglexerit: artem quoq; ipſam, cuius humani corporis anatome ſine controuerſia fundamentum eſt

Quid dictum libro ſuperiore.

Quid ſecundo libro dicetur.

Purgatio aduerſus eos, qui longiorem anatomes indagationem minus probāt

Anatomes cognitionis vtilitas & dignitas.

L.ij.

Liber XIII. Caput LXIIII.

syluestriū. Eliguntur rotundæ, tenues, duræ, perspicuæ, mediocris ambitus, lōgæ, et ex ala dextra. Ex ala dextra, ut exterius incuruentur: rotundæ melius seruāt duritiē, quoniam partes magis inuicem distant. Perspicuæ plerunque pinguedine carent: & ob id non respuunt atramentum: longæ diutius satisfaciunt, ut tenues melius: nam literarum etiam tenuiores uirgulas perficere & delineare possunt: ambitus mediocris efficit, ut commodius apprehendatur, quoniam non excedit magnitudine, & ut facilius deducatur. Atq; hæc omnia pennis generaliter conueniunt. Verùm quod superest, est ut doceamus: si quid desit, quomodo instaurandæ sint. Igitur si sub cinere calido absque igne semel aut bis deducatur, multis una succurritur incommodis: nam statim fricata exuit pinguedinem, & flexa incuruatur in quam partem uolueris (fit enim mollior) incuruatur autem in dextram (ut dixi) atque formatur in rotundum: inde refrigerata atque humido aqueo consumpto, siccatur, atque durescit. Præstantiores autem sunt quæ ex animali iam senescente habentur, atq; sponte deciderunt sub ueris initio: nam sic manēt, & densiores substantia sunt, nec friantur. Aptari consueuerunt in hanc formam, ut primùm pars quædam sensim detracta relinquat spatiū dehiscens hiásq;, pòst in cuspidem præceps deriuetur, sensímq; rursus terminetur. Tota uerò cauitas ambitum pennæ compleat. Sic ut longitudo circuitui, alius æquetur. Fiunt & ex argento æréq; pennæ eiusmodi, sed chartam rodere solent. Et ubi acies non respondeat, difficillimè restituuntur. Debent autem scindi per longum omnes, nec multum, tenuißimáq; scissura,

Pennarum qualitates.

Pennæ quomodo corrigantur.

Pennæ quomodo aptentur.

Vice versa: Antiqua italic with roman for the marginalia, Basel, 1557

07 ▶

By the Queene.

A Proclamation for bringing into the Realme of vnlawfull and seditious bookes.

Heras diuers bookes made or translated by certayne the Queenes Maiesties subiectes, for the more part remayning on the other syde of the sea, without lawfull licence, contayning sundry matters repugnaunt to trueth, derogatorie to the soueraigne estate of her Maiestie, and stirring and nourishing sedition in this Realme, are commonly in secrete sort here dispearsed by malicious persons among sundry her Maiesties subiectes, to thintent to drawe them to errour, and withdrawe them sediciously from their dueties and allegiance due to her Maiestie, as their onlye soueraigne. For redresse hereof, lyke as of late tyme some mylde example hath ben made in the starre chaumber at Westminster, in correction of certayne persons founde faultie in the secrete dispearsing, buying, and allowing of sundry of the sayde seditious bookes: So her Maiestie meaning of her clemencie neither to haue any aduauntage taken for thinges herein alredy past, nor any her honest and quiet subiectes to be entangled with the lyke hereafter for lacke of admonition in due tyme: wylleth and earnestlye chargeth all maner of persons, to forbeare vtterly from the vse or dealing with any such seditious bookes, made or translated by any person, contayning matter derogatorie to the soueraigne estate of her Maiestie, or impugning the orders and rites established by lawe for Christian religion and deuine seruice within this Realme, or otherwyse styrring and nourishing matter tending to sedition: and that such as alredy haue any of the sayde bookes, shall present, or cause to be presented the sayde bookes, within twentie and eyght dayes after the publishing of this proclamation, to the byshop of the diocesse, or ordinarie of the place, and to receaue of hym a testimoniall of the tyme of the deliuerie thereof: and without expresse licence in wryting of the sayde byshop or ordinarie, or some archbyshop, or other byshop of the Realme, not to kepe or reade any seditious bookes, vpon payne of her Maiesties greeuous indignation, and to be punished seuerely, as the qualitie and circumstaunces of the offence shall require and deserue.

Gyuen at her Maiesties pallaice of Westminster, the first day of March, 1568, the eleuenth yere of her Maiesties raigne.

God saue the Queene.

Imprinted at London in Powles

Churcheyarde by Richarde Jugge and John Cawood, Printers to the Queenes Maiestie.

Cum priuilegio Regiæ Maiestatis.

Fraktur combined with Antiqua for Latin terms, Helmstedt, 1697
09

English type foundries adopted these innovations and further added to their diversity |12|.

But a countercurrent was already becoming evident. With the emergence of Neoclassicism around 1700 and the typefaces designed by GIAMBATTISTA BODONI in Italy, the work of the typographic dynasty of DIDOT in France, which included FIRMIN DIDOT, the work of JUSTUS ERICH WALBAUM in Germany, and RICHARD AUSTIN in Great Britain, a new simplicity and rigor developed, at least in book typography.

Parallel to this development, the rich diversity of type design and typography continued – particularly in Great Britain under the influence of industrialization and the associated demand for striking designs. There seemed to be no more limitations in the nineteenth century. The example of a jobbing print from England with the new type forms *Egyptian* (slab serif) and *Grotesque* (sans serif) |13|, a book title design from Spain |14|, and a typographics textbook from Austria with a rounded arrangement in a contoured Grotesque confirm this |15|. Historicism and free typographical arranging approaches subsequently brought the excessive combination of typefaces to a preliminary final peak.[13]

The next countercurrent emerged in the period after 1870 – again starting in England – with the aim of drawing on arts and craft traditions and their qualities. One expression of this was the founding of the *Arts and Crafts Exhibition Society* in 1887 by its first and second presidents, WALTER CRANE and WILLIAM MORRIS. In the field of book art this reclaiming of tradition was illustrated by typography's embrace of the late Middle Ages and the early Renaissance. One of the examples drawn on was the incunables printed by NICOLAS JENSON in Venice, including his reprint of the *Pliny* edition of 1476. In his 1893 lecture *The Ideal Book,* WILLIAM MORRIS pointed out that even an unadorned book could be beautiful if it was, as it were, architectural.[14] Around the turn of the century EMERY WALKER and THOMAS JAMES COBDEN-SANDERSON of *Doves Press* took MORRIS at his word. Manual letterpress printing in Germany and the USA also adopted the limitation to one typeface. "The movement against typeface combination was significantly promoted [in Germany] by the title rules published in 1881 by the Leipzig Typographic Society, which stated that the key requirement for a good titling was the use of *one* typeface."[15]

Antiqua roman, italic, and decorated variants, Pierre-Simon Fournier, Paris, 1764

10 ▼

Towards the end of the nineteenth century, the combination of typefaces was generally frowned upon. In 1898, for instance, the Swiss journal *Schweizer Graphische Mitteilungen* published an article titled "Uniform Type Selection: A Contribution to the Simplification of Jobbing Setting", which included the following: "[…] But it is not only from the standpoint of stylish and tasteful configuration that a uniform typeface is advisable; it also makes sense for practical reasons. How many typesetters have not found the choice of typefaces for hitherto 'combined' uses a particular torture, one that demands a great deal of time, many corrections, and a large selection of titling and decorated typefaces. Multiple series, of which only a few sizes are usually available in letterpress printing – among which the ones one needs most of all are usually lacking – must be replaced by a few but complete series."[16] The last sentence implies one of the reasons – apart from aesthetic ones – for the variety in the use of typefaces in the nineteenth century.

In 1904, that is, six years later, a contributor to the same journal posed the question: "Given the current, almost universally cultivated uniformity in the selection of typefaces, is the use of *decorated type* permitted?"[17] According to the author this question was causing controversy in typesetting and book printing circles. A few lines later in the text he endorses those typesetters supporting the combination of decorated type with other typefaces, adding the rhetorical question, "And why shouldn't this be allowed? In my view there is no reason why it should not, especially if the decorated typefaces used in such combinations exhibit the same or a similar character as the other typefaces."[18]

In the 1910s the combination of typefaces was once again seen as in keeping with the times: "Our current, nervously hastening age demands more than ever a certain level of variety, including when it comes to printed matter. […] While there was hitherto an aspiration to realize the possibility of setting printed material not only in uniform characters but also in only one typeface series, the latest approach takes different directions. *Contrasts in the text appearance* – that is the motto of the day. […] The works of illustrators, painters, and hand lettering artists have left us printers far behind. Measuring ourselves against them in the field of drawn or written works would in general be a questionable undertaking from the outset, because these graphic designers have such an advantage due to their academic or applied arts training that we could never come up to their level. We must therefore

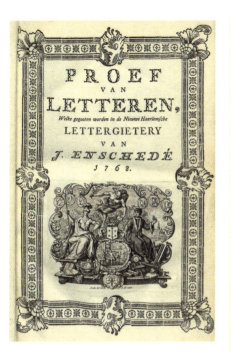

Antiqua roman, italic, and decorated variants: type specimen, Haarlem, 1768
11 ▲

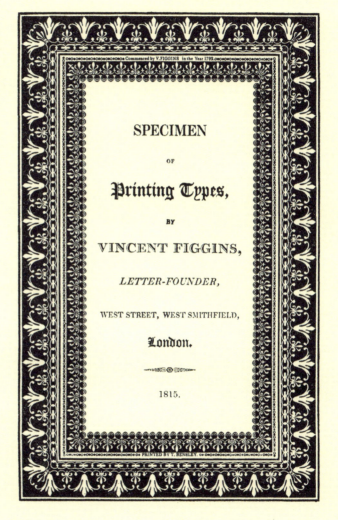

Combination of Antiqua with decorated variants and Textura: type specimen, London, 1815
12 ▶

13 Various typefaces including Egyptian and Grotesque: event information, Brighton, 19th century

14 Various typefaces with decorated typefaces and Script: book title, Valencia, 1836

Various typefaces including decorated Grotesque and Latin: textbook title page, Vienna, 1882

Futurist typographic onomatopoeia by F. T. Marinetti: book cover, Milan, 1914
16 ◀

Dadaism and multiple typefaces: sound poem by Hugo Ball, Berlin, 1920
17 ▶

Dada journal, cover no. 1, Tristan Tzara / Ilja Zdanévitch (?), Paris, 1922
18 ▶

Surrealist photo-text collage by Georges Hugnet: book page, Paris, 1936
19

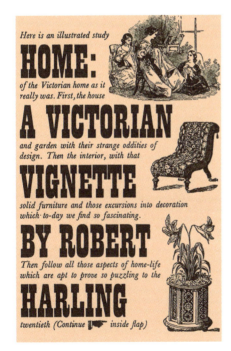

Antiqua italic and Italienne *Playbill* – Robert Harling: book jacket, London, 1938
20

Jan Tschichold:

Typographische Gestaltung

Benno Schwabe & Co . Basel 1935

Script, Egyptian, and Antiqua: title page by Jan Tschichold, Basel, 1935

Blackletter and Grotesque: advertisement for a German type foundry, 1934
22 ▼

Script and Egyptian: another strongly contrasting advertisement for the foundry, 1936
23 ▼▼

Groups of possible typeface combinations: page from a textbook by Paul Renner, Berlin, 1948
24 ▲

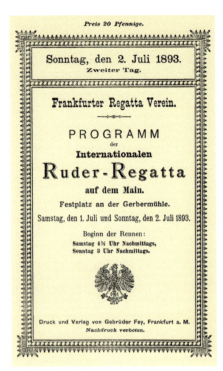

Comparison of multiplicity and uniformity by Karl Klingspor, Frankfurt a. M., 1949

25

make every effort to elevate the standing of typesetting, to awaken the interest of all participating parties by means of design that is as varied as possible, and thereby to regain ground we have lost to illustrators and hand lettering artists."[19]

In the meantime, typesetters and letterpress printers were facing new competition. The emergence of the consumer goods industry towards the end of the nineteenth century generated new professions such as poster artist, lithographer, graphic artist, etc. In addition, numerous applied arts schools were established. And with the advent of Art Nouveau, which aimed to unify all design fields, painters, architects, writers, and so on discovered the field of type and book design for themselves. It was writers such as Filippo Tommaso Marinetti who spoke out in favor of a diversity of typefaces. In 1913, in one of his Futurist manifestos under the heading 'Typographic Revolution', he wrote, "I have initiated a typographical revolution directed against the bestial, nauseating sort of book that contains passéist poetry and verse à la D'Annunzio – handmade paper that imitates models of the seventeenth century, festooned with helmets, Minervas, Apollos, decorative capitals in red ink with loops and squiggles, vegetables, mythological ribbons from missals, epigraphs, and Roman numerals. The book must be the Futurist expression of Futurist thought. Not only that. My revolution is directed against the so-called typographical harmony of the page, which is contrary to the flux and reflux, the leaps and bursts of style that run through the page itself. For that reason we will use, in the very same page, *three or four different colors of ink,* and as many as twenty different typographic fonts if necessary. For examples: *italic* for a series of swift or similar sensations, *boldface* for violent onomatopoeias, etc. The typographical revolution and the multicolored variety in the letters will mean that I can double the expressive force of words."[20]

The motivations for the combination of typefaces were thus now different. Through their differences, typefaces should visualize different forms of expression. Changes in typefaces thus accorded with a divergence of meaning or a different tone, as shown by Marinetti's war-glorifying, onomatopoeic book cover of 1914 |16|. At the other end of the political spectrum, Dadaists such as Richard Huelsenbeck and Hugo Ball used typeface diversity with the positive intention of "bringing the war to an end with nothing." The onomatopoeic poem *Karawane,* which was performed at the Cabaret

Voltaire in Zurich in 1916, appeared in printed form in 1920 | **17** |.²¹ In 1936, the surrealist GEORGES HUGNET achieved a congruence between pictorial and type diversity with his photo-text collages | **19** |.²²

Alongside those artistic approaches to typefaces that aimed for exclusivity, the typesetting trade sought a viable method for handling everyday work in book typography, jobbing setting, and commercial graphics. There was a corresponding aspiration among professionals to see guidelines formulated for the use of typefaces. In 1927, JUSTINIAN FRISCH wrote in his publication *Geist und Zweck der Schrift – Ihre Aufgaben in der Werbekunst* (Spirit and purpose of type: its role in commercial art), "Not so long ago, professionals regarded it as impermissible to use several styles in a setting pattern. Uniformity of type was a law that could be seen as an excessive reaction to the anarchic period (circa 1870 to 1900) in which typefaces were mixed together at will. Today things are different. Neither random combination nor strict uniformity is the rule. Rather, certain norms of taste have developed, among which the most important are: 1. Typefaces of a similar character should not be used with one another […] 2. Typefaces with entirely different characters can and should be used with one another, but it should be ensured that they contrast as strongly as possible in terms of typographic color and size. […] One must ensure that the heavier, more complicated, more open typeface is prominent, while the simpler, stricter, sleeker typeface plays a lesser role. […] 3. With every serif type one can readily use the associated italic form. One must merely avoid clusters and preferably use the two forms alternately. 4. Typefaces that by nature require different techniques should not be combined. […]"²³

In JAN TSCHICHOLD's 1928 book *Die Neue Typographie* (*The New Typography*, 1995), typeface combination was not treated as an independent topic.²⁴ The book was shaped by his goal of propagating sans serif as the sole *typeface of the time*. The situation was different in his book *Typographische Gestaltung*, published in 1935 (*Asymmetric Typography*, 1967).²⁵ The title page alone, with its type triad in three finely graded typographic colors, can be understood as a clear statement | **21** |. In the same year, he published an article on the topic in the Swiss typographic magazine *Typographische Monatsblätter*. In the essay, he wrote, with reference to the typographic change in the period around 1900, "The slogan 'unity of type' was the healthy countermovement

Multiplicity of typefaces: advertising poster by Alexander Girard, New York, 1961
26 ▼

Grotesque and Antiqua: *twen* magazine by Willy Fleckhaus, Munich, 1962
27 ▶

Sex Pistols album cover (front and back) by Jamie Reid, London, 1977

28

Antiqua italic and
Grotesque: newspaper
head redesign
by David Hillman,
England, 1988
29

Grotesque and
Antiqua: specialist
book by Jost Hochuli,
St. Gallen, 1996
30

that led to the improvement of jobbing prints and books. An article should be set using only *one* typeface: for running text, headings, and the title in the case of books, and likewise for everything in the case of jobbing prints. [...] This method has the advantage of almost automatically producing uniformity, but the disadvantage that it cannot cater to all demands for differentiation of the typographic appearance. We can adopt the good aspects of this approach: using only one typeface in different sizes; at the same time we should not hesitate to use the italic, semibold, and bold versions of the type. Accordingly, *today* 'unity of type' means setting work using only one particular set of typeface series. However, narrow and wide cuts are categorized as different typeface versions. For me, this form of typesetting gives me great confidence in printed matter that is uniform within itself. Nevertheless, works typeset in this way are not necessarily good, since the selection of typefaces is only a part of the problem facing typography. [...] Undoubtedly, the method of 'unity of type' leads to a certain monotony, which contradicts the aim of many printed works. The demands for rapid comprehension and characterization that are placed on printed matter today in turn demand lively contrasts that can be generated not only by size and brightness differences (for example, regular versus bold or black) but also by lively formal opposites (for example, heavy Antiqua versus Script). However, there are lovely and unlovely, delicate and rough contrasts, and it therefore cannot be a matter of indifference to us what contrast we employ. The feeling for this must be acquired through cumulative practice."[26]

In his 1948 textbook *Die Kunst der Typographie* (*The Art of Typography*, 1998) PAUL RENNER presented another robust guide to typeface combination (the table |24| was not included in the first edition published in 1939).[27] This provoked a response from KARL KLINGSPOR, one of the two owners of the Klingspor type foundry, who, in his specialist book *Über Schönheit von Schrift und Druck* (On the beauty of type and printing), made an unambiguous plea for uniformity |25|.[28] Modern applications of this idea of reduced typeface use are found in Swiss typography (International Style) around the middle of the twentieth century. One notable example is the excellent trilingual specialist book *Typographie* by EMIL RUDER, published in 1967.[29] Nevertheless, various works from the 1930s promoted a diverse approach |20|22|23| – which influenced WILLY FLECKHAUS in his design concept of the magazine *twen* from 1950 onwards |27| and DAVID HILLMAN in his 1988 redesign of *The Guardian* newspaper |29|. Book designer JOST HOCHULI occasionally also used such a typeface combination |30|.[30] Multiplicity, that is, plural typeface use, has since then repeatedly exerted an influence, for example on work by ALEXANDER GIRARD in 1961 |26|, the punk typography of JAMIE REID in 1977 |28|, and finally the retro book jacket designed by PETER MENDELSUND in 2004 |31|.

Singular, paucal, and plural typeface usage usually follow one another in waves and without doubt within an interplay between craft and art. It is above all multiplicity, that is, plural combination, that is frowned upon by opponents of typeface combination and a subject of controversy among its proponents.

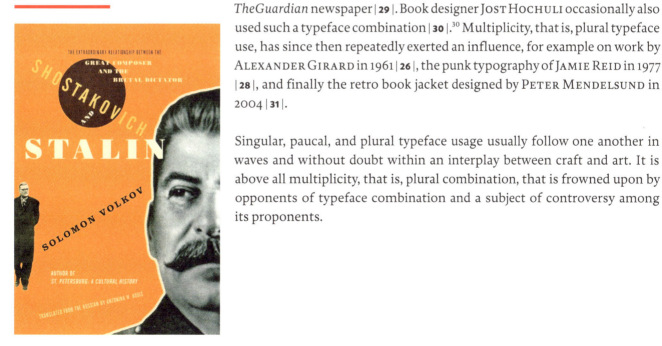

Typeface diversity: retro-style book jacket by Peter Mendelsund, New York, 2004
31

A typology of type

Developing a typology of type is to some extent hindered by terminological ambiguity. Even within the graphics profession, numerous terms are inconsistently defined and not standardized in every case. Deviations from other publications are therefore unavoidable here.

Writing

What is understood by writing differs according to the professional field under discussion. In the graphics industry we associate writing with a type, typeface, or font, all of which on a general level refer to the entirety of all characters (glyphs) within a defined group, that is, all kinds of letters, numerals, punctuation marks, symbols, and empty spaces.

In a more comprehensive sense and yet in as brief a formulation as possible, writing refers to a "system of graphical signs used for the purpose of human communication."[1] In linguistics a distinction is made between, on the one hand, a supra-linguistic inventory of signs, that is, the script, whose individual element is the character or symbol, and, on the other hand, the language specific design, that is, the writing system, which is governed by at least one set of rules (orthography) and the basic unit of which is the grapheme.[2] In the written form of a language, the number of phonemes (sounds) ideally corresponds to the number of graphemes (signs). However, this is generally not the case, either in German or in English.[3]

Writing system

In this publication the term writing system refers to the different kinds and forms of the transcription of language.[4]

A primary distinction can be made between two fundamentally different systems of writing and their variants:

1. *Logography* (Greek *logos*, idea): pictographic symbols, ideographic symbols, abstract logographic symbols; and 2. *Phonography* (Greek *phonē*, tone, sound): segmental writing (signs for sound segments), syllabic writing (syllabary), alphabetic writing (lettering).[5]

We use both logographic and phonographic signs. Logographic signs are much more common than we might think, whether they appear in the daily newspaper or in a specialist magazine for chemistry or meteorology. Everyday logograms include % (percent), @ (at), $ (dollar), and £ (pound) along with numerals, mathematical symbols, and punctuation marks.[6]

On a secondary level, the term *writing system* helps distinguish particular writing and linguistic cultures. For example, we speak of the Latin alphabet. When combining type – this applies to every writing system and even more to combinations of typefaces from different writing systems – the same

ελληνικό	Greek
Кирилица	Cyrillic
Latina	Latin
Հայերէն	Armenian
বাংলা ভাষা	Bengali
देवनागरी	Devanagari
ᎪᎨᏗ	Ethiopic
ქართული ენა	Georgian
יִ֣רְבְּעָ֗תִּ֒י ־בֶ֖ ־ק֑י ־לֵֽ֖א	Hebrew
മലയാളലിപി	Malayalam
සිංහල	Sinhala
தமிழ்	Tamil
อักษรไทย	Thai

Noto Sans | Noto Sans 'Language' – *Regular*

Google fonts for a wide range of writing systems (selection)

01 ▲

Typeface category

Typeface categories for three text classes: title, body text, and emphasis text

02 ▼

TITLING TYPEFACE
Text typeface
Emphasis typeface

Golden Cockerel · Titling | Regular | *Italic*

question is raised: how clear must the formal analogies and how pronounced can or should the contrasts be? The criteria developed here for the Latin alphabet can also be largely applied to very closely related writing systems such as Greek and Cyrillic, which are written upright and from left to right. Upright writing systems written from right to left, such as Hebrew, Arabic, and Persian, raise more differentiated questions, as do 'hanging' writing systems in the Indic (Brahmic) script, such as Devanagari and Bengali, which are also written from left to right. And in Chinese and Japanese writing systems – the latter being itself a convention based on combination – the case is even more complex, because these systems can combine vertical and horizontal and right-to-left and left-to-right reading directions.

In the age of globalization, multilingualism is playing an increasingly important role, which is having an impact on the corporate typefaces used to build company identities and in communication between enterprises as well as for signage. In airports this has long been common practice, of course. As a result we have increasingly seen the development – in part as cooperative ventures – of multiple, comprehensive typefaces incorporating many writing systems, such as Andron, Arial Unicode MS, Fedra, Nimbus, and Noto | **01** |. The fact that the same digital technology is being used all over the world has of course contributed a great deal to the development of such universal typefaces.

In this book typeface category is understood as referring to the differentiation of typefaces according to their use. For example, different typefaces can be assigned to the *text class* (title, text, footnote, etc.), the *reading mode* (look at, read, consult), or *media* and field of applications (poster, book, newspaper, magazine, advertisement, correspondence, screen, etc.).[7]

Type foundries traditionally divided their often thick type specimen books into typeface categories (among other subdivisions). Possible categories included *text* or *body typefaces*,[8] which included all serif typefaces for book, newspaper, and magazine settings; *emphasis typefaces* such as italic, bold, black, etc.; *titling typefaces* consisting only of uppercase letters | **02** | as well as somewhat lighter, slender and therefore more elegant variants of text typefaces (display typefaces) | **03** |; *jobbing* and *advertising typefaces* such as sans serif, slab serif, and decorated typefaces; *correspondence* or *card typefaces*,

41

| In larger point sizes the finer and narrower display version has a more elegant effect **03** ▼ | The font styles of one family used as typeface categories for four text classes **04** ▼▼ |

Regular with *Italic*
Display with *Italic*
Regular with *Italic* for body text

Bulmer · Display | Italic Display | Regular | Italic

Dateline: Bold with *Italic*
Bold Display *Italic*
Body text in Regular with *Italic*
Footnotes and marginal notes in Semibold with *Italic*

Bulmer · Bold | Bold Display | Regular | Semibold

| Typeface categories specially designed for different kinds of printed matter **05** ▼ | Typeface categories for three different reading modes: looking at, reading, consulting **06** ▼▼ |

Poster typeface
Advertising typeface
Book typeface
Correspondence typeface
CARD TYPEFACE

Latin | City | Aldus | Shelley Script | Président

Display typeface narrow
Display typeface hairline
Body text book typeface
Body text newspaper typeface
Agate typeface

Ellington | Bauer Bodoni | Arno | Swift | Amasis

type usually used for letterheads, business and greeting cards, etc. | **05** |, such as script (particularly calligraphic type), so-called engraving typefaces (often pure uppercase typefaces), and typewriter typefaces (monospace); and *poster typefaces,* a category covering the large point sizes (around 5 picas/60 points), which were sometimes published in a separate specimen book due to the fact that they were made out of wood or synthetic material rather than lead. A revised categorization would include additional typeface categories such as *signage type, corporate type, screen type,* etc.

Typeface category does not refer to classification groups such as Antiqua, Egyptian, Grotesque, or Latin, since these are better grouped under the term *type form* (→*Type form:* p. 45).

The following explanatory categorization of reading modes leads to a modified structure of typeface categories.[9] A distinction is made here between display typefaces, text typefaces, and agate typefaces | **06** |. Although this categorization is related to the distinction between display, text, and caption sizes (→*Type size:* p. 74), it should not be confused with it.

Display typefaces are designed for title sizes. Font styles described as *display* usually have a somewhat smaller width than body text typefaces | **03** |; the strokes of the letters also tend to be finer. In the case of Antiqua typefaces of the Neoclassicism class there is often an increased stroke contrast, which makes for a more elegant impression. Deep cuts (notches) and clear tapering at the curve connections to the stem are normally not used in titling typefaces.

However, the term *display typeface* also covers another aspect, which actually aims at the opposite: typefaces intended to be conspicuous. This refers to faces whose design has something special, unusual, attractive, or disturbing about it. Their appearance (→*Type appearance:* p. 49) is designed above all to be seen and only secondarily to be read. Typical examples are *decorated typefaces* and *graphic typefaces* | **07** |.

Text typefaces are designed for extended, continuous, linear reading and are therefore supposed to tire the eyes as little as possible. This is ensured by the use of letters in a familiar form and width, as well as by a tranquil, even type appearance. In addition, a horizontal orientation with a clearly defined,

Display type include an immense number of decorated and graphic typefaces
07

Decorated type
Graphic typeface

Viva | Russel Square

A large x-height provides greater legibility in the case of very small point sizes
08

Typeface	Franklin Gothic
Typeface	News Gothic
Typeface	Trade Gothic
Typeface	Antique Olive
Typeface	Vectora
Typeface	Verdana
Typeface	Hollander
Typeface	Swift

Diverse fonts: 5.1 – 5.6 pt (all same cap height)

Change in the principle of form and counterform in the case of *Minuscule 2*
09

Microgram
Microgram
Microgram
Microgram
Micr▪gram
Micr▪gram
Micr▪gram
Micr▪gram

Minuscule 3 | Minuscule 2 – in 9 pt, 4.7 pt, 3 pt, 2 pt

Ink traps absorb surplus ink; counters remain open in small point sizes
10

Notc
Notch

Bell Centennial · Address

moderate x-height is additionally conducive to reading; as a result, the middle letter band is clearly defined and strengthens the line structure | **06** |. Serifs on the stems also promote the horizontal aspect. The majority of body texts (running texts) are consequently set in serif fonts, mostly in Antiqua of the Renaissance or Baroque class (→*Type form / Class:* p. 95). The vertically dominant orientation of the Neoclassicism class of typefaces, on the other hand, deflects from the primary reading direction. Moreover, the fine hairlines are less suited to long periods of reading, particularly when the stroke contrast is very high, which gives rise to a flickering text appearance.

Newspaper typefaces often have (starkly) shortened descenders | **06** |, which allows the number of lines per column to be increased. In addition, the letters (in the case of a normal character width) tend to have a somewhat narrower shape – particularly the uppercase letters – which makes for a better typesetting quality in the narrow justified columns. Compared to this, in book typography, with their usually wider columns, text typefaces are used in which the generosity of uppercase letters is given full scope.

Agate typefaces are typefaces developed especially for the reading of shorter texts. Their areas of application are packaging, package inserts, timetables, stock market reports, encyclopedias, etc., but unfortunately they are too seldom used in these contexts. The typefaces must be clearly legible in very small point sizes from a considerable distance, and the characters must be quickly and clearly comprehensible. They are drawn more heavily, simply, and with reduced stroke contrast. In comparison to text typefaces, their x-height is somewhat higher. In addition, the counters (inner spaces of characters) are given as open a form as possible | **06** |. Better character recognition in small point sizes is also helped by a somewhat increased typeface width.

Well-known Grotesque typefaces with a large x-height are Franklin Gothic and News Gothic, both by MORRIS FULLER BENTON, Trade Gothic by JACKSON BURKE, Antique Olive by ROGER EXCOFFON, Vectora by ADRIAN FRUTIGER, and Verdana by MATTHEW CARTER. Notable serif typefaces are Hollander, Swift, and Gulliver by GERARD UNGER | **08** |. THOMAS HUOT-MARCHAND's Minuscule, with a very unusual 2-point cut, was especially designed for extremely small point sizes | **09** | and was rightly given a design award by the Type Directors Club TDC in New York in 2007.

Theme	Tool Make	Impression Epoch
Cartoon	Brush	3d
Christmas	Chisel	Bizarre
Comic	Marker	Casual
Graffity	Pen	Classic
Halloween	Pencil	Curly
Holidays	Typewriter	Digital
Horror		Elegant
Kids	Hand-drawn	Fancy
Party	Led	Foreign
School	Pixel	Grunge
Sci-fi	Sketch	Historical
Tattoo	Stencil	Informal
Wedding	Woodcut	Retro
Western		Romantic
		Square
		Techno
		Vintage
		Art Deco
		Art Nouveau
		Arts and Crafts
		Victorian

List of possible typeface categories, grouped by keywords (selection)
11 ▲

Several agate typefaces exhibit clear or even overemphasized notches in the junctures, such as the Bell Centennial, a 1978 telephone book face by MATTHEW CARTER | 10 |. The design was made necessary by, among other things, the difficult conditions involved in telephone book printing: thin paper, runny ink, and the highest possible printing speed. Newer typefaces use such ink traps to create a striking, fashionable effect.

Today it is common to list typeface categories using tags | 11 |, as can be seen on websites such as FontShop, MyFonts, Fontspring, etc. The keywords can relate to *theme* (Christmas, comic, holidays, horror, kids, sci-fi, wedding, etc.), *impression* (bizarre, classic, digital, elegant, fancy, romantic, technoid, etc.), *epoch* (Art Nouveau, Expressionism, Art Deco, etc.), *tool* (felt-tip, brush, etc.), or *method of production* (hand-drawn, sketched, carved in wood, etc.). But since this form of classification is not standardized, this well-intentioned approach nearly always leads to arbitrariness.

Typeface genre

Division into two typeface genres: round form and broken form (Blackletter)
12 ▼

Simplified textura: formal approximation of Blackletter to Grotesque
13 ▼▼

Round form
𝔅𝔯𝔬𝔨𝔢𝔫 𝔣𝔬𝔯𝔪

Adobe Garamond | Wittenberger Fraktur

𝔅𝔩𝔞𝔠𝔨𝔩𝔢𝔱𝔱𝔢𝔯 𝔗𝔢𝔵𝔱𝔲𝔯𝔞
Geometric Grotesque
𝔖𝔦𝔪𝔭𝔩𝔦𝔣𝔦𝔢𝔡 𝔗𝔢𝔵𝔱𝔲𝔯𝔞

Fette Gotisch | Kabel | Tannenberg

The term typeface genre refers to a main division of Latin typefaces into two formally, cultural-historically, and geographically different groups: round form and broken form.

The genre *round form typefaces* is based on lettering from Greek and Roman antiquity and encompasses all typefaces with round curves. In German textbooks they are commonly referred to as *Antiqua,* although in this case the term refers exclusively to a segment of serif typefaces. The round form typefaces include Glyphic, Script, Antiqua (blunt serifs), Egyptian (slab serifs), Grotesque (sans serifs), Latin (pointed or wedge-shaped serifs), and their italic forms as well as decorated variants. Gotico-Antiqua, a transitional form between Blackletter and Antiqua, also belongs to this category.

In the Middle Ages breaks were introduced to the curves of letters, leading to the development of a second typeface genre. The genre *broken form typefaces* encompassed the four main groups of Blackletter typefaces: Textura, Rotunda, Schwabacher, and Fraktur.

Apart from Rotunda, the dominant book script of the Gothic period, Blackletter was unable to assert itself in the Romance-language region and had little sustained effect – quite the opposite to its influence north of the Alps, particularly in the German-language region. Here, both forms developed in parallel, although over the course of centuries there was an attempt to modify broken form in the direction of round form typefaces – in terms of both typographic color (blackness) |12| and, in part, letterforms. A similar example can be seen in modernized or *Simplified textura,* an alteration of Textura in the direction of Grotesque between 1920 and 1940 |13|.

The combination of the two typeface genres can be observed from the sixteenth century onwards in German-language nonfiction books set in Fraktur, in which words originating from Latin were set in Antiqua (→p. 23 | **09** |).

Type form

Typefaces can also be divided into classification groups based on the type forms. The literature of the different languages and countries also uses other terms for this category, such as style and typeface class, but these are used differently here.

Seven classification groups are used to distinguish type forms: *Glyphic, Script, Blackletter, Antiqua, Egyptian, Grotesque,* and *Latin.* Chapter 4 (→p. 83) is devoted to classification groups, and in chapter 6 type form (→*Type form:* p. 166) and type style (→*Type style:* p. 172) are looked at in more detail.

Typeface

In the graphics industry, the terms typeface and type are often used synonymously. Here the terms refer to set type as opposed to lettering and handwriting.

Set type is distinguished from handwriting by its standardization, which also applies to script typefaces |14|. How well a type (from the Greek *týpos,* 'blow, imprint, model') is developed depends on the design concept, the planned field of use, and probably also its success on the market. Thus, a poster type requires a smaller range of characters than a newspaper type; a type for botany, different characters than a type for a dictionary. On the other hand, to typeset the UN Charter on Human Rights requires typefaces for numerous writing systems, which increases the character set or font styles enormously. Such a typeface also offers advantages for texts with multiple levels of hierarchy and emphasis, whereas a correspondence typeface can get by with a single font. For each kind of application, therefore, the most suitable typeface should be found.

From today's perspective it is surprising to discover that typefaces have not always had names. Well into the eighteenth century such names were not required, because each printing workshop had only a small number of typefaces. A label such as *older, new,* or *modern* sufficed.

A Script typeface can take on a handwritten appearance
14 ▼

Typeface
Typeface
𝒯𝓎𝓅𝑒𝒻𝒶𝒸𝑒

Warnock | Jaguar

Is this Akzidenz Grotesk?
Is this Akzidenz Grotesk?
Is this Akzidenz Grotesk?

Akzidenz Grotesk BQ | Basic Commercial LT | Gothic 725 BT

Typefaces of the same origin – disparate forms and names from three type foundries **15** ▶	
Grotesques by Swiss designers – with altered names in the Bitstream catalog **16** ▶	**Univers! Helvetica!** Zurich BT │ Swiss 721 BT

Today's names are usually short, pleasant to the ear, easy to remember, and easy to pronounce. At best they include letters characteristic of the type. A typeface can be named after its designer, for example Garamond, Caslon, Baskerville, Bodoni, Walbaum, Gill, Frutiger. It can represent a dedication to an important figure: Aldus, Dante, Sabon; to a wife: Caecilia; an institution: Berkeley; a location: Basilia; or a country: Helvetica. Other names often evoke a meaning or an association, for example: Futura or Avenir; refer to a specific formal feature of the type: Trinité or Swift; integrate the classification: EgyptienneF; or point to a possible application: Lexicon. There are also purely fantasy names.

For historical reasons, the same typeface can have different names (and vary slightly in appearance) |**15**|**16**|. Conversely, different typefaces, mostly due to ignorance, can have the same name. Legal issues may influence a name since the typeface name is subject to copyright, although this is seldom the case for *type design* (→*Type appearance:* p. 49) because letter shapes are considered public goods.[10] Even renowned type foundries have exploited this fact in order to avoid paying licensing fees and have selected typeface names that sound as similar as possible to the original.[11] This has given them the possibility of positioning imitations in the same parts of alphabetical listings. It is therefore advisable, today more than ever, to be cautious when considering offerings of freely available and very cheap font collections – from both a legal and a quality perspective. On the other hand, the immense number of typefaces currently available that can in part barely be distinguished from one another has in the meantime made the question of the original (and of originality) seem almost irrelevant.

Abbreviations are often added to typeface names that refer to the foundry's name |**17**|, as are suffixes such as *Pro, Std,* and *Com,* which provide a general indication of the character scope (→*Type format:* p. 80).

Abbreviation added to typeface names by different type foundries (selection) **17** ▼

AT	Agfa Type
BE/BQ	H. Berthold AG / Berthold Quality
BT	Bitstream
DTL	Dutch Type Library
EF	Elsner + Flake
EL	Esselte Letraset
FF	FontFont
HTF	Hoefler Type Foundry
ITC	International Typeface Corporation
LF	LucasFonts
LP	LetterPerfect
LT/LH	Linotype / Linotype-Hell
MS	Microsoft
MT	Monotype
PT	Paratype
SG	Scangraphic
URW	Unternehmensberatung Rubow Weber

Type family

A type family comprises all the font styles associated with a typeface name. Where emphasis is required in a text, it is recommended that the first option should be to employ the associated font styles. Such combinations are the simplest and often the best solution.

Whereas in the early period of printing, around the middle of the fifteenth century, typefaces were individual fonts in, at best, different sizes, the following three centuries produced typefaces with a small number of different font styles (→*Type family – triad:* p. 133). Although the nineteenth century then brought an incredible growth in the number of typefaces – above all, emphasis and commercial or jobbing typefaces – their shared characteristic tended to be the same classification group rather than formally coordinated *type appearance,* which is how we understand the concept of a type family today. The extremely comprehensive type specimen books produced between 1870 and 1930 commonly point to a sequence defined by the same stroke weight, width, and slant rather than a name designation. The increasing merger of type foundries – a reaction to, among other things, the rapidly growing competition coming from the mechanical hot metal typesetting systems Linotype, Monotype, Ludlow, and Intertype – in the decades before and after 1900 brought an increasing categorization of different compatible typefaces under a single name. Examples include Akzidenz Grotesk from 1898 onwards and Helvetica from 1956, whose font styles originate from several type designers and type foundries across several decades.[12]

The beginning of the twentieth century saw the emergence of the first genuine type families, which were soon significantly expanded, as in the case of Venus Grotesk, produced by the Bauer Type Foundry in Frankfurt am Main. Around 1914 this *extended type family* already comprised thirteen font styles combining three widths and four weights in upright and slanted variants.[13] In 1927 a further font style was added,[14] and later also a left-leaning oblique (backslanted) for cartography. Other examples include Friedrich Bauer's Genzsch-Antiqua, which was developed between 1906 and 1910 by the Genzsch & Heyse type foundry, based in Hamburg and Munich, and comprised seven font styles: roman, italic, bold, bold italic, condensed bold, condensed black, and black. However, the term type family still did not always correspond to our current understanding, as is evident in the type specimen book issued by the American Type Founders in 1923. Frederic William Goudy's font styles of Goudy Catalogue and Goudy Handtooled | **18** | are referred to as a family and

---

Actually one type family – with two and today even three names
18 ▼

Regular *Italic*
Bold ***Bold Italic***
Handtooled

Goudy Catalogue | Goudy MT | Handtooled

Two type families – different names and differences in the letter design
19 ▼

CRW CRW CRW CRW
CRW CRW
CRW

Goudy Catalogue | Goudy Old Style

summarized on one page but are not named. Moreover, the font styles of Goudy Old Style |**19**|, which diverges somewhat from the other styles in terms of shape, is included in the group.[15]

Following their successful launch onto the market, Grotesque typefaces in particular were quickly developed into extended type families. Nevertheless, the first extended type family that was systematically developed from the ground up and recognized as such was not created until 1953, when Swiss type designer ADRIAN FRUTIGER developed Univers with what were originally twenty-one font styles for the Paris-based Deberny & Peignot type foundry (→ *Extended type family:* p. 134). It subsequently provided the model for other families such as Neue Helvetica.

Today, the ease of digitally generating intermediate font styles (interpolations) and expanded font styles (extrapolations) has led to type designers' creating extremely comprehensive type families, in part with a very large number of font styles. We are thus increasingly seeing the emergence of *type superfamilies* (→ *Superfamily:* p. 137).

Font style

Font style refers to the *posture* of a typeface and combines type width, type weight, and type slant (as well as any embellishment). These three parameters, which are inherent aspects of every typeface, are an essential foundation of typeface combinations.

Many typefaces consist of a single font, and in such cases the terms *typeface* and *font style* are synonymous. When two or more font styles form a unit, they are referred to as a type family. Differentiation here is based on font style attributes such as regular, italic, bold, condensed, extended, etc. |**20**|. However, typefaces with only one font are also given a font style attribute, even though 'regular' is not always accurate |**20**|.

Designations of font styles can be quite long depending on whether the description of the visual traits requires two or three attributes. And even if font style attributes have now become oriented to an international quasi-standard, they continue to vary because there is no real norm. For example, in the case of Frutiger LT, the sequence of font style attributes is different from, and not as good as, that of Neue Frutiger LT, which is produced by the same foundry |**21**|. Listing width/weight/slant in alphabetical order has the advantage for type families with several widths in that all condensed and all extended styles are listed one under the other, which makes for a better overview.

Font styles as part of the family (right); font with confusing style attribute (below)
|**20**|

Freddo · *Regular*

Regular
Italic
Medium
Bold
Bold Italic

Basilia

Typefaces from the same foundry – different sequence of font style attributes
|**21**|

Black Condensed *Italic*
Condensed Black *Italic*

Frutiger LT | Neue Frutiger LT

Typeface series

Letterpress typeface
Impressum light series:
6–36 PT
(reduced to 90%)
22 ▼

Photomechanische Ton- und Farbwertkorrekturen
Abenteuer und Heimkehr des Odysseus
Catalogue et devis sur demande
Estadio Santiago Bernabeu
Münchner Chronik
Salón de Fumar
Kathedrale
Literatur

Typeface series refers to all point sizes of a font style as a whole. The term originated from the letterpress era, with its strictly graduated point sizes, which sometimes exhibit clear individual features in their appearance. Of late the term has come to mean the entirety of design scales in digital typesetting.

In letterpress printing the following point sizes (→*Point size:* p. 70) are common: 6, 7, 8, 9, 10, 12, 14, 16, 20, 24, 28, 36, 48, 60, 72, 84 points (PT). Depending on the font style, the number varies, and where needed further (small, intermediate, and larger) point sizes may be used. Together, all the point sizes of a font style make up the typeface series |22|.

Well into the eighteenth century, designations of point sizes included terms such as Brilliant, Diamond, Pearl, Nonpareil, etc., which in a very grand way expressed the value attached to the smallest point sizes. They could still be found in textbooks up until the end of the letterpress era, in the 1980s. The lack of uniformity in the use of designations in different countries, however, was a source of confusion.[16] In the nineteenth century, the point was adopted as the unit of measurement for size indication (→*Measurement systems:* p. 69), although for a long time this system was not uniformly standardized or precisely applied.

With the scaling of point size – earlier in phototypesetting from the photographic matrix (disc or grid), and with later technologies and today's digital typesetting from the digital data – the term typeface series became obsolete. However, to some degree, the former quality is now finding its way back into type matter, with different type sizes again being given a different design (→*Design size:* p. 75 / →*Opticals:* p. 78).

Type appearance

In typography the term type appearance refers to the design of characters – in the form defined for reproduction in all its facets. The term *type design* is also used in this context.

In the process of developing a typeface – from draft to final drawing, from repeated revisions to the end phase of final font generation – changes are constantly being made to the design of the characters and thereby to the type appearance. An original in the proper sense therefore doesn't exist. Even today, with largely or completely digitally designed and produced typefaces, the appearance changes when the typefaces are rendered; depending on the technology used, the screen resolution, the medium or type of printing and

VU

Downstroke
Main stroke
Thick stroke

Upstroke
Hairline
Thin stroke

NZ

Downstroke
Diagonal
Thick stroke

Spine

S

HT

Crossbar

Bar

EFL

Arm

K

Arm
Joint
Leg

WM

Juncture overlap

Transition
Bracket

Hook

JQ

Tail

R

Leg curved

jf

Hook

Arc

hn

Shoulder

Ear

rs

Beak

ß

Ligature long-s / round-s

mw

Juncture tapered

bpdq

Juncture broadened

z

Joint acute

Typology of character design: uppercase, lowercase, text figures (old style figures)
23 ▲

Legacy Serif

0124753968

Figure height: x-height | Descender | Ascender

T T T
Garamond Premier | Cochin | Vendôme

Different formulations in the diverse details of letter design
24 ▲

Classical modulation of strokes: thick stem and downstrokes, thin bars and upstrokes
25 ▼

Modulation of strokes in static Grotesque: rare (top) and normal (bottom)
26 ▼▼

H VM NZ Uu
H VM NZ Uu
Legacy Serif | Legacy Sans

H VM NZ Uu
H VM NZ Uu
Franklin Gothic | Akzidenz Grotesk

Changing stroke modulation with z – normal (top), rare (middle, bottom)
27 ▶

Zz Zz
Zz Zz
Zz Zz
Legacy Serif | Adobe Jenson | Wilke – *Roman, Italic*

substrate, and the display size. Ultimately, however, a distinction must be made between *type appearance* and *text appearance*. The former term refers to the design of all characters, including letters, figures (numerals), punctuation marks, and symbols. The latter term refers to the typeface in text composition and layout, in the use of point size, tracking, word spacing and leading (line spacing), and measure.

A variety of elements influence the appearance of a typeface, elements that are found in different letters of the Latin alphabet in different combinations: basic or original form, typeface width, weight and slant, rhythm (character width), proportion, axis, stroke contrast, stroke and curve form, stroke and curve terminals, instroke and outstroke, junctures, fill, outline, etc. Some of these elements are more striking than others, and depending on the typeface they are completely or minimally redesigned |**24**|. A typological consideration of letterforms |**23**| and character heights |**28**| of the Latin alphabet is very helpful for our understanding of typefaces. Particular note needs to be taken of the allocation of stems and hairlines in the letters and numerals. This distribution is based on three essential aspects:

1. The writing tool (such as, flat brush, broad nib pen): through its width and writing angle it creates a difference between the stem (thick stroke) and the hairline (thin stroke), thereby emphasizing the stroke contrast.
2. In the case of diagonal letters, the principle of conscious writing in, as much as possible, a single movement. In accordance with the direction of our writing, the diagonal downstrokes tend to proceed from the upper left to the lower right, while the diagonal upstrokes go from the lower left to the upper right.
3. The rule that letters exhibiting different directions must always include thick and thin elements – although not in the same number and quantity: the downstrokes are kept thick and the upstrokes, bars, and arms thin.

These aspects explain the stroke modulation in all letters: the difference in the verticals in Uu, the correspondence of the diagonals in Kk, Vv, and Xx – and even the similarity of the differently oriented diagonals in N, Z. Here, as in the case of M, the principle of 'writing' in a single movement applies. The allocation of thick and thin is thus actually 'standardized' |**25**|. But there is no rule without an exception, as shown by M, N, U in most Grotesques |**26**| and Antiqua lowercase-z |**27**|.

Basic typeface heights for uppercase (capitals), lowercase, and small caps
28 ▶

Stroke allocation is different in the case of numerals because of their origin in India or the Arab world. In Arabic type, the horizontals are stressed more than the verticals (in contrast to Latin type), which is still evident in the numerals 2,5,7 | **23** |.

Typeface character

The impression – the look and feel – conveyed by a typeface is known as typeface character. Since viewing the mere appearance of a typeface without any knowledge of word content can evoke associations, contradictions between form and content need to be avoided.

Although the zeitgeist changes, there is a fundamental consensus that not every typeface harmonizes with every statement. For instance, an ultrabold slab serif does not suggest anything light or fine, such as nylon stockings. And a playful script does not fit something stable like scaffolding, nor is a geometric Grotesque a fit for a wilderness | **29** |.

This realization is based on experience accumulated in the practice of typography, particularly in the field of advertising, and was confirmed by scientific research in the twentieth century. Terms introduced to characterize this aspect of typography include ANNA BERLINER's *Atmosphärenwert* (atmospheric value) in 1920[17] and KARLFRIED VON DÜRCKHEIM's *Anmutungsqualität* (impressionist quality) in 1932.[18] The concept of *connotation*, developed and published in 1957 by the psychologist CHARLES E. OSGOOD and his colleagues, is based on the difference between connotative (affective quality) and denotive (factual quality).[19] The concept of the *semantic differential* and the related process of *polarity profiles* were developed by PETER R. HOFSTÄTTER in 1957 to analyze connotative meanings, that is, subjective, associative, and emotional attributes. These ideas were applied to typographical analyses by DIRK WENDT in 1968.[20]

Degrees of correspondence between typeface character and word meaning
29 ▼

Wilderness
Wilderness
Wilderness
Wilderness

Humana Script | Jaguar | Icone | Avenir

3

Basic shapes | Measurements

Latin	Greek			Phoenician			Hebrew			Arabic		
A	A	[a/a:]	Alpha	𐤀	[ʔ]	'Ālep	א	[ʔ]	'Alef	ا	[a]	'Alif
B	B	[b]	Beta	𐤁	[b]	Bēt	ב	[v]	Bet	ب	[b]	Bā'
C G	Γ	[g/ŋ]	Gamma	𐤂	[g]	Gīml	ג	[g]	Gimel	ج	[ʤ]	Jīm
D	Δ	[d]	Delta	𐤃	[d]	Dālet	ד	[d]	Dalet	د	[d]	Dāl
E	E	[e]	Epsilon	𐤄	[h]	H'ē	ה	[h/ʔ]	He	ه	[ħ]	Hā'
F	F	[w]	Digamma	𐤅	[w]	Wāw	ו	[v/w]	Vav	و	[w]	Wāw
Z	I	[zd]	Zeta	𐤆	[z]	Zajin	ז	[z]	Zayin	ز	[z]	Zāy
H	H	[ɛ:]	Eta	𐤇	[ħ]	Hēt	ח	[x/χ]	Het	ح	[ħ]	Ḥā'
	Θ	[tʰ]	Theta	𐤈	[tˤ]	Ṭēt	ט	[t]	Tet	ط	[tˤ]	Ṭā
I J	I	[i/i:]	Iota	𐤉	[j]	Jōd	י	[j]	Yod	ي	[j]	Yā'
K	K	[k]	Kappa	𐤊	[k]	Kāp	כ	[k]	Kaf	ك	[k]	Kāf
L	Λ	[l]	Lambda	𐤋	[l]	Lāmed	ל	[l]	Lamed	ل	[l]	Lām
M	M	[m]	Mu	𐤌	[m]	Mēm	מ	[m]	Mem	م	[m]	Mīm
N	N	[n]	Nu	𐤍	[n]	Nūn	נ	[n]	Nun	ن	[n]	Nūn
	Ξ	[ks]	Xi	𐤎	[s]	Śāmek	ס	[s]	Samekh	س	[s]	Sīn
O	O	[o]	Omicron	𐤏	[ʕ]	'Ajin	ע	[ʔ]	'Ayin	ع	[ʕ]	'Ayn
P	Π	[p]	Pi	𐤐	[p]	Pē	פ	[f]	Pe	ف	[f]	Fā'
	M	[s]	San	𐤑	[sˤ]	Ṣādē	צ	[ts]	Tsadi	ص	[sˤ]	Ṣād
Q	Ϙ	[k]	Koppa	𐤒	[q]	Qōp	ק	[k]	Qof	ق	[k]	Qāf
R	P	[r]	Rho	𐤓	[r]	Rēs	ר	[ɣ/ʁ]	Resh	ر	[r]	Rā'
S	Σ	[s]	Sigma	𐤔	[ʃ]	Sīn	ש	[ʃ]	Sin/Shin	ش	[ʃ]	Shīn
T	T	[t]	Tau	𐤕	[t]	Tāw	ת	[t]	Tav	ت	[t]	Tā'
V Y U W	Y	[y/y:]	Upsilon							ث	[θ]	Thā'
	Φ	[pʰ]	Phi							خ	[χ]	Khā'
X	X	[kʰ]	Chi							ذ	[z]	Zā
	Ψ	[ps]	Psi							ض	[dˤ]	Ḍād
	Ω	[ɔ:]	Omega							ظ	[ð]	Ẓā'
										غ	[ʁ]	Ghayn

Phoenician alphabet (middle) – the basis of the European and Semitic alphabets
01

Basic shapes

The basic geometric shapes of the *square, circle,* and *triangle* have a particular importance in the development of a system of signs – whether the signs concerned are symbols, letters, pictograms, or company logos. These basic shapes can provide a starting point, the actual design of a character, or the frame for a design.

The Greek, Latin, and Cyrillic alphabets are writing systems (→*Writing system:* p. 40) based on basic geometric shapes. In a somewhat different way – in that they heavily emphasize the square or right angle – this also applies to Hebrew script[1] and the Indic (Brahmic) script Devanagari. All these systems of writing originate from the Phoenician alphabet |**01**|.

The Phoenician writing system is a right-to-left 22-character consonant script |**02**|.[2] It was used between the eleventh and fifth centuries BCE in the different language regions of the Levant, an area on the east coast of the Mediterranean stretching from the Sinai peninsula in the south to the border region of modern Syria and Turkey in the north. It is thought that from the ninth century BCE onwards the Greek culture gradually adopted the Phoenician alphabet, reshaped it, and extended the number of phonetic symbols to suit their respective language needs. Consonant characters that did not have any phonetic equivalents in Ancient Greek were used to represent vowels |**01**|. In the beginning, local (epichoric) character sets developed that featured different forms. Depending on the region, the Greek alphabet comprised between 24 and 27 characters. Initially, Ancient Greek

Old Phoenician script with right-to-left reading direction – Mesha Stele, 842 BCE
02 ▶

Bidirectional lines (right left right) – Idameneus inscription, 6th century BCE
03

Greek lapidary – part of the trilingual Decree of Canopus, Egypt, 238 BCE
04

Development of pronounced stroke terminals in Greek/Roman glyphics
05

INZISE
INZISE
INZISE

Syntax Lapidar | Lithos | Rusticana

INZISE
INZISE

Syntax Lapidar Serif | Trajan

was written right to left, later bidirectionally (boustrophedon) – alternative lines with mirrored letterforms | **03** | – and then left to right.[3]

Around the eighth century BCE the Romans adopted the Old Italic alphabet, which evolved from the Greek alphabet. Letters for which there was no need in Latin were either omitted or repurposed to serve Latin language needs. The resulting standardized Latin alphabet comprised 21 letters. The letter K was retained, although over time it was rendered redundant by the homonymous C and very rarely used. Q was also retained but only found in the QV connection as a labiovelar [k^w].[4] Also included was G, which was created in the third century BCE by adding a vertical stroke to C. It was placed in the seventh position, supplanting the omitted Z, which had originally occupied this position in another form (I) in the western Greek alphabet. The letter Y was not retained, although Y and Z were later introduced for the writing of Greek names and placed at the end of the 23-letter alphabet | **01** |.[5]

The rounded form of V was not originally an element of the Latin alphabet. The U design was first developed at the beginning of the first century through the writing process. Much later, towards the end of the first millennium, the letters J and W were adopted from the Germanic languages, the J in order to distinguish the consonantal from the vocalic I, the W as a non-syllabic U-phoneme. Conversely, the phonetic value of W goes back to the Phoenician *Waw* | **01** |. In the early Greek alphabet its rounded cup shape changed to Y with the phonetic value [u], which in turn changed to V. Through the duplication of V – as expressed in the name in Italian *(doppia vu)*, French *(double vé)*, and English *(double-u)* – W was rendered in the form of a ligature in the early Middle Ages.[6] Here, apart from the accent marks added later, the development of the Latin alphabet comes to its end – an incomplete end because in the diverse national languages phonemes and graphemes only correspond to a certain extent.[7]

Formal changes in ancient inscriptions are evident above all in the terminals of characters. The earliest inscriptions were carved into stone, resulting in terminals that were narrower than, or at most of equal width to, the stroke. They later became wider terminals | **05** |, resulting in the formation of short serifs. Inscriptions that were first painted on with a flat brush and then cut out with a hammer and chisel also featured a stroke contrast | **06** |.

The Ancient Greek | **04** | and Latin | **06** | alphabets have only *one* character set, which today we call capitals (majuscule, uppercase). In their most elegant

Inscription on the base of Trajan's column, Rome, 113 CE (Replica)
06 ▲

Trajan

Basis for the capital shapes: square, circle, triangle and their double-storey shapes
07 ▲

execution, their design incorporates the basic geometric shapes of the square, circle, and triangle – either as whole, double, or partial shapes.[8] The rhythm of the lettering is here shaped in particular by the relative widths of the basic shape and the double-storey shape |**07**| (→*Rhythm*: p. 176).

In the context of type design, the concept of 'geometric' should not be equated with 'mathematically equal'. In accordance with the laws of optics, the circle and the triangle need to be drawn somewhat larger than the square. The upper and lower edges of rounded and pointed shapes overshoot the cap line and baseline, since otherwise the characters would not optically form a straight line. Moreover, in the case of the stacked double-storey shapes, the lower part is enlarged so that it does not appear too small in comparison with the upper one |**07**|. The thickness of the strokes also varies: at their broadest points the curves are somewhat thicker than the downstrokes; these are in turn thicker than the upstrokes; vertical strokes are thicker than horizontal ones. And to offset differences in height when looking at tablets from below, the Romans made the letters in the descending lines progressively smaller |**06**|.

The development of the writing process over subsequent centuries saw the evolution of lowercase letters (minuscules), which were divided into

Roman book scripts, 3rd to 6th century: Capitalis quadrata, Uncial, Half-uncial
08 ▲ | ▲▶ | ▲▶▶

Roman majuscule cursive, 2nd century, Roman minuscule cursive, 6th century
09 ▶ | ▶▶

From the majuscule to minuscule form – reduction of the number of gestures: 4, 3, 2, 1
10 ▼

carefully written *book scripts* |08| and more quickly written *cursive scripts* |09|. While *Roman capitalis monumentalis* |06| as an inscriptional script and *Capitalis quadrata* |08| as a book script remained pure majuscule scripts, the *Roman uncial* |08| of the fourth and fifth centuries already included individual minuscule forms as well as ascenders and descenders. In the case of the *Roman half-uncial* |08| of the fifth and sixth centuries, majuscule forms were in the minority, and they were completely replaced in the *Carolingian minuscule* |12| that emerged in the eighth and ninth centuries.

In his *Theorie der Gestenreduktion*[9] (Theory of gestural reduction), the distinguished Swiss type designer ADRIAN FRUTIGER analyzes this development and concludes that writing the majuscule E requires four gestures, one

Irish-Anglo-Saxon half-uncial, 8th century – static style due to a flat pen angle
11 ▲

Conclusion of the change to lowercase – Carolingian minuscule, 9th century
12 ▲

Humanistic minuscule and cursive, 16th century – basis for Antiqua roman / italic
13 ▲▲ | ▶

HIT	UJ
EFL	BPR
OQCS	GD
VMWX	AZ YKN

nlhrm a	u ij ft
oec s	bpdq g
vwy x	z k

Syntax

Possible order of the letterforms based on formal affinity – square, circle, triangle
14 ▲ | ▲▲

Change from angular majuscule form to minuscule form with curves
15 ▼

AEFHMNTV
aefhmntu

vertical and three horizontal. In between these four movements the nib is lifted from the writing surface and placed on it again in another position. Joining the vertical stroke (stem) with the bottom horizontal stroke (arm) thus reduces the number of gestures | **10** |. This minimization is taken even further with the use in Uncial script of a C form with a stroke in the middle | **08** | and finally with the writing of the letter in a single movement, as seen in the minuscule e.

At the same time the alphabetical canon of forms changed. Whereas the original majuscules combined the basic shapes of the square, circle, and triangle in roughly equal measure (U, J and W came later) | **14** |, the majority of minuscule forms featured curves | **15** |.

Handwritten Bible, ca. 1450 (far left) and Gutenberg Bible, *B42-Type,* ca. 1454 (left)
16 ◀◀|◀

Counters and letter-spacing – Blackletter, Antiqua: adjusted; Grotesque: unadjusted
17 ▼

mínímum

minimum

minimum

Humanistic type (Antiqua old style), Nicolas Jenson, Venice, 1470
18 ▶

VSEBIVM Pamphili de euangelica præparatione latinum ex græco beatiſſime pater iuſſu tuo effeci . Nam quom eum uirum tum eloquétia: tũ multaꝗ rerum peritia: et ĩgenii mirabili flumine ex his quæ iam traducta ſunt præſtātiſſimum ſanctitas tua iudicet: atꝗ ideo quæcũꝗ apud græcos ipſius opera extét latina facere iſtituerit: euangelicã præpationẽ quæ in urbe forte reperta eſt: primum aggreſſi traduximus. Quo quidem in libro quaſi quodam in ſpeculo uariam atꝗ multiplicem doctrinã illius uiri licet admirari. Cuncta enim quæ ante ipſũ facta ĩuentaꝗ fuerunt quæ tamen græce ſcripta tũc inueniŕetur : multo certius atque diſtinctius ipſis etiam auctoribus qui ſcripſerunt percepiſſe mihi uidetur. Ita quom conſtet nihil fere præclarum unq̃ geſtum fuiſſe quod illis temporibus græce ſcriptum non extaret: nihil in rebus magnis naturaꝗ abditis quod a philoſophis non eſſet explicatum: omnia ille tum memoriæ tenacitate: tũ mẽtis p̃cepit acumine: ac ut apes ſolent ſingulis inſidere floribus: indeꝗ quod ad rem ſuam conducit colligere: nõ aliter ille undiꝗ certiora ueriſimilioraue deligẽs mirabilem ſibi atꝗ inauditũ ſcientiæ cumulum confecit: multiplices uariaſꝗ philoſophorum ſectas nõ ignorauit: infinitos pene gentium omnium religionis errores tenuit: orbis terrarum hiſtoriam ſerie ſua diſpoſitam ſolus cognouit & cæteris tradidit. Nam quom non eſſet neſcius geſtaꝗ rerum hiſtoriam titubare ſãctiſſime pater niſi diſtincta tẽporibus pateat. Quippe quom natura tẽporis faciat ut quæ ĩ tẽpore fuerunt niſi quando fuerũt ſcias: nec fuiſſe qdem ꝓpter confuſionem uideantur: eo ingenio: ſtudio: induſtria huic incubuit rei: ut omnium ſcriptorum peritiam in unum congeſtam facile ſupauerit: diſtĩctiuſꝗ cuncta ipſis ſuis ut diximus cognouerit auctoribus. Conferendo enim inter ſe ſingulos: ueritatem quæ ab omnibus ſimul emergebat: nec ab ullo exprimebatur: conſecutus eſt. Quæ omnia ab aliis quæ ſcripſit & ab hoc opere perſpicere licet. Quod ille ideo ſuſcepit: quoniam quom apud gentiũ præclaros philoſophia uiros nobiliſſimus eſſet: ac priſcã paternamꝗ deorũ religionem catholicæ ueritatis amore cõtempſerit: partim accuſātibus ſuum propoſitum reſpondere: partim noſtra pro uiribus ſuis uoluit cõfirmare. Itaꝗ ĩ duas uniuerſum partis negotium partitus eſt: quarum primam quæ nunc traducta nobis eſt: qua illis

Greek inscription, letters aligned in columns, Athens, ca. mid-5th century BCE
19 ▲

From the Middle Ages onwards, majuscules gradually won back lost terrain. They were now no longer used only as versals (initial letters) and for titles but also to mark the beginning of a sentence and for proper nouns within a text.[10] Mixed ways of writing became established. And with the development of *Humanistic minuscule* |13| and *Humanistic cursive* |13| in the fifteenth and sixteenth centuries, scripts emerged that provided the basis for the upright *roman* and slanted *italic* font styles of the Antiqua typeface.

Among the basic geometric shapes, the *square* has a particular status in the case of lettering, since it also serves as a standardized frame (bounding box) (→*Em quad:* p. 65). This principle is apparent in Greek antiquity above all in official documents from Athens during the fifth and fourth centuries BCE, which are stoichidon (from the Greek stoichos: row, order).[11] Irrespective of their width, all the characters are centered under one another – without any regard for word boundaries |19|.

Chinese script has a strong connection with the square, which was already used in early script forms as a systemic unit |20|.[12] The Korean script Hangul is particularly worth mentioning |21|. On the one hand, the square, circle, and triangle form the basis of the characters; on the other, the square is again the systemic unit or spatial module. Mayan high culture (in what is now Mexico and Guatemala) also used a modular system |22|. In this case the different characters can be combined into units forming a square, vertical rectangle, or horizontal rectangle.[13] In spite of temporal, geographical,

Qingshan, inscription in stone, China, 219 BCE (copy) – the script module is the square

20

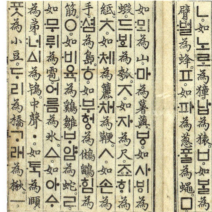

Traditional Hangul, Hunminjeongeum, Korea, 1446 – explanations in Chinese

21

Mayan inscription – the elements fit into a uniform character width

22

and cultural differences as well as obvious differences in character design, all three writing systems cited here share a modular structure and adhere to the principle of monospacing.

Em quad

The em quad is the basic unit of measurement in typography. Its advantage lies in the fact that, irrespective of numerical size, it remains what it is: a square with the edge length of the point size. The em quad is thus a fixed quantity – the square – as well as a flexible quantity because it increases with the point size.

The role of the em quad as the basic unit of measurement has become ambiguous in digital typesetting because it does not exist in material form as it does in metal typesetting. Although the quad and its proportional parts (a half, third, quarter, sixth, eighth, and ¹⁄₂₄-quad) still exist as fixed *white spaces*[14] (em space, en space, third space, quarter space, sixth space, thin space and hair space) and in the form of the *em dash* and *en dash* |**23**|, but they correspond to these widths in only a few typefaces. The height of the em quad is decisive for the point size (→*Point size:* p.70) but only to a limited extent for the height of the actual face (→*Font size:* p.72).

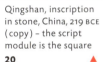

Em and en dashes, in between are fixed spaces from em space to hair space

23

Kabel LT · *Book:* 24 pt

Em quad: 6 pt | 8 pt | 10 pt | 12 pt | 18 pt | 24 pt

Em quad (square) and position of letters in different point sizes
24 ▶

Whereas in traditional typesetting font size is measured in *points,* in the case of digital typefaces the basic unit of measurement is UPM – units per em. Normally the em quad corresponds to a grid of 1000×1000 UPM.[15]

Body width

Body width refers to the set width of a character, that is, the width of the letter design along with the width of the sidebearings. Without these left and right sidebearings, the faces would touch one another.

In *proportional typefaces,* with their individual character widths, the square is decisive as a point of departure but is only present to a limited extent. In text type it is the majuscules H and N in which the proportions of the letter design refer to the square, as well as the majuscules M and W, the width of which approximates the em quad width | **25** |. Otherwise, neither the em quad nor the typographic system of measurement plays a role in character widths (→*Measurement systems:* p. 69). Each character has its own width, which is determined by optical aspects and coordinated with all other characters. As a result, the body width, and thus its UPM number, differs from character to character.

The situation is different with *monospace typefaces,* which derive from the typewriter. Absolutely all the characters, including the word space, exhibit the same width in their vertical arrangement | **26** |. When setting such fonts it is important to set the *kerning* from metric to zero to ensure the characters are actually positioned one below the other.

Individual body widths in proportional typefaces – M and W are almost of quad width
25 ▶▶

Proportional typeface (different widths), monospace typeface (equal body width)
26 ▶

Width
Width

Rockwell | Courier

Freya · *Medium* – body widths: H 849 UPM (units per em) | M 963 UPM | W 1013 UPM

Kerning

The determination of the left sidebearing and right sidebearing of characters and thus of the distance between characters is known in type production as fitting or kerning. However, this general kerning inherent in a typeface does not always suffice, since good typography often requires further manual kerning.

The spacing between characters is based on the determination of the sidebearings as an element of the width of every character. More precisely: The spaces between characters are each composed of the right sidebearing of a character and the left sidebearing of the one following it. In order to attain the goal of a type appearance that is as balanced as possible in optical terms – which means, to achieve an even typographic color without the formation of patches in the text due to spacing set too loose or too tight – the sidebearings need to be adjusted to the character design. In the case of vertical strokes, the space is a little wider than in the case of curves, in the case of diagonal strokes it is much narrower | **27** |. For this reason asymmetrical characters can exhibit very different UPM values for left and right sidebearings. Sometimes letters even require an overhang (kern), that is, a *negative sidebearing* | **28** |. Apart from this general kerning | **29** | fitting a typeface also includes an additional *pair kerning* for critical character pairs | **30** | as in the case of letters such as T, V, W, which optically have large sidebearings.

The default kerning integrated in fonts, which Adobe calls *metrics kerning*, ensures a homogeneous appearance in professionally fitted fonts with correctly selected tracking (→*Tracking:* p. 68). An interesting development in the software field is *optical kerning*. However, its use sometimes leads to a reduction in quality because the software alters defined spacing. Letter pairs such as ft, rf, rt, tt, etc., may be pulled apart in an unappealing way, while others may be pushed closer together.

In addition to the default spacing, *optical balancing* of the character spaces by *manually kerning* the particular word image is definitely required for word marks, all caps text, and setting in large point sizes. Such balancing needs to take into account that all spaces need to be perceived as equal in terms of their blackness. It is evenness of color that leads to balanced word images, rather than the same distance or same space between letters.[16] A well-trained eye – combined with perseverance – helps to determine the UPM value correctly | **31** |.

The sidebearings vary in the case of the vertical stroke, curve, and diagonal stroke
27 ▼

Letters with overhang: negative sidebearing on the left side at j and on the right side at f
28 ▼

Checking fitting: each letter is positioned between two n, two o, two H, and two O
29 ▼

nnnooonon
nanbncndnenfngnhninjnknlnmnnnonpn
nqnrnsntnunvnwnxnynznænœnßn
oaobocodoeofogohoiojokolomonooopo
oqorosotouovowoxoyozoæoœoßo

HHHOOOHOH
HAHBHCHDHEHFHGHHHIHJHKH
HLHMHNHOHPHQHRHSHTHUHVH
HWHXHYHZHÆHŒH
OAOBOCODOEOFOGOHOIOJOKO
OLOMONOOOPOQOROSOTOUOVO
OWOXOYOZOÆOŒ

Without and with pair kerning: negative right sidebearing of T in relation to e
30 ▶

Metrics kerning, optical kerning – and manual kerning adjusted to the word image
31 ▶

Tracking

Point size without and with adjustment of the letterspacing (metrics kerning)
32 ▼

Harmony
Harmony
Harmony
Harmony

Myriad: 32 pt | 18 pt | 9 pt | 6 pt – tracking 0

Harmony
Harmony
Harmony
Harmony

Myriad: tracking –15 | –4 | +12 | +60

Harmony 0	**Harmony** +18
Harmony 0	Harmony 18
Harmony 0	Harmony 18

New Baskerville · *Bold* | *Semibold* | *Roman*: 9.7 pt

Harmony 0	**Harmony** +15
Harmony 0	Harmony 30
Harmony 0	Harmony 50

Neue Helvetica · *Bold* | *Regular* | *Light*: 9 pt

The lighter the typeface (larger counters), the looser the tracking required
33 ▲

For optimal readability, every typeface requires its own, correct letterspacing or tracking. This means that the defined character spaces must be increased or decreased overall – taking into account the point size, display size, color, printing substrate, and medium.

When casting metal sorts, type foundries took into account the fact that letterspacing, for reasons of readability, had to be adapted to the typeface and to each point size. Because of the material of which they were made, it was either not possible or very laborious to set the letters closer together or wider apart.[17] In metal typesetting, the spacing of the type is thus in principle determined by *body width*.

In the case of digital fonts, the adjustment of tracking is left up to the user. Unfortunately, type producers have failed to offer support and set a letterspacing value of zero (default setting) at a defined point size, which would establish a standard. We therefore do not know what point size is correctly set at a tracking value of zero. Correct tracking values thus have to be determined by protracted, comparative investigation – for every typeface, every point size |**32**|, and every font style |**33**|. When combining different fonts in word marks, letterspacing also needs to be adjusted with reference to the kind of combination.

When specifying tracking, the following basics apply:
Typefaces require *looser tracking*
– the smaller the point size;
– the lighter the weight (regular, book, light, etc.), due to larger counters;
– the wider the width (extended, wide, etc.), due to larger counters;
– in the case of reversed-out, due to bright type radiates into dark spaces;
– in the case of larger reading distances, due to the type appears denser.

Typefaces require *tighter tracking*
– the larger the point size;
– the heavier the weight (bold, black, etc.), due to narrower counters;
– the narrower the width (condensed, etc.), due to narrower counters.

Unlike *metrics kerning, optical kerning* automatically adapts tracking to point sizes. However, manual adjustment to achieve the correct values is almost always necessary, because here too the zero value is rarely consistent in each case. Metrics kerning is preferable, and optical kerning should only be used where extremely precise checking and comparison is possible.

Measurement systems

In the digital age, the traditional typographic systems of measurement continue to exist, albeit with minor differences. Points (pica and inch), the em quad (including UPM), millimeters, and pixels represent four co-existing and equally important systems of measurement.

The smallest typographical unit of measurement in metal typesetting is the point.[18] The version used in continental Europe is the *Didot point* (named after François-Ambroise and Firmin Didot), with 12 points making up one *cicero*. In the English-speaking world the corresponding typographic measures are the *point* and the *pica*. These systems of measurement are based on the duodecimal system (base 12), which has the advantage of five whole-number divisions (:2/:3/:4/:6/:12); however, the two systems do not exactly correspond |**34**|. In modern digital typesetting, yet another unit of measurement is used, the inch-based PostScript or *DTP point*. It is slightly bigger than the pica point but smaller than the Didot point |**34**|.

In metal typesetting, the traditional unit of measurement is used as a standard not only for type but also for the typography – for the vertical dimension or column height as well as for the horizontal dimension or line length (measure). However, newer technologies have long used the decimal system in layouts – except in the case of point size (→*Point size:* p.70) and leading – at least in countries using the metric system. In screen media such as websites, the pixel is the standard unit of measurement (→*Pixel:* p.78).

Current and traditional typographic systems of measurement (conversion table)

34

Em quad	*Type / Setting parameter*	
	Fixed white space	
Units per em	*Character / Setting parameter*	
	Width, Kerning, Tracking	
Point	*Type / Setting parameter*	
	Point size, Leading, Baseline shift	
Percent	*Type / Setting parameter*	
	Word spacing, Letterspacing, Glyph scaling	
Millimeter Inch	*Setting / Size parameter* Indent, Hyphenation zone, Column width, Gutter, Line length (Measure), Type area (Grid), Margins, Page size	
Pixel	*Type / Setting / Size parameter* Point size, Leading, Segment size, Page size	

	Didot-Point	Pica-Point	Inch	DTP-Point	Millimeter	Pixel
Didot-Point (p)						
1 Point		1.0703	0.0148	1.0660	0.3760	1.4213
1 Cicero = 12 Point		12.8438	0.1777	12.7559	4.5128	17.0078
Pica-Point (PT)						
1 Point	0.9345		0.0138 (≈ 1/72)	0.9962	0.3513	1.3283
1 Pica = 12 Point	11.2148		0.1660 (≈ 1/6)	11.9951	4.2163	15.9402
1 Inch = 6 Pica	67.2891				25.4	95.6413
DTP-Point (pt)						
1 Point	0.9380	1.0037	0.0138 (= 1/72)		0.3528	1.3333
1 Pica = 12 Point	11.2569	12.0484	0.1666 (= 1/6)		4.2333	16
1 Inch = 6 Pica	67.5415				25.4	96
Millimeter						
1 mm	2.6591	2.8460	0.0394	2.8346		3.7795
1 cm = 10 mm	26.5911	28.4609	0.3937	28.3465		37.7952
Pixel (Px) at 96 dpi						
1 Pixel	0.7035	0.7528	0.0104	0.75	0.2645	

Values rounded to four decimal places

Point size

Point size refers to the height of type. However, what is meant here is not the visible height of the type appearance but the vertical extension of the background, which is invisible in digital fonts. It is thus a *numerical* quantity.

There are only two mathematically predefined measures for the creation of digital fonts. As already explained, one of the standard measures of typographic letters is the *em quad* (a square with the same dimensions as the point size). However, in the realm of digital typefaces, the size of the em quad, the technical term for which is *body size* |35|, has become an almost irrelevant measure with regard to the visible type appearance. It describes only a mathematical and no longer additionally a physical and optical height. For this reason we speak of *virtual body size* in the case of digital type.

On the other hand, the *baseline* is a predetermined measure, which in all professionally produced typefaces corresponds to the y-coordinate zero |36|; however, this does not mean that this position is fixed in relation to the em quad size (→*Font size:* p.72). Due to the zero coordinate, however, the baseline is the only actually defined *visible* measure for digital fonts. As the guide to combining typefaces will show, this can lead to considerable problems (→*Heights:* p.167).

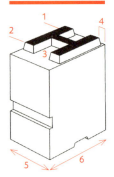

Schematic drawing of a metal type – and terms relevant for digital fonts
35 ▼

In digital typesetting, different point sizes automatically align on the baseline
36 ▶

Unit of measurement: UPM
1 Face
2 Baseline
3 Counter
4 Left and right sidebearings
5 Width
  Body width

Unit of measurement: Point
6 Point size
  Body size
  Em quad size

Hfgx Hfgx Hfgx Hfgx Hfgx Hfgx

Minion: 12 pt | 16 pt | 20 pt | 24 pt | 28 pt | 32 pt

In order to make point size more easily understandable as a measure – and the problems arising from this today – we need to look once again to metal typesetting. The advantage here lies in the fact that the physical presence of body size in metal typesetting means that it is both visible and tactile. Moreover, in this context point size is also measurable with a line gauge (typographic ruler) |37|.

What is measured here is not the type appearance but, for practical reasons, the size of the metal base on which the type face is cast. In metal typesetting the number of points (PT) is thus a measure of the nonprinting but visible part of the type |35|. There are two other reasons that make body size seem to be the logical defining measure in metal typesetting. It provides a constant

Line gauge – top:
2-point units, ciceros;
middle: concordance
(4 ciceros);
bottom: mm, cm
37

and systematized measure and, at the same time, it includes the minimum interval to the next line. In terms of typographic measures, the body size is thus the constant, the type face the variable.

Although the body size remained present in only virtual terms, most manufacturers of typesetting machines, including later technologies such as analog and digital phototypesetting, remained tied to the traditional specification point size. This is astounding, because the disappearance of physical body size meant the loss of the only constant, which made measuring typefaces much more difficult. One exception was the Fonderies Deberny & Peignot in Paris and their Lumitype phototypesetting machine (an adaptation of the Photon phototypesetting machine), which was codeveloped by ADRIAN FRUTIGER and which featured a uniform cap height.[19]
Unfortunately, in the 1980s hardware and software companies as well as foundries working on the development of desktop publishing (DTP) continued to apply the existing principle of body size to point size. They thereby missed the (unique) opportunity in the development of digital typesetting to establish a visible height such as the cap or x-height as measure of the point size. The defined, systematically graduated point sizes in metal typesetting were subsequently replaced in digital typesetting by a variable scale – in Adobe InDesign currently from 0.1 to 1296 point (pt) accurate to three decimal places. However, this development makes it all but impossible to precisely define the point size based solely on the type appearance.
When combining typefaces, the lack of a standardization of the cap height or x-height results in the need for laborious adaptation. Possible sources of help can be found in the layout software VivaDesigner[20] and a number of (computer) scripts.[21]

In regards to point size, digital typefaces run the risk of losing all visible standardization because the face size does not have to be oriented to the body size. However, in the case of most of the text faces in use, it can be assumed that the body size is almost filled out – from the upper edge of the ascender to the lower edge of the descender |**35**|. Even if unsatisfactory, the point size can thus be gauged approximately using the so-called *fg-height*.

Font size

Font size refers to an *optical* quantity, unlike point size, which refers to a numerical quantity. The fg-height is decisive for the vertical dimension; however, the most distinctive aspects of the font size are the cap height and, above all, due to its common occurrence, the x-height.

Type appearances can have very diverse dimensions. The em quad, with its height of 1000 UPM, therefore says little about the font size in two respects:
1. The cap height and the height of lowercase letters (ascender, x-height, and descender, which together make up the fg-height) are freely determinable individually and in relation to one another, which in optical terms leads to different height effects (→*Heights:* p. 167).
2. The position of the baseline is freely determinable in relation to the em quad height. This means that although the baseline always assumes the zero value on the y-coordinate, this zero value can have a different position in each font. The distance above the zero value is defined by a positive value, the distance below by a negative value. Together, the two absolute values make up the 1000 units of the em quad or the virtual body size |**38**|.

Same coordinates, different positioning – height: 1000 units; baseline: y = 0
38 ▶

Freya: ascender 752 UPM, descender –248 UPM | Serifa: ascender 654 UPM, descender –346 UPM

Nonstandardized baseline in metal typesetting for the same point size (body size)
39 ▲

This is not an innovation of the digital age – on the contrary. Up until the standardization of the baseline in 1905, it was normal in metal typesetting for the baseline to assume different positions in relation to the body height |**39**|.[22] It was the *universal baseline* that first ensured that typefaces of the same point size maintained the same baseline and different point sizes could be relatively quickly aligned with standardized leads and reglets |**40**|. However, the low position of the baseline led to short descenders. In some cases, the upper curve of the lowercase f and the lower curve of the g poked over

German standard line (round form typefaces)

Standardized baseline in metal typesetting created by equalizing positions with leads

40 ▲

Different fonts are also automatically aligned with the baseline

41 ▶

Card typeface in metal typesetting – three type appearances with the same point size

42 ▶

the edge of the body. This is also possible in the case of digital fonts and even common in the case of capitals with accents. But the reverse case is also common: the face or printing form does not always extend to the edges of the body height. In the case of many metal and digital typefaces, the entire em quad height is thus not reached by the fg-height. The em quad height can be exceeded above and fallen short of below, or vice versa.

Typefaces with the same point size have always exhibited differences in the vertical dimension of the type appearance. However, for the optical size of the type appearance, the overall height is less decisive than the x-height and the cap height. Accordingly, Cochin with its low x-height appears significantly smaller than Hollander with its pronounced x-height | **41** |. While there is no standard for cap height or x-height (although a fixed height would be helpful), no values have been defined for the height ratios of the letters, which in fact has a positive effect.

Cochin | Minion | Hollander – each 32 pt

The fact that the complexity of point size and font size can lead to confusion is also shown by the conceptual approach to handset metal type, in which the same point size accommodates systematically graduated visual sizes. In France these are labeled with the numbered term *œil* (eye) | **42** |.[23]

Président · œil 1 | 2 | 3 – simulation in 48 pt

Unlike a setting with different point sizes in one line, these faces cast on the same body size do not require the use of leads, which above all benefited typesetters. However, the type foundries also profited from this development, because it reduced the number of point sizes that needed to be cast. In addition, these faces offered a kind of substitute for the production of genuine small caps. It was thus often *card typefaces* (faces for greeting and business cards) that were cast in such a method.

Same point size, increasing x-height with increasing weight

43 ▶

HzHzHzHzHz

Meta · Normal | Book | Medium | Bold | Black – each 48 pt

It would be premature to speak of a universally valid standard for type design. However, it is increasingly the case that the font styles of Grotesques exhibit diverging x-heights. This is the result of an optical correction, because the heavier a font style is, the smaller the counters (interior spaces). The increase in x-height corresponding to increasing weight somewhat counteracts this perceived decrease in size | **43** |.

Type size

Unlike point size, which has a numerical quantity – type size, same as font size, is an optical measure. However, while font size has to do with type design, type size has to do with typography. In this book, type size refers to different application sizes used in typesetting, namely *agate size,* *text size,* **and** *display size.*

Type size is often – including in technical terminology – equated with point size. However, the term *type size* actually refers to a range of sizes and not to a precise numerical value.

In text setting, type sizes are traditionally divided into three size groups: agate sizes 4–8 pt; text sizes 8–12 pt; and display sizes over 12 pt (→*Design size:* p.75). This corresponds to three fundamentally different reading modes: consultation reading, linear reading, and display reading.[24] The size indications relate to the normal reading distance of two-thirds of an arm length. Of course, in poster design, wayfinding, and road signage, with its greater reading distance, type sizes increase.

Apart from the different sizes intrinsic to the type appearance, typography also involves other optical size factors: amount of text, position, surroundings, and color. For example, short titles appear slightly smaller than a large amount of text set in the same typeface and point size; a word surrounded by a great deal of white space appears smaller than the same word in a tight space or smaller format | **44** |; black type on a white background seems minimally smaller than white type on a black background. Matching all these optical phenomena with typographic examples is beyond the scope of this publication.

Phänomena

Phänomena

Type surrounded by a lot of white space appears slightly smaller than on a tight-fitting background

44 ▲

Design size

Design size indicates the type-size range for which a typeface has been designed. Since the advent of phototypesetting, most typefaces have had only one design for all point sizes, and this also applies to digital faces. However, in terms of legibility and aesthetics, this is a compromise.

In metal type, the situation was different. Every point size had its own design, the formal details of which took into account how the typeface was to be applied and its requirements for optimal legibility, as well as its ability to please the eye. The production of each point size involved adaptations of type width, stroke weights, and stroke contrasts to achieve harmony between legibility and the beauty of the type design – with a strong emphasis on the first in the case of agate and text sizes, and on the second in the case of display sizes (→*Type size:* p.74). At the same time, punch cutters also aspired to contribute to an *aesthetic quality in the text composition* with an *aesthetic quality in the type appearance*. For example, in large point sizes a narrower type width has not only a more elegant effect but also the advantage of allowing for more letters in title lines. In smaller point sizes, on the other hand, an expanded width makes for better legibility.

In metal type, the smaller point sizes were therefore cut wider in comparison with the medium point sizes |45|. The x-height is elevated, enlarging the counters; the stroke contrast is reduced and letters appear more robust. The tracking (letterspacing) is also looser. On the other hand, large point

Metal type in two point sizes – weight, proportions and letterspacing differ
45 ▶

Monumentalität

Monumental

Berthold Akzidenz Grotesk · *medium*: 8 p | 8 p enlarged to 48 p (large image scaled: 82%)

Monumentalität

Monumentalität

Berthold Akzidenz Grotesk · *medium*: 48 p downsized to 8 p | 48 p (large image scaled: 82%)

Digital font – tracking is increased in small point size and decreased in large one
46 ▶

Monumentalität

Monumentalität

Berthold Akzidenz Grotesk · *medium*: 8.5 pt, tracking +10 | 48 pt, tracking −30

Metal typeface in three point sizes with different degrees of formal intricacy **47** ▼	Digital font with only one design for seamless scaling of all point sizes **48** ▼▼

Wilhelm-Klingspor-Schrift: 10 p | 16 p | 48 p

Wilhelm Klingspor Gotisch: 12 pt | 18.5 pt | 55 pt

sizes have a lower x-height, are finer and thinner, and their stroke contrast is clearer; this lends them a more elegant effect, as shown by the example of Wilhelm-Klingspor-Schrift | **47** | – a quality that today is all too rare | **48** |.

Up until the end of the nineteenth century – and in some cases even much later – punch cutters cut each letterform by hand. In 1884 the development of the pantograph as a tool for type production by the American LINN BOYD BENTON made the production process far easier. Now, only *one* brass template was required for each character in order to drill all point sizes. At the same time, optical adaptations continued to remain possible.

With the emergence of phototypesetting in the 1930s and its wider use from the 1950s onwards, only one character drawing was produced as a template. A medium size was usually chosen as the design size, often 12 pt or 18 pt. In the case of most typefaces taken from metal typesetting and phototypesetting and reworked as digital fonts, such a design size can therefore be adopted; a design size of around 6 pt may also be used sometimes for agate faces, and a size of around 40 pt for display faces.

In contrast to metal typesetting, in phototypesetting there was no change in form for the individual point sizes. Photographic exposure was based on the template, without the necessary optical adaptations. This required compromises in character drawing in order to make possible an acceptable reproduction in the point sizes from 6 to 72 pt, for the type image was exposed from the negative plate onto film material or photographic paper only through linear scaling with the help of lenses.

Notable exceptions were the neoclassical Antiquas, for example Bodoni and Didot with their very thin hairlines, the reproduction of which required great sensitivity. Occasionally, two or three design sizes were produced for these typefaces. Some manufacturers of phototypesetting machines, such as the traditional German type foundry H. Berthold AG, also made specially revised display faces available.

In relation to design sizes, type professionals may also be aware of the typefaces created by the phototypesetting machine manufacturer Scangraphic. Two designs were created there for digital laser-setting: the Bodytext fonts for point sizes from 4 to 72 pt – ideally up to 18 pt – and the Supertype fonts for sizes from 12 to 360 pt. These fonts remain available as the SB version (body type) and the SH version (headline type) | **49** |.[25]

Two design sizes – junctures in Scangraphic fonts with and without notches
49 ▼

Clearface Gothic · *Bold:* Bodytext | SB 66 pt

Clearface Gothic · *Bold:* Supertype | SH 66 pt

Unfortunately, most digital faces hitherto had only one design for continuously variable scaling from extremely small to extremely large type | **50** |, which is not ideal since the quality of a font is shown in a relatively limited scope of applications and sizes. Type designers are certainly aware of this and take it into consideration when designing and reworking letterforms, which leads to a compromise. A font in agate size can thus seem too delicate or too light; however, in a display size it may not seem elegant enough. Or, in smaller point sizes a font exhibits a strong and yet open appearance, while in a poster size the same font appears unharmonious, with excessive differences in thickness between main strokes and hairlines, pronounced notches (ink traps), and too much tapering at junctures of curves and strokes, and at joints of two strokes. However, in small point sizes, particularly in the case of acute-angled counters | **49** |, the notches are necessary in order to counteract optical aggregation. This also enables the counters to remain open when exposed and printed, since they tend to lose their definition and take on a rounded fill.

For some time now, the market has again been producing more faces comprising several design sizes. One example is the International Typeface Corporation's ITC Bodoni, with its three design sizes | **51** |.

Bodoni versions in one design size – for medium (left) and large point sizes
50 ▶|▶▶

Bodoni version in three design sizes for agate, text, and display sizes
51 ▼

Harmony
Harmony
Harmony
Harmony

Bodoni LT: 36 pt | 24 pt | 12 pt | 6 pt

Harmony
Harmony
Harmony
Harmony

Bauer Bodoni: 36 pt | 24 pt | 12 pt | 6 pt

Harmony
Harmony
Harmony
Harmony

ITC Bodoni · Six | Twelve | Seventytwo: 36 pt | 24 pt | 12 pt | 6 pt

Harmony
Harmony
Harmony
Harmony

Harmony
Harmony
Harmony
Harmony

Opticals

Opticals can be understood as an extension of *design sizes*. Employing up to six optical sizes, they facilitate an improved type appearance in the different type sizes. This enables digital type to reconnect with the quality of typeface series in metal typesetting.

Adobe Systems Inc. has been a particularly significant contributor to such improvements in digital type creation. Since 1987 the software producer has maintained a well-developed type library, which now contains many fonts with optical sizes. Here, the company has made use of its own development of multiple master technology (→*Multiple master:* p. 141). In typefaces with opticals, type sizes are divided into a scale of four to six sizes: Caption 6–8.5 pt; Small Text 8.5–11 pt; Text 11–14 pt; Subhead 14–24 pt; Display 24–72 pt; Poster 72 pt and larger | **52** | **53** |. Expansion at Adobe Systems has been particularly due to the efforts of type designer and director of type development Robert Slimbach, who has contributed many well-structured type families, including Arno, Brioso, Cronos, Garamond Premier, Kepler, Minion, Sanvito, and Warnock. Thus, a quality of the typeface series in metal typesetting is successfully returning to modern typography (→*Typeface series:* p. 49). However, typefaces with several design sizes remain the exception.

Four normal opticals: differences in stroke thickness, width, and pointedness
52 ▼

Display Harmony
Subhead Harmony
Regular Harmony
Caption Harmony

Warnock · Opticals: 18 pt

Less harmony between type sizes in scaling compared with opticals
53

Regular Harmony   *Display* Harmony
Regular Harmony   *Subhead* Harmony
Regular Harmony   *Regular* Harmony
Regular Harmony   *Caption* Harmony

Warnock · *Regular* | Warnock · Opticals: 28 pt | 18 pt | 10 pt | 6 pt

Pixel

Digital type is basically generated using pixels: in laser printing, commercial printing, and on a monitor. The jagged edge (jaggies) is inherent in the technology and visible or not depending on the resolution.

Digitization from the mid-1960s onwards lent renewed significance to the square with reference to type. A character no longer corresponded to an interconnected form, as in metal typesetting and phototypesetting, but instead was composed of a large number of square pixels | **54** |. Type thereby became aligned with the image, the reproduction of which for printing is converted into a halftone (pattern of dots). In historical terms, this technique in a sense formed a connection with the mosaics of Greek antiquity.[26]

Bitmap fonts show that digital fonts generally consist of pixels **54** ▼	However, this technological progress reduced the rendition quality – with pixilated curves and diagonals exhibiting clearly visible jagged edges. This was also the case at the beginning of the desktop publishing era in the mid-1980s, which saw the introduction of dot matrix printers with a very low resolution of 72 dpi (dots per inch) and laser printers with 300 dpi; since then, 600 and 1200 dpi have become commonplace. For press quality, 2400 dpi or higher has long been seen as the norm. Little by little, this process of development came to confirm type designer Adrian Frutiger's conviction that it was not that type design had to adapt to technology but that technology had to meet the needs of type design.[27]

For displays with a low resolution – bitmap fonts with 18 pixel fg-height **55** ▶	Bitmap-Fonts **Bitmap-Fonts** Emperor 15	Emigre 15	Accordingly, the phase of bitmap fonts was rather short. However, it was with these fonts that Zuzana Ličko established her reputation as a type designer and shaped the early phase of desktop publishing stylistically. Her pixel fonts, including Emperor, Oakland, Universal, and Emigre |**55**|, have been published since 1985 by Emigre, the American type foundry she established with Rudy VanderLans. In terms of good readability on monitors, bitmap fonts remained an important alternative for some time, providing sharpness in text sizes even at very low resolutions. Font families were produced such as Unibody 8, published by Underware in Holland in 2003, which even includes a sufficient number of font styles for emphasis in body texts |**56**|.

For sophisticated display on monitors – bitmap font family with 10 pixel fg-height **56** ▶	ABCDEFGHIJKLMNOPQRSTUVWXYZ 1234567890 abcdefghijklmnopqrstuvwxyz ABCDEFGHIJKLMNOPQRSTUVWXYZ 1234567890 ABCDEFGHIJKLMNOPQRSTUVWXYZ 1234567890 abcdefghijklmnopqrstuvwxyz **ABCDEFGHIJKLMNOPQRSTUVWXYZ 1234567890** **abcdefghijklmnopqrstuvwxyz** **ABCDEFGHIJKLMNOPQRSTUVWXYZ 1234567890** **abcdefghijklmnopqrstuvwxyz** Unibody 8 · Regular	sc	Italic	Bold	Black

Monitor pixels (LCD) consist of three sub-pixels in the additive primary colors **57** ▶		On monitors and displays, the pixel structure is still discernible, although the quality has improved enormously. Type rendering is increasingly gaining precision. A decisive improvement is provided by sub-pixel rendering,[28] which allows for the control of each part of an LCD pixel in the three additive colors of red, green, and blue rather than the entire square pixel |**57**|.

Type format

There is currently an international standard for generating digital fonts in the printing field, the type format OpenType. The format allows for two different ways of describing the character design: Bézier functions (PostScript) and square B-splines (TrueType). In both cases, character design is structured by outlines.

The better-known method is the Bézier function, because it is used in vector graphics and layout software such as Adobe Illustrator and InDesign to draw and to convert type into paths. There are three types of anchor points (nodes): a smooth point with double-sided handles, a cusp point with one-sided handles, and a corner point without handles. The anchor points are placed at the extremes where the direction changes; the direction and length of the handles describe the form of the curve | **58** |. Counters are punched out by the opposing path directions of the outer and inner outlines and thereby become transparent.

Starting in the 1970s, JOHN WARNOCK developed – initially at Xerox and from 1982 at his own company, Adobe Systems Inc. – a page description language dubbed PostScript. This made possible the combined representation of type and image on the monitor of the Apple Macintosh as well as – in collaboration with, among others, the font distributor Linotype – output on a laser printer and on a high-resolution imagesetter. In computer magazines the new technology known as desktop publishing was advertised with the acronym WYSIWYG: what you see is what you get. Even though this was something of an exaggeration and the quality of such printing has since improved enormously, the development of PostScript nevertheless represented immense progress compared with the devices offered by traditional phototypesetting machine manufacturers. The latter were incapable of producing an image, and monitors for the most part displayed text only in monospace fonts.

With PostScript, Adobe Systems Inc. also established a new font format. The PostScript Type 1 fonts contained three files per font style: for monitor displays a bitmap font (Suitcase), an outline or vector font for reproduction on printers and imagesetters, and a file for numerical values (Adobe Font Metrics .afm). Unlike the bitmap font, the vector font with its Bézier curves is scalable without the loss of quality.

For a long time Adobe refused to disclose the coding of PostScript, and as a result Apple and Microsoft turned to the font format TrueType. Initially

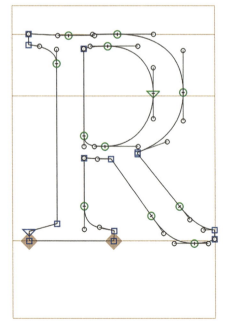

Bézier curve drawing of the *Freya* Medium R – from the Glyphs font software
58 ▼

installed primarily on devices using the Windows operating system – and therefore not in the graphics industry – it soon found acceptance in mixed contexts. Its advantage over PostScript Type 1 was that the same data could be used for monitor displays and printer outputs. In addition, the quality of type display on monitors was significantly better.

The year 2000 saw the release of the first typefaces in a new cross-platform font format, the result of a collaborative effort by Adobe and Microsoft. The OpenType format contains both PostScript fonts (.otf) and TrueType fonts (.ttf). The compatibility of the same font file is therefore guaranteed when using Mac OS and Windows. In addition, compared with the two older formats, the new one offers a glyph set that extends the original 256 code points (2^8) to a current 65,536 code points (2^{16}). *Glyph* refers to all design variants of a character, that is, uppercase, small cap, lowercase, swash letter, and positional (initial, medial, final, isolated) forms; then tabular figure or numeral, lining figure, text or old style figure, fraction, etc. Moreover, OpenType allows for the programmable context-dependent use of glyphs.

The extension of the number of glyphs in the various writing systems allows for – based on the international Unicode standard – the integration of all known linguistic and special characters in the fonts. The Unicode/ISO character set now comprises more than 100,000 glyphs, and a single OpenType font no longer suffices to incorporate all the characters. More decisive here, however, is the fact that the coding of glyphs is standardized. The release of Unicode 2.0 in 1996 expanded the number of code points to more than 1.1 million, divided into 17 levels of 2^{16} code points each to ensure that access can be guaranteed to all glyphs.

However, an OpenType font is not synonymous with the more than 256 glyphs. The existing character inventory has often been transferred unchanged into the new font format. Fonts with the name affixes *Std* and *Com*, unlike those with *Pro,* offer no or only a limited extension of the character set. For font use on websites, the Web Open Font Format (WOFF) has been developed, which, thanks to compression, offers short loading times.

Typeface classification

Typeface classification systems

The aim of every classification is the grouping and arrangement of a large, sometimes confusing array of things according to certain criteria. When it comes to the classification of typefaces, there are, roughly speaking, two different approaches: a formal-historical one and a purely formal one, and both of them include the writing tools.

The task of classifying typefaces always has to address the question of how detailed the differences between categories should be. If there are only a few categories and classifications are correspondingly broad, the number of typefaces within the respective groups will be immense and difficult to comprehend. If there are many categories and therefore more refined distinctions, the clarity within categories will be greater, but there will be more decisions to be made regarding allocation and thus ambiguous cases. Even for specialists, the allocation of some typefaces to only one group is not completely satisfactory. This can in part be explained by the fact that type designers keep a lookout for gaps in the typeface repertoire and design faces that defy clear attribution in that they combine elements from different classification groups. In this context, a distinction can be made between *hybrids* and *fusions*. The letter design of hybrid typefaces, such as the semi serif version of Rotis by OTL AICHER, uses elements taken from different classification groups | 01 |. But, in the case of fusion typefaces, the upper and lowercase letters do not belong to the same classification group. Examples are Kallos and Gilgamesh with Antiqua majuscules and Script minuscules based on the Carolingian or Humanistic minuscule | 02 |. Borders and delimitations can thus also provide ideas for new type designs. And it is innovations of this kind that enrich the array of typefaces – while at the same time raising questions about classification systems. Allocation to groups repeatedly raises the question of the weighting that should be given to the features of a typeface, which – as implied above – can lead to different opinions and to justifiably different classifications.

The type specimen books produced in the decades before and after 1900 are for the most part divided according to type form and kind of application. First to appear are the faces commonly used for book, newspaper, and magazine settings, the so-called text or body typefaces. In type specimen books from the German-language region, serif typefaces are listed after Blackletter faces. These are followed by the jobbing and advertising typefaces from the

---

Hybrid forms:
Grotesque and Script,
Glyphic and Script,
Antiqua and Grotesque

01 ▼

ABCDEG abcdefghik
ABCDEG abcdefghik
ABCDEG abcdefghik

Sassoon Infant | Finnegan | Rotis Semi Serif

Fused forms:
uppercase letters
in Antiqua with lower-
case letters in Script

02 ▼

ABCDEG abcdefghik
ABCDEG abcdefghik

Kallos | Gilgamesh

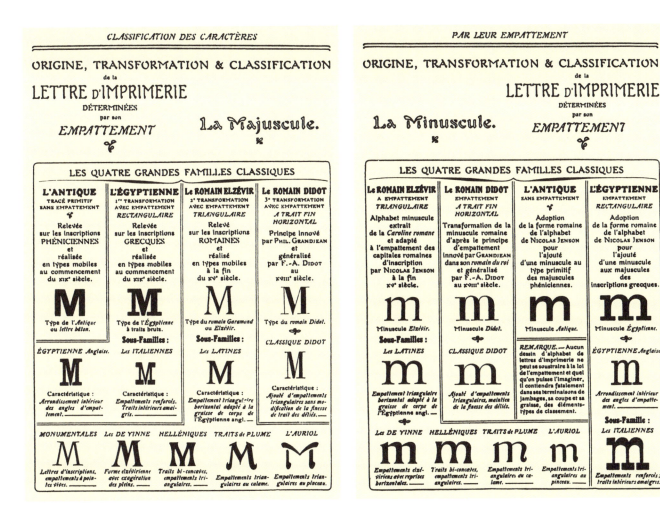

Classification system by Francis Thibaudeau, 1924 – structured according to serif forms

03 ▲|▲▶

Egyptian, Latin, and Grotesque groups, the typefaces of industrialization. Next are Script, correspondence, and business card typefaces, and last up are the poster typefaces. In some cases, cursive font styles have their own registers. However, the number and sequence of the registers as well as the terms used are very diverse.

What is probably the first dedicated classification of typefaces |**03**| is found in the second volume of *La Lettre d'imprimerie* by FRANCIS THIBAUDEAU, published in Paris in 1921.[1] Taking the differences between serif forms as his

Classification system by Maximilien Vox, 1955 – nine groups, four with subdivisions

04 ▶

Classification system by Maximilien Vox, 1963 – nine groups divided into three segments

05 ▶

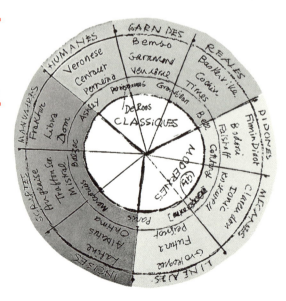

Classification system by Aldo Novarese, 1958 – ten groups with incised faces at the beginning

06 ▼

Lapidari

Medioevali

Veneziani

ATypI 1962	France 1963	Germany 1964 – DIN 16518	Italy 1965	Netherlands 1965	UK | USA 1967 – BS 2961	Spain 1969	Portugal 1969
I	Humanes	Venezianische Renaissance Antiqua	Veneziani	Humanen	Humanist *Venetian*	Humanos	Humanos
II	Garaldes	Französische Renaissance Antiqua	Elzeviri	Garalden	Garalde *Old Style / Old Face*	Garaldos	Garaldos
III	Réales	Barock Antiqua	Transizionali	Realen	Transitional *Transition*	Reales	Reals
IV	Didones	Klassizistische Antiqua	Bodoniani	Didonen	Didone *Modern / Neoclassical*	Didones	Didonis
V	Mécanes	Serifenbetonte Linear A. *Egyptienne*	Egiziani	Mechanen	Slab Serif *Egyptian / Antique*	Mecones	Meconos
VI	Linéales	Serifenlose Linear A. *Grotesk*	Lineari	Linearen	Lineale / Sans Serif *Grotesque / Gothic*	Lineales	Lineals
VII	Incises	Antiqua-Varianten	Lapidari	Incisen	Glyphic	Incisos	Incisos
VIII	Scriptes	Schreibschriften	Scritti	Scripten	Script	Escrituras	Escriturais
IX	Manuaires	Handschriftliche Antiqua	Fantasie	Manuaren	Graphic	Manuales	Manuales
X a		Gotisch (Textur)			Blackletter		
b		Rundgotisch (Rotunda)					
c		Schwabacher					
d		Fraktur					
e		Fraktur-Varianten					

Italics: former designations

Language-specific typeface classifications according to the ATypI standard
07

Transizionali

Bodoniani

Scritti

Ornati

Egiziani

Lineari

Fantasie

Typeface classification by Maximilien Vox, 1963 – nine groups with examples **08** ▼

Humanes
Centaur

Garaldes
Garamond

Réales
Baskerville

Didones
Firmin Didot

Mécanes
Ionic

Linéales
Futura

Incises
Albertus

Scriptes
Mistral

Manuaires
Fraktur

reference point, the author divides typefaces into four groups with subgroups. His two overview tables (in the book *Manuel français de typographie moderne*, published in 1924, they are supplemented by two examples under the heading *Classification des caractères par leur empattement*) established a milestone in the formal analysis of typefaces.[2]

In the 1960s, the typeface classifications formulated by the French typography expert MAXIMILIEN VOX in 1954, 1955 |**04**| and 1963 |**05**|**08**| provided the basis for the establishment – by the Association Typographique Internationale (ATypI) – of both the number of groups and their sequence.[3] The typefaces are organized according to formal features (the design of stroke terminals is a particular feature here), the chronology of the original form design, and, not least, the importance of the respective typefaces at the time. Accordingly, the groups of serif typefaces are found at the beginning of the ATypI classification rather than, as might be expected, the Glyphic (incised) typefaces, which are the origin of uppercase letters (capitals/majuscules), or the script typefaces, which are the origin of our lowercase letters (minuscules), or the group of Blackletter typefaces that were the first to be used by JOHANNES GUTENBERG as text faces.

The typeface classification system published by Italian type designer ALDO NOVARESE in 1958 took a different approach, positioning the *Scritti* (Scripts) in sixth place, the *Lapidari* (Glyphic) at the beginning, and the *Medioevali* (Blackletter) in second place |**06**|.[4] ADRIAN FRUTIGER also positioned the *Manuaires* with Blackletter typefaces at the beginning of his classification system for the Lumitype phototypesetting machine.[5]

The ATypI classification system |**07**| owes its success, on the one hand, to the initiative and preparatory work of MAXIMILIEN VOX and, on the other, to the involvement of well-known figures from the world of typography.[6] Although a range of concepts were formulated both from within and from outside the committee, the classification approach that was selected subsequently established itself in many European countries. However, in spite of this standard, complete uniformity is still lacking. The category names have been adapted to different languages and in some cases even different terms are used. In the German-speaking region, there is yet another aspect: With the DIN 16518 typeface classification system |**07**| a version was formed that deviates significantly in one point from the original idea. Unlike in other countries, group VII does not have a name that establishes a link to (ancient) inscriptions (incised, lapidary, glyphic), but has instead inexplicably been named *Antiqua variants*. This has become a catchall for all typefaces that cannot be, or at least cannot easily be, allocated to another group.[7]

Criticism of the ATypI classification, which is diverse and in part fundamental, is justified. The sequence of groups and their names are often judged to exhibit little historical coherence.[8] The classification of typefaces in accordance with DIN 16518 refers to four epochs, namely Gothic, Renaissance, Baroque, and Neoclassicism. Despite their conspicuous features, later styles such as Art Nouveau are not considered.

However, there is a more significant deficit of quite a different kind that continues to hinder an understanding of the formal connection between the typefaces from the fifteenth to eighteenth centuries (Antiqua) and the typefaces of the nineteenth and twentieth centuries (Egyptian, Grotesque, and Latin). The ATypI classification system distinguishes between *axis* and *stroke contrast* only in the case of serif typefaces (Antiquas), and features four groups based on these features; however, for slab serifs (Egyptians) and sans serifs (Grotesques) this is not the case. This is further proof that the quantity of available typefaces and their importance for typesetting at the time were decisive factors for the formation of the groups.

EUGEN NERDINGER chose a different focus for his detailed analysis of type design and, in his informative *Buchstabenbuch* (Letter book), published in 1955, distinguished between dynamic and static type styles (supplemented by so-called preforms).[9] This allowed for a chronological consideration of typefaces, one that was independent of classification groups.

This distinction based on form and style is presented with great clarity by ERICH SCHULZ-ANKER in his 1969 brochure on the Syntax typeface by the Swiss type designer HANS EDUARD MEIER.[10] The schema depicted here | **09** | and the lettering comparisons | **10** | **11** | vividly illustrate the elementary principles of typefaces. The comparisons make clear the common features as well as the differences, including between Sabon, as the representative of the Renaissance Antiqua, and Syntax. The former is characterized by stroke difference with serifs and a dynamic form principle, the latter by stroke similarity without serifs and likewise a dynamic form principle. Defining these qualities also makes clear their obvious differences from and commonalities with typefaces defined by a static form principle, such as the neoclassical Antiqua Madison and Grotesque Helvetica.

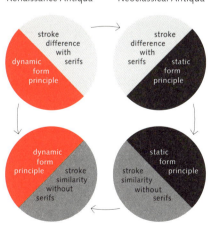

Historical development from the Antiqua of the 16th century to the sans serif of the 20th
09

Renaissance Antiqua — Neoclassical Antiqua

Dynamic Sans serif — Static Grotesque

| **Stroke difference with serifs (top), stroke similarity without serifs (bottom)** | **Comparison of Antiqua and Grotesque – dynamic style (left), static style (right)** |
| 10 ▼ | 11 ▶ |

aes aes
aes aes

Sabon | Syntax   Madison | Helvetica

BCDEGJKMOPRS   BCDEGJKMOPRS
BCDEGJKMOPRS   BCDEGJKMOPRS
abcdefghjkmopstß   abcdefghjkmopstß
abcdefghjkmopstß   abcdefghjkmopstß

Sabon | Syntax   Madison | Helvetica

A more extended form of this approach is found in the work of typography teacher GERRIT NOORDZIJ, whose books *Letterletter* and *The Stroke – Theory of Writing* are informative studies of writing in a visual sense and the typeface forms.[11] Based on his studies of lettering published in 1985, he shows and explains his cube of interpolation. Using 61 (of 125) different versions of lowercase e presented in a spatial arrangement, the author renders visible the variability of flowing transitions between typefaces: in accordance with the weight (from light to black), stroke contrast (from modulated to unmodulated), and principle of curve form, axis, and stress (from dynamic to static) | 12 |. In doing so, he anticipates the principle of multiple master fonts with their different design axes, which were developed only a few years later (→*Multiple master:* p. 141).

Also worth mentioning is the proposal formulated by HANS RUDOLF BOSSHARD in 1980.[12] He reduced the number of groups proposed by the ATypI classification to seven and formed subgroups for each of these groups. For example, sans serif faces are divided into three subgroups: *original Grotesque* (Akzidenz Grotesk), *geometric Grotesque* (Futura), and *sans serif Antiqua* (Gill Sans). Today these groups are referred to as static, geometric, and dynamic Grotesque. He positioned Blackletter faces at the beginning of his classification of Latin typefaces, after making this position available by merging Venetian Renaissance Antiqua and French Renaissance Antiqua into one group with two subgroups. He also combined the groups *Schreibschriften* (Scripts) and *Handschriftliche Antiqua* (script-like typefaces) and dispensed with Antiqua variants.

From the mid-1980s onwards, the design of typefaces on and for personal computers using Fontographer software and, at the end of the same decade, the emergence of digital marketing independent of producers by FontShop

Noordzij cube –
x|y|z-axis: increase,
decrease, straightening
of the axis of contrast

12 ▶

in Berlin led to the development of an extraordinary range of new fonts in a very short time. This led to a renewed questioning of the existing ATypI classification system. But in this case, unlike previous proposals, the result was not a reordering with the possibility of extension but rather a reduction to only six groups: *Serif, Sans, Slab serif, Script, Display,* and *Blackletter*.[13] This facilitated the rapid allocation of typefaces, reduced the number of questionable cases, and made classification simpler for those with less training in the field. However, specialists found that this approach lacked both historical context and an overview of the diversity involved. According to GEORG KURT SCHAUER, GERRIT NOORDZIJ had already developed a system without

Classification system based on form, stroke contrast, and style by Indra Kupferschmid
| 13 | ▼ |

	Serif		Sans serif		Script
	Stroke contrast				
	yes	no	yes	no	
dynamic					
static					
geometric					
fancy/decorative					

Hans Peter Willberg's typeface classification according to form and style
| 14 | ▼ |

Form

Antiqua
Grotesque
Egyptian
Script
𝔉𝔯𝔞𝔨𝔱𝔲𝔯

Style

Dynamic Dynamic
Static Static
Geometric Geometric
Decorative 𝐃𝐄𝐂𝐎𝐑𝐀𝐓𝐈𝐕𝐄

a chronological aspect in 1968 with his groupings based on writing implements.[14] INDRA KUPFERSCHMID took the same approach in 1999.[15] Her matrix organized around *form*, *style,* and *stroke contrast* divides typefaces into columns for serifs and sans serifs – in each case with and without stroke contrast – and scripts |13|. The rows of the matrix are divided into type styles based on their derivation from writing with three different implements (tools): dynamic (broad nib pen, diagonal axis), static (pointed nib pen, vertical axis), and geometric (round nib pen, no stroke contrast). There is also a fourth style, labeled fancy/decorative.

In 2001, HANS PETER WILLBERG presented a classification system that took a related approach |14| but set aside the fundamental aspect of stroke contrast and focused on the formulation of variant groups.[16] He divided typefaces into five groups based on type form: The first group, *Antiqua* (serif), are typefaces based on the formal principles of the fifteenth to eighteenth centuries. The second group, *Grotesque* (sans serif), and also the third group, *Egyptian* (slab serif), are typefaces used for setting from the early nineteenth century onwards. The fourth group, *Script,* comprises faces based on formal scripts and on casual scripts. The fifth group, *Fraktur,* comprises the Blackletter typefaces. Glyphic typefaces do not really play a role in this classification system – they are labeled as variants.

WILLBERG adopted his style subdivisions from KUPFERSCHMID: dynamic, static, geometric, and decorative. The fact that *decorative* should not be defined on the same level as the other type styles becomes understandable when we consider the following: from every type form – whether Glyphic, Script, Antiqua, Egyptian, or Grotesque, etc., whether dynamic or static in terms of type style, whether with round or flat curves, whether with high, distinct, noticeable, or no stroke contrast, whether proportional or monospace in terms of width – decorated variants can be derived: contoured, outlined, inlined, engraved, three-dimensional, shaded, embellished (ornamented), etc. It is only if the matrix has a separate level for *decorated types* that these can be positioned identically. Only in this way can the kinship between basic form and decorated version be made clear |16|17|.

Pro typeface classification

The aim of the Pro typeface classification system is to improve on existing classification systems. Using the four features *type form, attribute, stroke contrast,* and *type style* – and maintaining historical connections – the intention is to facilitate a more precise and comprehensive classification of typefaces.

This concept of typeface classification system draws on both the formal-historical approach of MAXIMILIEN VOX, and thus on the ATypI classification system |07|, as well as the stylistic approach based on the principle of form devised by the artistic director of the D. Stempel AG type foundry in Frankfurt am Main, ERICH SCHULZ-ANKER |09|.[17] Both methods are useful and valuable for an understanding of Latin typefaces; they are consistent and can be combined in a way that leaves in place the historical aspect and detailed categorization of the ATypI classification system. At the same time, subdivisions based on type form, stroke contrast, and type style are afforded an appropriate status, which is particularly helpful when it comes to typeface combinations.

Unlike the ATypI classification system, the new matrix of the Pro typeface classification system |15| begins with the segment in the lower left of the Vox wheel from 1963 |05|, namely incised or glyphic typefaces, the inscriptional lettering form of Roman antiquity. In this sense, it dispenses with the relevance of classification groups to actual typesetting. The number of

The new classification: level subdivision by form, attribute, stroke contrast, and style
15 ▼

Pro typeface classification

Type form	I Glyphic				II Script				III Blackletter				IV Antiqua				V Egyptian				VI Grotesque				VII Latin			
Attribute	*Waisted stroke*		*Flare serif*		*Separated finials*		*Joined finials*		*Round curve*		*Flat curve*		*Round curve*		*Flat curve*		*Round curve*		*Flat curve*		*Round curve*		*Flat curve*		*Round curve*		*Flat curve*	
Stroke contrast	S.d.	S.s.	S.d.	S.s.	S.d.	S.s.	S.d.	S.s.	S.d.	S.s.	S.d.	S.s.	S.d.		S.d.		S.d.	S.s.	S.d.	S.s.	S.d.	S.s.	S.d.	S.s.	S.d.	S.s.	S.d.	S.s.
Type style **dynamic** strongly moderately slightly																												
static																												
geometric																												
eccentric																												

S.d. = Stroke difference   S.s. = Stroke similarity

The four virtual levels of the Pro typeface classification (extended version)
16 ▼

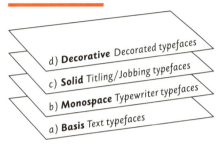

Relating decorated and text faces: a connection between the Decorative and Basis levels
17 ▼

Havonsberg
Havonsberg

Viva | Utopia

groups is reduced through combination, and names are in part changed. At the same time, the Latins, the third relevant group of text faces from the nineteenth century, are now given explicit consideration.

The extension of the ATypI classification system has several aspects:
1. The additional formal division according to *attribute,* including the distinction between *round curve* and *flat curve,* which is the basis of the categorization of technoid-looking types.
2. The systematic and continuous integration of stroke contrast, which is divided into two subgroups: *stroke difference* for typefaces with a noticeable stroke contrast and *stroke similarity* for typefaces with minimal or no stroke contrast (monolinear).
3. The systematic and continuous division of *type style* into *dynamic, static, geometric,* and the new category of *eccentric* for typefaces that partly or wholly deviate from the classical notion of the optical center and the concentric circle. Examples are often seen in Art Nouveau typefaces.
4. The intended positioning of typefaces on several levels | **16** |: text faces on the *Basis* level; monospace (typewriter) faces on the *Monospace* level; titling, display, and jobbing faces as well as fancy faces (graphic typefaces) on the *Solid* level, and decorated faces on the *Decorative* level | **17** |. If it proves appropriate, two levels could be introduced for decorated typefaces, one for text and one for display faces.
Other writing systems for non-Latin languages have not yet been positioned in the matrix, since they often conform to quite different criteria.

The extent to which this roughly sketched concept of levels calls into question the classification system comprehensively presented here remains to be seen. It should be noted that it is quite legitimate not to use all the divisions in the new typeface classification system; the differentiation based on *attribute* could be dispensed with, and the three subgroups relating to dynamic style could be reduced to one group. The actual function of the system should always be kept in mind: to provide a better overview of the available typefaces. It should serve to promote increased knowledge, better description, and thereby a better understanding of the diversity of typefaces and their design; this will ultimately result in better use of type by making the process of finding appropriate alternatives more efficient.

Type form | Class

Type form is generally to be understood as referring to the design, that is, the appearance of a type. In this book, type form serves as a basic criterion for group formation in the typeface classification system.

Categorization based on type form uses seven main classification groups: I: Glyphic, II: Script, III: Blackletter, IV: Antiqua, V: Egyptian, VI: Grotesque, and VII: Latin (for descriptions, see *Classification groups:* →pp. 97–115). The selected sequence is based on historical derivation. It traces an arc from ancient incised lettering and the development of our majuscule forms to written lettering and the development of minuscule forms, to the first printed letters in the Middle Ages and the book typefaces of the modern era, to the type forms of the nineteenth century.

Assignment to form groups, as previously, is based (albeit not exclusively) on one primary, obvious formal feature: *stroke terminals*.

An additional, more refined historical division into subgroups based on *class* is made in the case of Blackletter and Antiqua. In the latter classification group, distinctions are made between Humanism, Renaissance, Baroque, Neoclassicism, and Art Nouveau classes.

Attribute

The additional differentiation of type form based on attributes facilitates a more refined division of typefaces. Depending on the classification group, a different form-specific attribute is conceivable, but a limitation to three features seems sufficient.

Allocation to a subgroup depends on a certain criterion. The following attribute pairs are used; for five of the seven classification groups, the curve form serves as an attribute.

I: Glyphic (→pp. 98/99)
Waisted stroke terminal progressively broadening out of the stroke
Flare serif implied serif or a short end stroke

II: Script (→pp. 100/101)
Separated finials unconnected letterforms
Joined finials (joins) majority of connected letterforms

III–VII: Blackletter, Antiqua, Egyptian, Grotesque, Latin (→pp. 102–115)
Round curve circle, ellipse, oval
Flat curve superellipse, stadium, rounded corner rectangle …

Stroke contrast

Stroke contrast refers to the thickness relationship between the downstroke or main stroke (stem) and the upstroke (hairline). Distinctions are made between typefaces with *stroke difference* (noticeable stroke contrast) and *stroke similarity* (minimal or no stroke contrast).

The appearance of typefaces is fundamentally influenced by stroke contrast. Appropriately, this obvious distinguishing feature is used for all seven classification groups (and not, as hitherto, only for Antiqua). Although in the case of stroke contrast there is a high diversity of differentiation – from high contrast to monolinear – the division into two subgroups facilitates quick allocation. The regular font style serves as a reference.

Type style

The meaning of type style is directly connected with the classification of art historical stylistic movements. The definition of style within the context of type design as secondary to type form has also been around for some time.

There are four groups for dividing text typefaces according to style: dynamic, static, geometric, and eccentric. The determination of style is made with reference to as many as possible of the following distinguishing features: in the case of lowercase, with reference to the axis, counterforms, and instrokes, as well as possible features of movement transferred from writing into the printed letter; in the case of uppercase, with particular reference to the axis and letter proportions.

dynamic   The proportions of H and E are clearly distinguishable, since they are based on the square and the double-storey square. This gives rise to a lively rhythm. The round form is based on a circle. The finial of the lowercase e points to the following letter and appears to open the letter up. Depending on the degree of dynamism, the angle of the axis ranges from strongly diagonal to almost vertical; the counterform ranges from clearly asymmetrical to almost symmetrical; the changes in direction of the inner and outer curves range from clearly to discernibly diagonally offset; and the instroke ranges from strongly rising to almost flat. Sometimes asymmetrical stroke terminals generate a clear movement in the writing and reading direction.

The observer's gaze tends to be directed into the horizontal, giving rise to an impression of progress and providing good to very good reading flow.

static   The proportions of H and E conform to a double-storey rectangle. The former lively rhythm is thereby changed to a more regular beat. The round form tends optically to an ellipse, and the finial of the lowercase e refers back to the vertical, thereby creating a narrow aperture and closing the letter. The changes in direction of the inner and outer curve at the shoulder are almost aligned, and the instroke is almost or completely flat.
The observer's gaze is directed into the vertical, which creates an impression of stagnancy and minimizes reading flow. In the case of typefaces with a static style, larger leading (line spacing) is essential.

geometric   The proportions of H and E can tend to extremes because they are usually based on the square and on the half-width double-storey square. As a result, the rhythm of the typeface is very lively. The round form comes very close to a circle, and the finial of the lowercase e suggests this formation. The axis, insofar as it is discernible at all, is vertical, the counterform is often (but not necessarily) symmetrical, the changes in direction of the inner and outer curve are almost aligned, and the instroke is almost always flat.
Now and again, the observer's gaze gets caught in the counter of the wide curvatures, which can bring reading flow to a halt. In the case of typefaces with a geometric style, larger leading (line spacing) is necessary.

eccentric   The middle strokes of H and E are deliberately offset from the optical center: upwards or sometimes downwards. The round form sometimes takes on an oval shape. The stroke and curve forms can range from austere to organic and floral.
The observer's gaze tends to be drawn to particular individual forms, which can make for somewhat agitated, halting reading flow.

Classification groups
Descriptions / tables

On the following pages, the typeface classification groups are discussed and presented in detail in terms of their definition based on *type form* and with reference to the additional distinguishing features *attribute, stroke contrast,* and *type style.*
The four features, type form, attribute, stroke contrast and type style, along with other important criteria, are decisive for the quality of typeface combinations. Further explanation of this mechanism can be found in the following two chapters.

I
Glyphic

Type form
· **Glyphic**

Attribute
· **Waisted stroke**
· **Flare serif**
  End stroke

Stroke contrast
· **Stroke difference**
· **Stroke similarity**

Type style
· **dynamic**
· static
· geometric
· eccentric

HAVONSBERG
Waisted stroke: Rusticana

HAVONSBERG
Flare serif: Elan

HAVONSBERG
HAVONSBERG
Serif: Trajan | Arrus

HAVONSBERG
HAVONSBERG
End stroke: Sophia | Copperplate Gothic

Glyphic typefaces are derived from inscriptions on stone and metal. The letter design and proportions often exhibit a reference to ancient Roman inscriptions with their basic shapes and narrow double-storey shapes. The terminals of these typefaces are slightly broadened.

MAXIMILIAN VOX's arrangement of typeface categories in a wheel or circle is a particularly interesting approach | **05** |. His model indicates that there is a causal link between all forms of Latin typefaces and that all type forms refer to each other. The ongoing development of designs has seen a modification of forms from different epochs and not exclusively forms from the respectively preceding period. An awareness of this is helpful for an understanding of this typeface classification system. If Vox's classification wheel is read clockwise from dark to light, the Glyphic typefaces become the first classification group, which corresponds to the historically correct sequence. Glyphic typefaces represent the beginning of the development of the Roman alphabet. But they also represent a provisional conclusion of the definition of the majuscule letterforms. For this reason, the corresponding typesetting faces often do not contain a minuscule character set.

The original tool used to carve or engrave lettering was a stylus, which typically produced linear strokes, in part with tapering at the stroke and curve terminals. Later, between the third and first centuries BCE, the strokes of *Roman lapidary* (from the Latin *lapis,* meaning stone) underwent a process of waisting or in other words tapering/broadening or narrowing/widening (waisted stroke), resulting in the advent of expanded stroke and curve terminals (flare serif).[18]

Ancient Roman inscriptions reached their high point in the first century CE with the *Capitalis monumentalis* (→p. 59 | **06** |). In contrast to the Roman lapidary, the lettering was painted with a flat brush and then carved out with a hammer and chisel. Due to the writing implement used, the incised lettering is clearly distinct from older forms in terms of axis and stroke contrast. In addition, the terminals feature short, fine serifs. The most well-known adaptation of this face – due to its omnipresence on Hollywood posters – is Trajan (1989) by CAROL TWOMBLY. There is nothing here that points to the original creative process, although this is somewhat more the case with Arrus (1991) by RICHARD LIPTON, and decidedly so with Stevens Titling by RYUICHI TATENO and JOHN STEVENS, who use elements of calligraphic brushwork, and with Castellar by JOHN PETERS, with its reference to engraving.

Havonsberg
Havonsberg
Waisted stroke: Optima | Mentor

Havonsberg
Havonsberg
Havonsberg
Waisted stroke: Stellar | Skia | Formata

Havonsberg
Havonsberg
Flare serif: Tiepolo | Albertus

Havonsberg
Havonsberg
Flare serif: Laudatio | Friz Quadrata

Havonsberg
Havonsberg
Flare serif: Goudy Sans | Memo

The categorization of Glyphic typefaces is based on the attribute of *waisted stroke* with and without stroke contrast. Optima (1958) by Hermann Zapf and Mentor (2005) by Michael Harvey are distinguished by stroke difference, although there are also differences in type style between static and slightly dynamic. Formata (1989) by Bernd Möllenstädt tends towards the category of stroke similarity. Stellar (1929) by Robert Hunter Middleton and Skia (1993) by Matthew Carter, whose capitals refer to early ancient forms, can also be classed in terms of stroke similarity.

In contrast to waisted stroke with successive increases, *flared serif* has to do with clearly definable widenings of stroke terminals. Whether the terminal transition is bracketed or unbracketed plays no role here. Stroke difference is evident in Albertus (1932) by Berthold Wolpe and Tiepolo (1987) by Arthur Baker. Friz Quadrata (1978) by Ernst Friz and Laudatio (1982) by Friedrich Poppl exhibit a low level of stroke contrast and tend to stroke similarity. This category also includes Goudy Sans (1925) by Frederic William Goudy, and Elan (1985) and Memo (1998) by Albert Boton.

Copperplate Gothic (1901) by Frederic William Goudy features *end strokes,* terminals whose origins are found in the inscriptions of Roman antiquity. What is unusual here is that the widenings sometimes end at right angles not only to vertical and horizontal lines but also to diagonal strokes and curves. Such approaches can be seen, for example, in Adrian Frutiger's Rusticana, which is derived from ancient models. Although this is a typeface with waisted strokes, this kind of Roman lapidary also received flared serifs or end strokes in the process of further development. One example of this is Sophia by Matthew Carter.

Glyphic typefaces can be divided into the following attribute subgroups:
a) typefaces with *waisted stroke,* which usually exhibit a gradual tapering of the stem and a progressively broadening stroke and curve terminals;
b) typefaces with *flared serif* or short *end stroke,* in which the change from the stem – often not waisted – to the expanded stroke terminal is easily discernible (table →pp. 116/117).

A shared feature of Glyphic type form is their minimally broadened or flared stroke and curve terminals. This feature distinguishes Glyphic typefaces from both Antiqua and Grotesque typefaces.

II
Script

Type form
· **Script**

Attribute
· **Separated finials**
· **Joined finials (Joins)**

Stroke contrast
· **Stroke difference**
· **Stroke similarity**

Type style
· **dynamic**
· **static**
· **geometric**
· **eccentric**

HAVONSBERG
Roman majuscule cursive: Herculanum

HAVONSBERG
Capitalis rustica: Pompeijana

Havonsberg
Uncial: Neue Hammer Unziale

Havonsberg
Carolingian minuscule: Carolina

Havonsberg
Latin German Gothic script: Codex

Havonsberg
Humanistic minuscule: Sanvito

The lettering of antiquity also included scripts, which were scratched into beeswax with a stylus, or written with a flat brush or reed pen (calamus) on papyrus and parchment. The use of other tools – broad, pointed, and round nib pen, felt-tip pen, etc. – over subsequent centuries greatly influenced the form of such typefaces.

While Glyphic lettering engraved in stone and metal was meant for 'eternity' – which is expressed in the clarity of the letterforms – the scrolls and codices on papyrus and parchment and their scripts were meant at least for 'preservation'. A more transient form was fleeting handwriting whose primary purpose was not readability. Such writing was done on unfired clay and wooden panels coated with beeswax. The surfaces could be smoothed by dampening or warming them and then reused. However, it is mainly the other forms that inspired typefaces.

The Scripts can be divided into at least two general groups: carefully written book hand such as *Roman uncial, Roman half-uncial, Carolingian minuscule,* and *Humanistic minuscule;* and the more quickly written cursive and running hand. MAXIMILIEN VOX divided them into the groups 'Manuaires' and 'Scriptes'. The latter were used for notes, comments, and correspondence, and as official scripts. Handwritten letterforms were developed on the one hand as Scripts into text faces – derived, for example, from *Cancellaresca,* the official Italian script of the fifteenth century, and on the other hand as Antiquas into italics, which refer back to *Humanistic cursive* with its origins in the fifteenth century. From this time on, the broad nib pen faced competition from the pointed nib pen, which allowed for the highly contrastive strokes that became so typical of English formal metal engraving scripts in the eighteenth century. The twentieth century also produced casual scripts, which communicate spontaneity and individuality, although the imitation of writing actually contradicts the idea of set type.

In 1989, ADRIAN FRUTIGER devised the project 'Type before Gutenberg' for Linotype, the aim of which was to transport the early forms of Latin lettering into the digital age. He himself drew four typefaces, three of which are based on ancient scripts: Herculanum, Frutiger Capitalis, and Pompeijana. Script faces based on models from late antiquity such as Hammer Unziale (1955) by VICTOR HAMMER, from the Carolingian period such as Carolina (1990) by GOTTFRIED POTT, and from the Middle Ages such as Codex (1954) by GEORG TRUMP, either

Havonsberg
Havonsberg
Dynamic style: Lucida Calligraphy | Zapfino

Havonsberg
Havonsberg
Static style: Snell Roundhand | Bickham Script

Havonsberg
Havonsberg
Havonsberg
Separated finials: Pepita | Jaguar | Sunetta

Havonsberg
Havonsberg
Joined finials (joins): Mistral | Magneton

Havonsberg
Havonsberg
Havonsberg
Positional forms and alternates: Abelina

are part of the project or would fit with the concept. A script such as Sanvito (1993) by Robert Slimbach, the roots of which lie in humanism, would therefore be positioned in temporal proximity to Gutenberg.

Many typefaces belong to the two categories of *formal scripts:* broad nib pen scripts, which derive from Cancellaresca and have an affinity with Antiqua in a dynamic type style and which include Lucida Calligraphy (1991) by Charles Bigelow and Kris Holmes, and Zapfino (1998) by Hermann Zapf; and pointed nib pen scripts such as Snell Roundhand (1966) by Matthew Carter and Bickham Script by Richard Lipton, which can be combined with Antiqua in a static style.

Strongly contrasting with these are the ostensibly spontaneously dynamic brush scripts, referred to as *casual scripts,* which aspire to a more individual expression: Mistral (1953) and Choc (1955) by Roger Excoffon, Pepita (1959) by Imre Reiner, Time Script (1956) and Jaguar (1964) by Georg Trump, and Sunetta (2005) by Werner Schneider.

Script typefaces such as Zapfino, Abelina (2014) by Guille Vizzari and Yani Arabena, and Magneton (2017) by Mika Melvas have more of a handwritten character in that they offer alternative uppercase and lowercase letterforms. The font format OpenType allows for the definition of variants (alternates) and positional forms – such as initial, medial, final, and isolated forms – as well as the generation of stylistic sets. This allows for an automatic combination- and position-dependent exchange, reflecting the fact that, in writing, differences emerge in design and connections depending on the letter combination and position within a word. In Scripts with joins, many connections have to be standardized and defined extremely precisely, so that the letters can be coherently combined.

Script typefaces can be divided into the following attribute subgroups:
a) typefaces with *separated finials,* that is, the letterforms are not connected;
b) typefaces with *joined finials,* that is, for the most part the lowercase letters exhibit connections (table →pp. 118/119).

A shared feature of Script typefaces are the forms that are derived from handwriting or that recall writing by hand. The slanted Script form can be an expression of this but certainly does not have to be.

III
Blackletter

Type form
· Blackletter

Class
· **Rotunda**
· **Textura**
· **Schwabacher**
· **Fraktur**
· **Art Nouveau-Blackletter**
· **Simplified textura**

Attribute
· **Round curve**
· **Flat curve**

Stroke contrast
· **Stroke difference**
· **Stroke similarity**

Type style
· **dynamic**
· **static**
· **geometric**
· **eccentric**

Blackletter typefaces are based on handwritten manuscripts from the Gothic and early Renaissance periods. Unlike the scripts of late antiquity, the curve forms of the minuscules are no longer round but feature angles known as breaks. The design of the majuscules, which is related to the minuscule form, can be traced back to the Uncials.

During the Middle Ages, lettering changed in a way analogous to the development of architecture in the Gothic period, when, starting in France, the Romanesque rounded arch was replaced by the Gothic pointed arch. In Italy, *Rotunda,* with its less broken curves, became the most important form of lettering used in handwritten books and manuscripts and in printed matter for several centuries. North of the Alps, this class was also enthusiastically used. Here, however, handwritten Bible texts took on another starkly angled, compressed, and dark form. The text appearance was similar to woven textile, hence the name *Textura,* also known as *Textualis.* In his design of the B42-Type around 1450, JOHANNES GUTENBERG appropriated on such a model to cast the metal alloy characters with which he typeset his printed version of the Bible (→p. 62 | **16** |). The advantage of typesetting with cast individual letters as opposed to handwritten books and text pages carved into wooden panels was obvious: following printing, the characters could be set aside in a letter case and used for further typesetting. The new process was an immediate success, and over more than 500 years it provided access to knowledge for broad sections of the population in almost unchanged form.

Blackletter, with its broken curves and sharp angles, was further developed in Germany during the sixteenth century in parallel to round form typefaces and now became an independent branch of type history. The Blackletter classes *Schwabacher* and *Fraktur* provided two additional book faces, although it was the second that became dominant for setting text. Interestingly, neither of them featured slanted font styles (individual exceptions only emerged later), and as a result Schwabacher was used for emphasis in texts set in Fraktur.

Whereas the use of Blackletter was already declining in the fifteenth century in the Latinate language area *(Gotico-Antiqua),* Fraktur remained a dominant feature of German printed matter for centuries. In this language region, the two typeface genres were to some extent combined – Antiqua was used for words with Latin roots in texts set in Fraktur (→p. 23 | **09** |) – though the relationship between the two genres was more one of coexistence. Until well

Havonsberg
Rotunda: San Marco

Havonsberg
Textura / Textualis: Caslon Gotisch

Havonsberg
Schwabacher: Alte Schwabacher

Havonsberg
Fraktur: Luthersche Fraktur

Havonsberg
Art Nouveau-Blackletter: Eckmann

Havonsberg
Simplified Textura: Kursachsen (Blackhaus)

into the twentieth century, Fraktur maintained a status that was at least equal to that of Antiqua. From 1925 onwards, *Simplified textura,* a class of modernized Blackletter typefaces in elementary form similar to Grotesque, actually breathed new life into the typeface genre. It was a decree issued by the Nazi government in 1941 that brought an end to the widespread use of Blackletter.[19] Although it was some time before it finally disappeared as a text typeface, Blackletter remained stigmatized for decades.

Blackletter is still used today for the nameplates of tradition-conscious newspapers such as *The New York Times* and *The Washington Post* in the USA, *The Telegraph* in England, *Le Monde* in France, *Frankfurter Allgemeine Zeitung* in Germany, and *Neue Zürcher Zeitung* in Switzerland. With its down-to-earth character, Blackletter is also still used for word marks (for example, schnapps and beer) and – albeit less and less often – for lettering on buildings (in the case of 'Gasthof' [hotel], the round s is increasingly used in place of the f-like long s). Heavy metal bands, on the other hand, employ Blackletter as a tool of provocation. And the tattoos of star footballers? In the act of theatricalization, are they an expression of toughness, or are they simply decorative?

Blackletter typefaces can be divided into the following attribute subgroups:
a) typefaces with *round curves:* there are fewer pronounced breaks in the curve, and the round form is also clearly visible in the lowercase letters;
b) typefaces with *flat curves:* the breaking of the curve is very pronounced, and the curvatures can be replaced with straight lines (table →pp. 120/121).

A shared feature of Blackletter faces is the broken (angular) curve form, at least in the lowercase letters. The breaks can be positioned on the inner or outer curve form. Depending on the class of Blackletter, there are obvious differences in the instroke of the ascender (lowercase b) and in the number and design of breaks (lowercase o):
Rotunda – b: horizontal / o: angular to the above left and lower right,
Textura/Textualis – b: forked or diagonal / o: completely angular,
Schwabacher – b: pent-roof form / o: converging to point above and below,
Fraktur – b: forked / o: left side angular, right side rounded,
Art Nouveau-Blackletter – b: diverse, pent-roof form / o: hardly angular, oval,
Simplified textura – b: diagonal / o: interior rhomboid or right-angled.

IV
Antiqua

Type form
· **Antiqua**

Class
· **Humanism**
· **Renaissance**
· **Baroque**
· **Neoclassicism**
· **Art Nouveau**

Attribute
· **Round curve**
· **Flat curve**

Stroke contrast
· **Stroke difference**
   noticeable
   distinct
   high

Type style
· **dynamic**
   strongly
   moderately
   slightly
· **static**
· **eccentric**

The development of Antiqua began with the return to the round letterform. Three and a half centuries of constant stylistic change followed. Due to its legibility – in which serifs play an essential role – it has maintained its currency and quality as a book type.

In the middle of the fifteenth century, alternatives to Blackletter *Rotunda* began to emerge in Italy, at first tentatively with *Gothico-Antiqua*, a transitional face with angular and round forms, and then more comprehensively and rapidly with the development of *Antiqua*. The lowercase form of the upright *roman* font style was influenced by the carefully written *Humanistic minuscule* of the fifteenth century. However, the systematic attachment of serifs in the case of both alphabets was a feature of printing typefaces. This aspect is connected with *Capitalis monumentalis* and thus with antiquity, hence the name Antiqua.[20] The model for the slanted *italic* font style is the more quickly written *Humanistic cursive*.

In the ensuing epochs, Antiqua changed from a dynamic type style with diagonal stress axes and noticeable stroke contrast into a static type style with a vertical stress axis and high stroke contrast. In addition, there was a discernible change in proportions of the uppercase letters from the rhythm of the square/double-storey square of H/E to that of the adjusted rectangle. Under the influence of Art Nouveau at the end of the nineteenth century, the letters H/E and in part O etc. underwent a shift upwards or downwards from the optical center. This led to fundamental changes in the typeface character. Such deviations from the formal canon of antiquity are classed under the newly introduced eccentric type style.

Antiqua typefaces can be divided into the following attribute subgroups:
a) typefaces with *round curves:* in the case of a dynamic style, they are based on the form of a circle; in the case of a static style, the inner form, at least, changes to an ellipse;
b) typefaces with *flat curves:* at least along the vertical axes the curvatures are flatter, resulting in a flat ellipse or superellipse – described as squircle (table →pp. 122/123).

A shared feature of Antiqua typefaces are stroke terminals with clearly discernible serifs (in the roman font style) in a rather blunt and flat design, a tendency for round curve forms, and clear stroke contrasts.

Havonsberg
Havonsberg
Havonsberg
Adobe Jenson | Legacy Serif | Calluna

Antiqua – *strongly dynamic type style* (Humanism class)

Elements of writing with a broad nib pen and a strongly diagonal axis are easily discernible, including on the usually diagonal bar of the lowercase e, which is sometimes extended in a spur beyond the curve form. The typeface employed by the Frenchman NICOLAS JENSON in Venice in 1470 for the book *De evangelica praeparatione* by EUSEBIUS is regarded as an archetype of the Humanism class. His letterforms makes for a nicely consistent text appearance (→p.63 | **18** |). This applies particularly to the lowercase, whereas, from a contemporary point of view, the uppercase appear too dominant due to their size. However, the use of uppercase in Latin texts is restrained, with capitals used only for initial words, sentence beginnings, and proper nouns. Some 420 years later, the emergence of the Arts and Crafts movement around WILLIAM MORRIS and his Kelmscott Press ushered in an era of typographic revival, reinterpretation, and recuts of earlier typefaces. It is due to the initiative of MORRIS and his colleagues that type designers rediscovered the value of the Jenson typeface and that type families such as Centaur, Legacy Serif, and Calluna are being produced to this day.

Iomeb HOVE

Characteristics *serif* [I]: adnate (bracketed) or abrupt (unbracketed) *base* [I]: cupped (slightly concave) or flat *direction* [m]: mostly asymmetrical *stem* [I]: waisted or parallel *axis/stress* [o]: strongly diagonal *instroke* [m]: steeply rising *juncture* [m]: tendency to be angular *shoulder* [m]: extreme points strongly offset *bar* [e]: often diagonal *curve direction/aperture* [e]: opening *counter* [b]: asymmetrical *proportions* [HE]: usually very different *center position* [HE]: optical *stroke contrast* [V]: noticeable

Antiqua – *moderately dynamic type style* (Renaissance class)

From the sixteenth century onwards, Antiqua successively took on a form distinct from written lettering, and an increasing number of forms developed that were defined by the actual cutting of typefaces. In 1495 the punch cutter FRANCESCO GRIFFO designed a typeface for *De Aetna* – a book written by Cardinal PIETRO BEMBO and published by ALDUS MANUTIUS in Venice – that is generally regarded as a precursor of the drawn Antiqua. However, its slightly inwardly curved right-hand downward stroke in the lowercase m and the n and its asymmetrical serifs still refer to handwriting. Unlike the written form, the bar of the lowercase e appears almost horizontal. Another

Havonsberg
Havonsberg
Havonsberg
Bembo | Garamond – Adobe | Simoncini

Havonsberg
Havonsberg
Havonsberg
Lexicon | Dolly | Freya

difference from Jenson is that the capitals are proportionally narrower and somewhat shortened in relation to the ascender, which visibly improves their integration into the text appearance – an aspect that is particularly important for German text, where many words begin with a capital letter.

Iomeb HOVE

Characteristics *serif* [I]: adnate (bracketed) or abrupt (unbracketed) *base* [I]: cupped (slightly concave) or flat *direction* [m]: symmetrical *stem* [I]: waisted or parallel *axis/stress* [o]: moderately diagonal *instroke* [m]: rising *juncture* [m]: angular or rounded *shoulder* [m]: extreme points strongly offset *bar* [e]: horizontal *curve direction/aperture* [e]: opening *counter* [b]: asymmetrical *proportions* [HE]: usually very different *center position* [HE]: optical *stroke contrast* [V]: noticeable

The further development of Antiqua was led by France. By the 1530s typefaces were being developed there with narrower proportions and symmetrical serifs. Today these typefaces are mostly associated with the name GARAMONT. Following its revival in the 1920s, the tranquil text appearance produced by this class predestined it for book settings. Even more replicas and reinterpretations were produced on the basis of the newer design than on the basis of its predecessor: Bembo, Aldus, and Dante were inspired by ALDUS MANUTIUS; Stempel Garamond, Sabon, and Adobe Garamond (among others) were inspired by CLAUDE GARAMONT (whose form is regarded as an archetype). However, GARAMONT's name is applied too loosely in the case of some typefaces, for example Simoncini Garamond, which like other falsely named versions draws on the typeface created by JEAN JANNON in the seventeenth century – which is in turn easy to spot due to the somewhat hanging bowl of the lowercase a. Newer typefaces include Minion, Arno, Lexicon, Dolly, and Freya, whose text appearance is usually robust enough for today's smaller text sizes.

Antiqua – slightly dynamic type style (Baroque class)
From the mid-seventeenth century onwards, foundry typefaces were increasingly influenced by copperplate engraving. This is evident in the finer hairlines and the associated increasing stroke contrast (along with only slightly diagonal axes). Since in intaglio printing the letterform is engraved, fine strokes do not present any problems; on the contrary, they are an inherent part of the process. The situation was different with relief printing and thus with cutting the steel punches for typesetting. In this case, fine strokes were

Havonsberg
Havonsberg
Van Dijck | Adobe Caslon

Havonsberg
Havonsberg
Havonsberg
Baskerville | Bell | Wilke

Havonsberg
Times New Roman

a significant challenge since, like a ridge, they remained in place and the surroundings were removed.

Well-known typefaces of this class bear the names of CHRISTOFFEL VAN DIJCK and JOHANN MICHAEL FLEISCHMANN. Also worthy of mention is Romain du Roi by PHILIPPE GRANDJEAN, which is based on a grid structure. The center of development lay in the Netherlands and, in the eighteenth century, extended to England. There, WILLIAM CASLON the Elder established a foundry dynasty that was to last for over 200 years. Other outstanding typefaces in this class include those of JOHN BASKERVILLE and RICHARD AUSTIN, the latter of whom cut Bell for the JOHN BELL type foundry.

The book typography set in the original Caslon by the Chiswick Press around the mid-nineteenth century spurred the already mentioned return to earlier type designs among foundries. In the twentieth century, a particular status is occupied by Times New Roman, which was designed at Monotype Corporation by STANLEY MORISON and VICTOR LARDENT. Its quality in narrow columns is a standard for typefaces used in newspaper and magazine settings.

Baskerville is often presented as a Transitional or Baroque class archetype. In this context it is represented by the later Bell, which has a closer relationship to the transition from the dynamic to the static type style of the Neoclassicism class. More recent digital fonts, which can deviate from the standard classification features, include Wilke, Mrs Eaves, Utopia, Arnhem, and Freight.

Iomeb HOVE

Characteristics *serif* [I]: adnate (bracketed) or abrupt (unbracketed) *base* [I]: cupped (slightly concave) or flat *direction* [m]: symmetrical *stem* [I]: waisted or parallel *axis/stress* [o]: slightly diagonal (almost vertical) *instroke* [m]: slightly rising *juncture* [m]: rounded or angular *shoulder* [m]: extreme points slightly offset *bar* [e]: horizontal *curve direction/aperture* [e]: opening or nearly closing *counter* [b]: hardly asymmetrical *proportions* [HE]: hardly different *center position* [HE]: optical *stroke contrast* [V]: distinct

Antiqua – static style (Neoclassicism class)

The development of Antiqua came to a provisional end at the beginning of the nineteenth century. The names of the type designers involved are well-known: GIAMBATTISTA BODONI in Italy, FRANÇOIS AMBROISE DIDOT and FIRMIN DIDOT in France, WILLIAM BULMER in England, JUSTUS E. WALBAUM in Germany. On the one hand, this development seems in retrospect to have

Havonsberg
Havonsberg
Havonsberg
Bulmer | ITC Bodoni Twelve | Walbaum

Havonsberg
Havonsberg
Havonsberg
HTF Didot — L64 | L16 | L06

Havonsberg
Havonsberg
Tiemann | New Caledonia

Havonsberg
Iridium

Havonsberg
Havonsberg
Havonsberg
Photina | Basilia | Media

been continuous; on the other, the development of the Neoclassicism class should be understood as a paradigm shift – from a dynamic to a static style. The proportions of the letters were adjusted and the axis became completely vertical. The latter further increased the stroke contrast, which was taken to the limit in the case of title faces, which appear very elegant when printed on coated paper. Since Didot by FIRMIN DIDOT best illustrates the change from dynamic to static, it is shown here as the archetype of the Neoclassicism class.

Iomeb HOVE

Characteristics *serif* [I]: abrupt (unbracketed) or minimally adnate (bracketed) *base* [I]: tendency to be flat *direction* [m]: symmetrical *stem* [I]: parallel, rarely waisted *axis/stress* [o]: vertical *instroke* [m]: tendency to be flat *juncture* [m]: rounded *shoulder* [m]: extreme points nearly aligned *bar* [e]: horizontal *curve direction/aperture* [e]: closing *counter* [b]: symmetrical *proportions* [HE]: adjusted *center position* [HE]: optical *stroke contrast* [V]: high to extreme

The body text faces produced in the nineteenth century were extremely thin and therefore difficult to read, which towards the end of the century, as mentioned above, led to the revival of older typefaces. Those that proved their worth were subsequently reintegrated into the twentieth-century typeface canon. In addition, the many and diverse type foundries produced numerous redrawn versions (which explains the large number and formal diversity of, among others, Bodoni and Didot), reinterpretations such as the somewhat gentler Tiemann-Antiqua and Caledonia, and, later in phototypesetting, the waisted Iridium as well as Photina, Basilia, and Media.

Difficulties emerged in the 1950s with phototypesetting, and they have continued with digital setting in the present. The typefaces are scalable from one master template, which particularly decreases the quality of neoclassical faces due to their hairlines. These faces appear elegant in display sizes, when the hairlines are very fine, and are only pleasant to read when the hairlines are thick enough in the text sizes. For this reason, the foundry typefaces exhibit a different design in each of the different point sizes. In the phototypesetting version, companies sometimes still offered two or three design sizes. For digital setting, only one version is usually produced for continuous variable scaling from very small to extremely large. However, there are also faces such as HTF Didot and Monotype Walbaum that offer several optical sizes.

Havonsberg
Havonsberg
Marconi | Zapf Book

Havonsberg
Havonsberg
Havonsberg
Kennerley Old Style | Horley Old S. | Edwardian

An innovation that spread over the course of the twentieth century – and is therefore included in the new typeface classification system as an Antiqua attribute – is the change of the curve form from round to flat. A tendency in this direction is already evident around 1800 in the case of Prillwitz and Walbaum. It is notable that many typefaces with this feature were created in Germany. It is therefore not unreasonable to surmise that – along with other aspects – the curve form of Fraktur may have played a role here. From 1950 onwards, HERMANN ZAPF designed several Antiqua typefaces in a static style with flat curves, including Marconi and Zapf Book.

Antiqua – eccentric type style *(Art Nouveau class)*
The emergence of Art Nouveau at the end of the nineteenth century also brought about a stylistic change in type design. Faces in the eccentric type style – which were created primarily between the 1890s and 1920s and then again in the 1970s and 1980s – deviated from the hitherto customary order and rigor in terms of structure and, in part, formal design. Such deviation can involve the introduction of flourishes, elements that create a floral effect, such as curved strokes. Much more fundamental, however, is the renunciation of geometric symmetry. This is particularly clear in the upper-case H and E and also evident in other uppercase letters. The middle stroke is offset from the optical center upwards or, in a lesser number of cases, downwards. In some instances the bowl form changes from a symmetrical to an asymmetrical oval shape. The curves of letters do not systematically feature the same stress axis, which in some cases is diagonal, in others vertical/horizontal.

Representative of the Antiqua faces in the eccentric style are Kennerley Old Style (1911) by FREDERIC WILLIAM GOUDY, Horley Old Style (1925), which is similar and shown here, and Edwardian (1983).

Characteristics *serif* [I]: adnate (bracketed) or abrupt (unbracketed) *base* [I]: cupped (slightly concave) or flat *direction* [m]: tendency to be symmetrical *stem* [I]: parallel or waisted *axis/stress* [o]: diagonal, vertical or inconsistent *instroke* [m]: rising or flat *juncture* [m]: angular or rounded *shoulder* [m]: extreme points offset or nearly aligned *bar* [e]: diagonal or horizontal *curve direction/ aperture* [e]: tendency to be opening *counter* [b]: tendency to be asymmetrical *proportions* [HE]: adjusted *center position* [HE]: offset up or down *stroke contrast* [V]: tendency to be noticeable

V
Egyptian

Type form
- **Egyptian**

Attribute
- **Round curve**
- **Flat curve**

Stroke contrast
- **Stroke difference**
- **Stroke similarity**

Type style
- **dynamic**
- static
- geometric
- eccentric

Havonsberg
Havonsberg
Dynamic style: Joanna | Chaparral

Havonsberg
Havonsberg
Dynamic style: Lucida Fax | LinoLetter

Havonsberg
Havonsberg
Dynamic style: Caecilia | Oranda

Havonsberg
Dynamic style – flat curve: Raleigh

Industrialization created a need for new and different typefaces such as Egyptian, with its slab serifs. Its primary task was not to be pleasant to read or aesthetically pleasing, but above all to stand out.

One of the reasons for these new designs was that the industrial production of goods – which in Great Britain was already starting in the mid-eighteenth century – reversed the customary sequence of demand and manufacture. Now the manufacture of goods was for stock rather than a response to the demand of the individual customer. Thus, the interest of potential customers in stockpiled goods needed to be awakened. Another reason was that direct contact with the customer base was lost when production was moved from workshops in town centers to factories on the periphery. The new era therefore required advertising typefaces – for posters, pamphlets, packaging, and newspaper ads. The wealth of creative ideas to meet this need seems to have been unlimited. No idea was too bizarre, no effort too great – as shown by the extraordinary compilation presented by Nicolete Gray in her standard work *Nineteenth Century Ornamented Typefaces*.[21]

Along with fat face neoclassical Antiqua, including italic and ornamented font styles, three new groups of type forms were created in the nineteenth century: Egyptian with its slab serifs, Grotesque without serifs, and Latin with its pointed or wedge-shaped serifs. Just as interesting as the differences in the stroke and curve terminals are the common features. All three groups include typefaces with very obvious *stroke contrast* (stroke difference) and optically identical stroke thickness (stroke similarity). Moreover, they all also contain typefaces whose *type style* can be categorized as dynamic, static, geometric, or eccentric. And in all three cases differentiation based on the attributes, round curve and flat curve, helps to further define more detailed subgroups.

British foundries were at the forefront of this development, creating a large number of innovations. For example, in 1815 Vincent Figgins produced a type specimen, in which he showed a typeface dubbed 'Egyptian'. This name had no relation to the scripts of Egypt such as hieroglyphs. The name derives wholly from the spirit of the times, recalling the French frigate *Égyptienne*, which had the Rosetta Stone on board (→p. 13 | **01** |) when it was seized by the English and taken to Woolwich, London, in 1802.[22]

The style of early slab serif typefaces can be geometric, with a reduced stroke contrast and unbracketed transitions to the serifs – related faces include the

Havonsberg
Havonsberg
Havonsberg
Static style: Ionic | Clarendon | Egyptienne F

Havonsberg
Havonsberg
Static style: Venus Egyptienne | Serifa

Havonsberg
Static style – flat curve: Melior

Havonsberg
Havonsberg
Havonsberg
Geometric style: Rockwell | Memphis | Stymie

Havonsberg
Geometric style – flat curve: Cholla Slab

Havonsberg
Havonsberg
Eccentric style: Bramley | Belwe Mono

Havonsberg
Monospace: Courier

bold font style of Memphis (1929) by Rudolf Wolf and Stymie (1931) by Morris Fuller Benton; or the style can be static, with a noticeable stroke contrast and bracketed serif transitions, as in the case of the British typefaces Ionic (1844) and Clarendon (1848), which formed the basis for a number of newspaper typefaces. The far more well-known Clarendon designed by Hermann Eidenbenz and published by the Haas Type Foundry in Münchenstein, near Basel, in 1953 deviates considerably from the original. An early version developed prior to 1950 is Venus Egyptienne, which features a static style with little stroke contrast and was followed in 1967 by Adrian Frutiger's Serifa.

Slab serif typefaces in a dynamic style first appeared in the twentieth century. They include Joanna (1930) by Eric Gill, which features stroke contrast, and Caecilia (1990) by Peter Matthias Noordzij, which is without stroke contrast. Examples in the eccentric style include Bramley and the monolinear Belwe Mono.

The development of Egyptian as a typesetting face in the nineteenth century was accompanied by the design of fonts for typewriters. Typefaces with stroke similarity and slab serifs proved particularly suitable. In the case of typewriters, all letters are monospaced, and slab serifs helped to widen the narrower letters. These typefaces were created using the economical method of boring into metal, and as a result all strokes and curves exhibit the same weight and rounded terminals – a feature still exhibited by the digital version of Courier.

Egyptian typefaces can be divided into the following attribute subgroups: a) typefaces with *round curves* in all styles, with and without stroke contrast; b) typefaces with *flat curves* in all type styles, for example Melior (1952) by Hermann Zapf, which is in a static style,[23] Raleigh (1977) by Robert Norton, which is in a dynamic style, and Cholla (1998) by Sibylle Hagmann, with its distinctive transitions in a geometric style (table →pp. 124/125).

A shared feature of Egyptian typefaces is their emphasized serifs. In typefaces with stroke similarity, the serif weight is usually 50 percent or more of the stem weight; in those with stroke contrast, somewhat less. An unambiguous distinction from Antiqua is not always possible.

VI
Grotesque

Type form
· **Grotesque**

Attribute
· **Round curve**
· **Flat curve**

Stroke contrast
· **Stroke difference**
· **Stroke similarity**

Type style
· **dynamic**
· **static**
· **geometric**
· **eccentric**

Havonsberg
Havonsberg

Dynamic style: Johnston | Gill Sans

Havonsberg
Havonsberg
Havonsberg

Dynamic style: Syntax | Frutiger | Today Sans

Havonsberg

Dynamic style – flat curve: Zemestro

Following the production, in 1815, of the first slab serif typeface, the year 1816 saw the first sans serif typeface included in the range offered by an English foundry. However, Grotesque, as it was known, was not actually new. Since Greek antiquity, such a script had been used to inscribe stone and on coins, and it had thus been around for centuries.

In 1816 WILLIAM CASLON IV published a sans serif titling typeface in a geometric type style, the size specification and description of which was listed as *'Two lines english egyptian'*. A bold version published by VINCENT FIGGINS in 1830 was called *'sans-serif'*, and a condensed bold typeface published in 1834 by WILLIAM THOROWGOOD, which also included lowercase letters, was dubbed *'grotesque'*.[24] The three terms subsequently became established, although Egyptian remained the umbrella term for slab serif typefaces; typefaces without serifs were called both sans serif and Grotesque.

In the wake of the reduction of serifs to extremely fine hairlines in the eighteenth century and then their emphasis in 1815, the creation of new setting typefaces that did without serifs completely can be seen as a logical next step. Nevertheless, this was also a radical innovation. For centuries, type foundries had almost exclusively produced serif and Blackletter typefaces. And it is therefore understandable that the new typefaces would have been perceived as 'grotesque'. At the same time, it should be noted that the word *grotesque* comes from the Italian *grottesco*, which derives from *grotta*, meaning grotto or cave. The origin of these typefaces without serifs in inscriptions suggests a relationship to stone, while their condensed heavy cut implies a relationship to something dark. The term *Gothic* as it is commonly used in the USA can also be seen as having a reference to darkness, while in German there is the term *Steinschrift* (stone lettering).

The comprehensive set of Steinschrift/Grotesk typefaces published by the Leipzig type foundry Schelter & Giesecke with compressed, condensed, and (from 1870) three so-called extended font styles – all with minuscules – represents a milestone. A replica of this Grotesque face, which was used by the Bauhaus, can be seen in Bau by CHRISTIAN SCHWARTZ. Other Grotesque typefaces in a static style include Akzidenz Grotesk (1898) by the firm H. Berthold AG in Berlin and MORRIS FULLER BENTON's designs for American Type Founders (ATF): Franklin Gothic (1903), News Gothic, and Lightline Gothic (both 1908). Compared with the European Grotesque, the American version has a slightly higher x-height. Italic font styles were rare in the initial phase.

Havonsberg
Havonsberg
Havonsberg

Static style: Bau | AG Old Face | News Gothic

Havonsberg
Havonsberg
Havonsberg

Static style: Venus | Grotesque MT | Arial

Havonsberg
Havonsberg

Static style: Univers | Neue Haas Grotesk

Havonsberg

Static style – stroke difference: URW Imperial

Havonsberg

Static style – flat curve: Eurostile

Havonsberg
Havonsberg

Geometric style: Futura | Kabel

Havonsberg
Havonsberg
Havonsberg

Geometric style: Avenir | Brown | Effra

Precisely one hundred years after Caslon's uppercase alphabet, a successor was produced in the form of Edward Johnston's typeface for the London Underground. However, the two typefaces differ in one key aspect: in the case of Johnston, the curve terminals are not cut at a 90-degree angle (apart from the capital S). This was a departure from the geometric type style and initiated the dynamic style of sans serif. His colleague Eric Gill continued this style in 1927 with Gill Sans. Meanwhile, some geometric alternative letters were being produced for the European mainland. These designs were competing with the highly successful geometric sans serif; examples include Erbar (1926) and Futura (1927). After the Art Nouveau epoch, the emphasis was now on clarity. In contrast to the designs produced at the Bauhaus, Jakob Erbar and Paul Renner did not use a construction grid, preferring to employ the proportions of the *Roman capitalis monumentalis*.

In Switzerland, the rational design continued more or less unabated in the 1950s. An overriding aim was to design Grotesque typefaces with the greatest possible degree of uniformity and a neutral character that could, as contemporary typefaces, replace Antiqua.[25] Univers by Adrian Frutiger and Neue Haas Grotesk, later renamed Helvetica, by Max Miedinger are products of this approach. (Arial from 1982, which is based on Monotype Grotesque 215, which is in turn based on Venus Grotesk from 1907, also falls within this category.)

New standards were set by Adrian Frutiger – "Mr. Sans Serif" – with his slightly dynamic Frutiger (1976) and his geometric Avenir (1988). The latter type style also includes Brown (2007) by Aurèle Sack and Effra (2008) by Jonas Schudel, which uses dynamic curves for b, p, d, q. A dynamic style face in this group can be found in Hans Eduard Meier's Syntax (1968).

Sans serif faces with stroke contrast are widely used in the cosmetics field.

Grotesque typefaces can be divided into the following attribute subgroups: a) typefaces with *round curves* in all styles, with and without stroke contrast; b) typefaces with *flat curves* in a static type style, such as Eurostile (1962) by Aldo Novarese, or in a dynamic type style, such as Zemestro (2003) by David Farey and Klavika (2004) by Eric Olson (table →pp. 126/127).

A shared feature of Grotesque typefaces is their unwidened stroke terminals. In most cases downstrokes are horizontally cut, but they can also end diagonally. Symmetrically or asymmetrically rounded terminals are also possible.

113

VII
Latin

Type form
- Latin

Attribute
- Round curve
- Flat curve

Stroke contrast
- Stroke difference
- Stroke similarity

Type style
- dynamic
- static
- geometric
- eccentric

Poster face: Latin MT · Condensed | Latin Wide

Card face: Président

Decorated: Augustea Open | Phoebus | Cristal

Latin typefaces with their pointed or wedge-shaped serifs are, along with Egyptian and Grotesque, one of the three new letterforms of the nineteenth century. All three groups offer the same extensive range of possible variations in terms of both stroke contrast and type style.

Latin typefaces play a significant role in France, and it is probable that they emerged there in the middle of the nineteenth century. NICOLETE GRAY writes that the Dutch type historian Dr. GERRIT WILLEM OVINK refers to a *Latines grasses* on a type specimen sheet produced by the Laurent & Deberny type foundry in Paris in 1854 as the first typeface of this kind.[26] Up until the end of the 1800s, Latin typefaces increased in scope and variety to such an extent that in 1926 a two-volume type specimen book produced by the Deberny & Peignot type foundry included a section exclusively for Latins.[27] They were also included in the typeface classification system formulated by FRANCIS THIBAUDEAU, although not as an independent group like *Grotesque* and *Égyptienne* but as the first subgroup of *Elzévir*.[28] In France, the term generally refers to the older serif typefaces that are distinguished from the *Didot* group by their flat serifs.

Latin typefaces were also represented in other European markets – usually in identical versions – but did not enjoy the same status. In England, the type foundry Stephenson, Blake & Co. had six font styles bearing the name *Latin,* bold from wide to elongated as well as light.[29] There were two other names for typefaces with pointed serifs: *Antique* and *Runic*. All these terms imply a reference to lettering inscribed in stone – the first two to the Italian region of Latium and the capital Rome – as well as to antiquity. In Germany, Latin typefaces are for the most part referred to as *Renaissance* and *Etienne,* suggesting a much later epoch.[30]

Gradually the significance of these typefaces changed; even in France their status diminished over the course of the twentieth century. And with the decline of metal typesetting in the 1960s, they disappeared in their original form almost completely. They only retained a certain presence due to successful reinterpretations such as the unusually vivid Vendôme by FRANÇOIS GANEAU, which was released in 1951 by the Fonderie Olive in Marseilles. In the same year, a titling typeface named Augustea was produced in Italy by ALESSANDRO BUTTI and ALDO NOVARESE. At Deberny & Peignot, ADRIAN FRUTIGER designed three new Latin typefaces: the card face Initiales Président, the shadow face Initiales Phoebus, and his first text typeface, Méridien. The same

Havonsberg
Dynamic style: Vendôme

Havonsberg
Havonsberg
Dynamic style: Méridien | Veljovic

Havonsberg
Havonsberg
Havonsberg
Dynamic style: Trump Mediäval | Swift | Warnock

Havonsberg
Dynamic style: Celeste

Havonsberg
Static style: Versailles

Havonsberg
Eccentric style: Barcelona

foundry also released Initiales Cristal by RÉMY PEIGNOT.[31] The year 1984 saw the release of FRUTIGER'S Versailles, a static type style face that was more strongly oriented towards the original Latin faces of the nineteenth century.

The scope of the Latin type form is illustrated by the few typefaces that are mentioned here. They range from body text to display and decorated faces, and include versions with and without stroke contrast. In terms of type style, this group includes dynamic, static, and eccentric versions, an example of the latter being Barcelona (1981) by EDWARD BENGUIAT. They also cover the full range of possible serif weights, from very fine to very heavy. Moreover, the transition from stem to serif can be bracketed or unbracketed.

These are all reasons to accord Latin typefaces of the nineteenth century their own main group on the same level as Egyptian and Grotesque. This being the case, the question of delimitation from other groups needs to be addressed. In the case of Glyphic typefaces, the difference consists in the distinction between broadened stroke terminals: waisted strokes and flared serifs in the case of Glyphic typefaces and actual serifs in the case of Latins. The difference from Antiqua is evident in the serif forms, which tend to be blunt in the case of Antiqua and pointed (wedge-shaped serif) in the case of Latin. Latin typefaces with pronounced serifs have been hitherto allocated to the Egyptian group. Such a classification is obsolete in this context for two reasons. In principle, the weight of the serifs is directly correlated with stroke contrast. Latins with low or no stroke contrast normally exhibit heavier serifs, while those with noticeable to extreme stroke contrast have finer serifs. That said, there are always exceptions that proves the rule. Latins with exaggerated wedge serifs, which were also previously classed as Egyptian, are actually not text typefaces but jobbing and advertising faces. They are therefore positioned in the matrix on this level.

Latin typefaces can be divided into the following attribute subgroups:
a) typefaces with *round curves* in all styles, with and without stroke contrast;
b) typefaces with *flat curves* such as Calicanto (2019) by ALEJANDRO FREITEZ (table →pp. 128/129).

A shared feature of Latin typefaces is stroke and curve terminals with serifs that suggest a triangle (pointed serif/wedge-shaped serif). A diversity of stroke contrasts and styles as well as a diverse range of serif weights are also possible.

I Glyphic

	Attribute Waisted stroke Stroke difference	Stroke similarity
dynamic strongly	Lydian HOE oneb	Lithos HOE
moderately	Odense HOE oneb	Laudatio HOE oneb
slightly	Mentor Sans HOE oneb	Palatino Sans HOE oneb
static	Optima HOE oneb	
geometric		
eccentric		Shannon HOE oneb

| **Attribute Flare serif** | | **Glyphic** | I |
| Stroke difference | Stroke similarity | | |

Tiepolo

HOE oneb

dynamic
strongly

Cartesius

HOE oneb

Carter Sans

HOE oneb

moderately

Baker Signet

HOE oneb

Friz Quadrata

HOE oneb

slightly

Pompei

HOE oneb

Memo

HOE oneb

static

Brewery

HOE oneb

Serif Gothic

HOE oneb

geometric

Korinna

HOE oneb

eccentric

	II	**Script**	**Attribute** Separated finials Stroke difference	Stroke similarity

		Stroke difference	Stroke similarity
dynamic strongly		Sunetta HOE oneb	
moderately		Sanvito HOE oneb	Bradley Hand HOE oneb
slightly		Lucida Calligraphy HOE oneb	Flora HOE oneb
static		Redonda HOE oneb	Klepto HOE oneb
geometric			Reliq HOE oneb
eccentric		Papyrus HOE oneb	Stylus HOE oneb

| **Attribute Joined finials** Stroke difference | Stroke similarity | **Script** | II |

Stroke difference | Stroke similarity

	Mistral	**dynamic** strongly
Lucida Handwriting	Caflisch Script	moderately
Boscribe		slightly
Snell Roundhand	Monoline Script	**static**
	Kulukundis	geometric
		eccentric

		Attribute Round curve	
III	**Blackletter**	Stroke difference	Stroke similarity

dynamic
strongly

Rotunda
San Marco

𝕳𝕺𝕰 oneb

moderately

Schwabacher
Alte Schwabacher

𝕳𝕺𝕰 oneb

slightly

static

geometric

eccentric

Art Nouveau-Blackletter
Eckmann

𝕳𝕺𝕰 oneb

Attribute Flat curve Stroke difference	Stroke similarity	**Blackletter**	III

Textura
Caslon Gotisch

HOE oneb

dynamic
strongly

Fraktur
Walbaum Fraktur

HOE oneb

moderately

slightly

Fraktur
Unger Fraktur

HOE oneb

Simplified textura
Deutschmeister

HOE   oneb

static

Simplified textura
Kursachsen (Blackhaus)

HOE   oneb

geometric

eccentric

IV Antiqua

Attribute Round curve
Stroke difference

dynamic
strongly

Humanism class
Jenson

HOE oneb   *HOE oneb*

moderately

Renaissance class
Garamond

HOE oneb   *HOE oneb*

slightly

Baroque class
Bell

HOE oneb   *HOE oneb*

static

Neoclassicism class
Didot

HOE oneb   *HOE oneb*

geometric

eccentric

Art Nouveau class
Edwardian

HOE oneb

Attribute Flat curve
Stroke difference

Antiqua   IV

dynamic
strongly

moderately

Slimbach

slightly

HOE oneb   *HOE oneb*

Zapf Book

static

HOE oneb   *HOE oneb*

geometric

eccentric

V Egyptian

	Attribute Round curve Stroke difference		Stroke similarity
dynamic strongly			Mendoza HOE oneb
moderately	Chaparral HOE oneb		TheSerif HOE oneb
slightly	Excelsior HOE oneb		Amasis HOE oneb
static	Clarendon HOE oneb		Serifa HOE oneb
geometric			Rockwell HOE oneb
eccentric			Belwe Mono HOE oneb

		Egyptian V
Attribute Flat curve Stroke difference	Stroke similarity	

		dynamic strongly
Raleigh HOE oneb		
Pensum HOE oneb	Capita HOE oneb	moderately
Askan HOE oneb	Vista Slab HOE oneb	slightly
Scherzo HOE oneb	Rutherford HOE oneb	**static**
	City HOE oneb	**geometric**
		eccentric

	VI Grotesque	**Attribute Round curve** Stroke difference	Stroke similarity
dynamic strongly		Legacy Sans HOE oneb	Calluna Sans HOE oneb
moderately		Linex Sans HOE oneb	Gill Sans HOE oneb
slightly		Stone Sans HOE oneb	Frutiger HOE oneb
static		URW Imperial HOE oneb	AG Old Face HOE oneb
geometric		Luna HOE oneb	Futura HOE oneb
eccentric		Panache HOE oneb	Benguiat Gothic HOE oneb

Attribute Flat curve
Stroke difference

Stroke similarity

Grotesque VI

dynamic
strongly

Zemestro

HOE   oneb

moderately

Siro

HOE   oneb

Condor

HOE   oneb

Venn

HOE   oneb

slightly

Eurostile

HOE   oneb

static

Kaliber

HOE   oneb

geometric

House Sans

HOE   oneb

Scarlet

HOE   oneb

eccentric

		Attribute Round curve	
VII	**Latin**	Stroke difference	Stroke similarity

dynamic
strongly

Vendôme

HOE oneb

moderately

Swift

HOE oneb

slightly

Méridien

HOE oneb

static

Versailles

HOE oneb

Président

HOE

geometric

Lovato

HOE oneb

eccentric

Barcelona

HOE oneb

| | | Latin | VII |

Attribute Flat curve
Stroke difference   Stroke similarity

Origami

HOE oneb

dynamic
strongly

Krete

HOE oneb

moderately

Calicanto

HOE oneb

slightly

static

geometric

eccentric

Typeface concepts

5

Type family: dyad

Roman *Italic* Type
Roman *Italic* Type

Delphin | Poetica · *Chancery IV*

Original dyadic form: upright uppercase with slanted lowercase letters
01 ▲

Coordinated fonts (above), font styles from one typeface family (below)
02 ▼|▼▼

Roman *Italic*

Poliphilus · Regular | Blado Italic · *Regular*

Roman *Italic*

Bembo · Regular | *Italic*

Unlike italic, oblique is a slanted version of roman
03 ▼|▼▼

Design frame
Design frame

Caecilia · Roman | *Italic*

Design frame
Design frame

Glypha · Roman | *Oblique*

Although the mixed-case writing form actually represents a typeface combination, the coincidence of *majuscules* and *minuscules* is no longer perceived as such. Moreover, there is little awareness of the different origins of *roman* and *italic*. As a dyad, they provide the basis of the typeface family. In the tradition of typeface combination, the dyad plays a significant role.

Based on the lowercase letters of the Carolingian minuscule of the eight/ninth centuries in combination with the far older majuscules of the Capitalis monumentalis of the first century, the development of Humanistic minuscule in Italy in the fifteenth century saw the emergence of a book hand that corresponds very closely to today's character forms. It is the basis of *Antiqua,* or more precisely its *roman* font style. A good example is the balanced type appearance of Poliphili-Type (1499) by Francesco Griffo.

At the beginning of the sixteenth century, another form of Antiqua, which today is known as *italic,* was already starting to be used as a text typeface. It is based on Humanistic cursive, which was also used as a book hand from the fifteenth century onwards. In Venice in 1501, Aldus Manutius set his small-format book series in an italic face cut by Francesco Griffo. This spatially economical typeface – initially featuring upright majuscules – was used by Aldus Manutius for the body text in his books. Modern typefaces based on this dyad prototype are Delphin (1951) by the German type designer Georg Trump, Poetica (1992) by Robert Slimbach |**01**|, and Rialto (1999) by Giovanni de Faccio and Lui Karner. However, for the most part the italic font style is used as a secondary face in typography, for example on title pages and emphasis within text. Based on centuries of tradition, it is also used for *marginalia*(→p. 20 | **06** |), notes affixed to the book text.

Roman and italic are based on very different ways of writing. While roman faces stem from carefully written book hand, italic (like Script typefaces) originates from hand used for rapidly written correspondence. The alternative term *cursive* stems from the Latin *currere,* meaning to run or to hurry. The term courier has the same origin. Cursive thus refers to 'running' type. The typical feature of italics is not, as widely thought, slant, which is by no means essential. More decisive is the impression of a 'flowing' text appearance in the case of the unconnected letters. In addition, a traditional italic typeface is characterized by narrow proportions; it is finer, lighter, and often features a different design of the letters *a,e,f,g,k,p,v,w,x,y,z* | **02** |.

Obliques, on the other hand, have the same letterforms as romans but are slanted at an angle of 10 to 17 degrees to the right | **03** |. However, the claim that the oblique style are merely faces that have been slanted electronically is not correct. A well-crafted oblique is drawn separately, or at least optically corrected following modification; otherwise, the curve shapes appear to lack harmony. It is perhaps this misunderstanding that has led to the occasional mislabelling of oblique as italic.

Type family: triad

In basic terms, both Latin-based alphabets and book typography can also be related to the concept of the triad – even if this way of seeing things is of course highly simplified. For centuries the triad shaped the setting of book titles, and today the triad or tetrad provides the basic framework for book typefaces.

As already discussed (→*Basic shapes:* p. 57) the Latin majuscule alphabet is based on the triad of *square, circle,* and *triangle.* Later, the development of majuscule (uppercase letters) into minuscule forms (lowercase letters) gave rise to the triad of *ascender, x-height,* and *descender.* And in a very general sense, the character set of a typeface can be divided into *letters, figures (numbers),* and *punctuation marks* | **04** |.

Classic book typography also has a triadic idea. Traditionally set book titles consisted of *majuscules (caps), small caps,* and *minuscules,* as well as *roman, small caps,* and *italic* font styles, or, later, *regular, italic,* and *bold* styles. In the case of chapter opening pages, the triad consisted of *title, decorative initial letter (versal),* and *text.* Another kind of triad can be seen in the graduation of type sizes in book setting: *display size* for titles, *text size* for body copy, and *agate size* for footnotes | **04** | (→*Type size:* p. 74 / →*Design size:* p. 75). And last but not least, the organization of a book into *front matter, book body,* and *back matter* and of the book form (codex) into *cover, endleaves,* and *block* in each case also forms a triad.

Type families with *regular, italic, bold,* and *bold italic* styles can be characterized as tetrads (groups of four), as can those with *regular, italic, bold,* and *decorated* faces. In the first half of the twentieth century, book typefaces were often made up of four font styles, which is usually sufficient for a book setting.

Triadic forms in lettering and classic book typography
04 ▼

H O V
Square | Circle | Triangle

h o y
Ascender | x-height | Descender

Hov 123 .;?
Letters | Figures | Punctuation marks

HOV ʜᴏᴠ nov
Uppercase | Small caps | Lowercase

Hov ʜᴏᴠ *Hov*
Roman | Small caps | Italic

Hov *Hov* **Hov**
Regular | Italic | Bold

Title Text Note
Display size | Text size | Agate size

Extended type family

An extended type family is a well-developed family that includes not only different weights and their slants but also different widths, and which offers many possibilities for combinations. However, the *nature* of such combinations is oriented towards similarity, since the concept is based on *analogy* in terms of both type form and type style.

Beginning in 1953, the Swiss type designer ADRIAN FRUTIGER created the first systematically structured extended type family concept in the form of the Grotesque Univers for the Deberny & Peignot foundry in Paris. His system was highly acclaimed. Unlike older extended type families such as Venus Grotesk, Futura, and Gill Sans, which were successively expanded, Univers was conceived of as an extended family from the beginning and released as such into the market. Visualized using a schema |05| and equipped with a two-digit numbering system to promote better international comprehension of the font style names,[1] the family initially consisted of 21 font styles. The normal font style – indicated by the median number 55 – provides the reference point in terms of width, weight, and slant against which the other font styles are measured. The *widths* are ordered on the horizontal plane: extended, roman, condensed, and extra condensed (odd second digit in the two-digit number). Oblique styles are positioned to the right of the upright font style (even second digit in the two-digit number). The *weights* are positioned on the

Planning in totality: *Univers* concept with 21 font styles and a numbering system
05 ▼|▶

vertical axes with values increasing downward: extra light, light, book, bold, heavy, and black (first digit in the two-digit number). Asked in a conversation about the apparently unsystematic form of the schema, FRUTIGER responded by saying that, on the one hand, there was no need for certain font styles and that, on the other hand, diagonal combinations, for example the font styles 58 and 49, had also been taken into account. While all the original font styles on the horizontal axis exhibit the same stroke weight, their color values appear different due to the different widths of the counter spaces.² Later adaptations saw a departure from identical downstrokes in favor of optically adjusted stroke weights, as is usually the case in font design today. An extended digital version was produced for Linotype containing 27 font styles, and in 1998 a completely revised version was released with 59 font styles. As Linotype Univers, and from 2010 as Univers Next, the family now uses a three-digit numbering system.

For their Grotesque Knockout (1994), JONATHAN HOEFLER and TOBIAS FRERE-JONES chose names derived from boxing for the different font styles, with the nine weight classes from flyweight to heavyweight as well as sumo designating nine widths (in an additional four weights) | 06 |.

Knockout width designations – derived from boxing weight classes
06 ▶

Flyweight
Bantamweight
Featherweight
Lightweight
Welterweight
Middleweight
Cruiserweight
Heavyweight
Sumo

The designer effect

Do type designs by the same designer share certain characteristics, and, if so, does this make for particularly good combinations of these typefaces? It is often claimed in specialist publications that this is indeed the case. However, while there may well be a strong tendency in the direction of *analogy*, this in itself is not a guarantee of commonality. What is true here and what is false?

Arguments for the pervasiveness of a particular designer's style usually cite the work of well-known type designers such as ERIC GILL, HERMANN ZAPF, ADRIAN FRUTIGER, GERARD UNGER, and ROBERT SLIMBACH | 07 | and their

Almost identical height proportions in three typefaces by Zapf and Frutiger
07 ▶

Optima | Palatino | Melior

Hhxg Hhxg Hhxg

Univers | Serifa | Versailles

The superimposition of text typefaces by Adrian Frutiger reveals their analogies
08 ▶

'stylistic idiosyncrasies'[3] or 'signature styles'.[4] This conception is based on the probability of analogies within a body of creative work. FRUTIGER himself provided proof of such an analogous quality when, in 1980, he compared his text typefaces by superimposing them,[5] with the result that, with a few exceptions, forms and proportions proved astoundingly similar | **08** |. However, this result can by no means be generalized. Testing is always required! Even combinations of typefaces by FRUTIGER | **09** | **10** | and ZAPF | **11** | **12** | do not necessarily result in harmony.

Analogies can also be found between typefaces from the same period and from the same cultural sphere.[6] In addition, one can speak of analogous approaches taken by designers whose work draws on the same paradigm. Moreover, today an immense number of fonts are based on existing specimens from earlier periods (a fact that is too often not admitted).

Let us return to the question of type designs by the same individual and why, despite analogous designs, combinations do not always produce good results. One of the basic rules of typeface combination is that faces based on the same *type form* should not be combined with one another (→*Type form:* p. 166). For example, two typefaces from the Grotesque group or two from the Antiqua group will not fit together even if they originate from the same designer | **11** |.

Middle line: dynamic style is appropriate, but the uppercase F appears too narrow
09 ▼

Middle lines: the weights harmonize, but the widths are too different
10 ▶|▶▶

DesignFormen
DesignFormen
DesignFormen
Apollo – Univers | Frutiger | Avenir

DesignFormen
DesignFormen
DesignFormen
Centennial – Egyptienne F | Serifa | Glypha

DesignFormen
DesignFormen
DesignFormen
Centennial – Egyptienne F | Serifa | Glypha

Three other reasons are worth mentioning here:

1. The typefaces in question can be too similar, so that the difference between them is hardly discernible, or not discernible at all. If this is the case, there is no reason to combine them. The effort involved in doing so is wasted |11|.

2. They may be too dissimilar in terms of width |12| or stylistically too different in terms of other proportions, resulting in perceptual disruption that does not generate a positive tension.

3. They may appear to lack harmony due to too little contrast or a lack of interesting contrast, as is seen in the case of combinations in which the stroke contrast lacks differentiation. Juxtaposing weight gradations often fails to generate a succinct-enough contrast |12|.

Although the typefaces created by one designer will in many cases exhibit a high degree of similarity, effective typeface combination requires above all an expressive contrast and only secondarily an analogous trait.

Bad combination: analogy in form and weight, contrast in style and curve form

DesignFormen
Aldus – Melior

The search for suitable combinations: the *URW Grotesk* has five weights and widths

DesignFormen
DesignFormen
DesignFormen
Zapf Intl – URW Grotesk · *Light* | *Wide* | *Extra Wide*

Design**Formen**
Design**Formen**
Design**Formen**
Light – *Bold Extra Narrow* | *Bold Narrow* | *Bold*

DesignFormen
DesignFormen
DesignFormen
Medium – *Light Extra Wide* | *Regular Wide* | *Medium*

Superfamily

Superfamily refers to complementary type families from different classification groups. The concept is appealingly simple: *contrast* **in terms of** *type form,* **analogy** **in terms of** *type style* **and proportions. However, a different visual impression should not be expected in the case of combinations within the same superfamily.**

Although sans serif *extended type families* such as Venus Grotesk, Gill Sans, Futura, Univers, Helvetica, Frutiger, and others, with their numerous font styles in different *weights, slants,* and *widths,* are designed to meet a wide range of typographical requirements, these font styles still share a certain property. If a more familiar face for the body text is desired, then an appropriate second typeface must be found. This can take a considerable amount of time, especially since typeface parameters such as appropriate point size and correct tracking also need to be taken into account. The remedy is provided by the superfamily.

Analogies Analogies
Analogies Analogies
Century Old Style | News Gothic

Similar letterforms, but somewhat different x-heights and other proportions	Despite the similar nomenclature, only limited formal conformity
13 ▲	14 ▼ | ▼▼

Analogies **Analogies**
Clearface | Clearface Gothic

Analogies Analogies
Analogies Analogies
Benguiat | Benguiat Gothic

Uncompleted *Romulus* superfamily: the sans serif exists only as a sample face
15   ▶ | ▶▶

Early evidence of deliberately produced analogies in the letterforms and proportions of Antiqua and Grotesque can be seen in typefaces of American Type Founders. MORRIS FULLER BENTON, who worked for the firm, was one of the most productive type designers of the first half of the twentieth century. Similarities can be observed, for example, between his News Gothic (1908) and the Century Old Style | **13** | designed by his father, LINN BOYD BENTON, in 1894. A more obvious connection – emphasized by the typeface names – can be seen between his two families Clearface (1907) and Clearface Gothic from 1910 | **14** |. However, there are obvious differences in some of the letter designs and respective proportions.

Also worth mentioning here are two typefaces produced much later in the USA. In 1978, EDWARD BENGUIAT created Benguiat and a year later Benguiat Gothic | **14** |. Drawing on the prevailing zeitgeist, the letterforms contain neo-Art Nouveau elements. The obvious similarities between the two typeface families are matched by equally striking differences in their curve forms and proportions.

ABCDEFGHIJKLMNOPQRSTUVWXYZ
abcdefghijklmnopqrstuvwxyz fbffffifflfhfifkfl 1234567890

ABCDEFGHIJKLMNOPQRSTUVWXYZ
abcdefghijklmnopqrstuvwxyz ffffifflfifl 1234567890

Different names, but a consciously designed relationship in the regular font styles
16   ▼

Analogies Analogies
Analogies Analogies
Analogies
Demos | Praxis | Flora

Probably the first attempt to realize a typeface *superfamily* is Romulus | **15** | by JAN VAN KRIMPEN. The renowned Dutch book and type designer produced the first drawings of the roman version in 1931 and then added the roman sloped, the semi-bold, and the semi-bold condensed. He then went on to design the Cancellaresca Bastarda, a cursive face conspicuous for its pronounced ascenders and descenders, and Romulus Greek. Unfortunately, the light, roman, semi-bold, and bold font styles of the Romulus Sans serifs were only realized as 12-point sample cuts | **15** |.[7] This may be the reason why this superfamily is not frequently cited in discussions of this topic.

> Analogy as the goal of the superfamily – often with exceptions in the case of letters such as a and g
> |17|
> ▼

Analogies *Analogies*
Analogies *Analogies*

Lucida | Lucida Sans

In 1976 and 1977, another Dutchman, GERARD UNGER, designed two typefaces that refer to one another but have different names: Demos and Praxis |16|. They were joined in 1980 by Flora, an almost upright italic. It was developed in combination with the sans serif and can be seen as an alternative to its oblique. At the same time, the low majuscules provide it with a degree of autonomy.

In the 1980s, superfamilies were released into the market with uniform names. The similarity of the two to four type forms involved was a response to the content, media, technical, and design needs emerging above all in the field of corporate identity, corporate design, and in business culture. In the USA, for example, Lucida (1984/85) and Lucida Sans (1989/90) were designed by CHARLES BIGELOW and his partner KRIS HOLMES as a superfamily |17| for use in interoffice communication. Their project is particularly interesting because the fonts were also created for digital typesetting, which the development of the Apple Macintosh was now making possible. The initially very low resolution provided by monitors and printers was a challenge for type

ABCDEFGHIJKLMNOPQRSTUVWXYZ
12345 abcdefghijklmnopqrstuvwxyz 67890

ABCDEFGHIJKLMNOPQRSTUVWXYZ
12345 abcdefghijklmnopqrstuvwxyz 67890

ABCDEFGHIJKLMNOPQRSTUVWXYZ
12345 abcdefghijklmnopqrstuvwxyz 67890

ABCDEFGHIJKLMNOPQRSTUVWXYZ
12345 abcdefghijklmnopqrstuvwxyz 67890

ROMULUS SANS SERIFS

designers, who had to create faces that offered good legibility in text sizes. It is for this reason that the constantly augmented superfamily is characterized by large x-heights and open counters.

SUMNER STONE, the director of typography at Adobe Systems, also contributed to the early development of digital typesetting. His Stone Serif, Stone Sans, and Stone Informal | 18 |, which were released in 1987, represented a new concept of superfamily, in this case featuring 18 font styles. Here, Stone Informal plays a particular role as a mediating instance in formal terms between handwritten lettering and printed type.

A very different concept of superfamily was created by OTL AICHER in 1988. Drawing on the condensed Univers and Times New Roman, he designed four – in terms of the curve terminals of c/e and the two hybrid versions, idiosyncratic – type families: Rotis Sans, the two hybrids Rotis Semi Sans and Rotis Semi Serif, and Rotis Serif | 18 |.

In this period, corporate identity specialists increasingly adopted the view that large firms needed to be more independent and versatile when it came to selecting typefaces. They needed to move away from the monotony of 'off-the-rack' typefaces and acquire their own *corporate type*. The fact that the typeface requirements of firms were no longer met by one type family and certainly not by a single corporate typeface is evident in what agencies were marketing. A good example is the superfamily Corporate A·S·E | 18 | designed by KURT WEIDEMANN for Daimler-Benz AG and their car brand Mercedes. Its Antiqua, Sans serif, and Egyptian typeface trilogy was created between 1984 and 1990.[8] Several years later, the originally exclusive type family was made generally available.

In superfamilies the different concepts of Antiqua and Grotesque are fixed elements

18 ▼

Analogies *Analogies*
Analogies *Analogies*
Analogies *Analogies*

Stone · Serif | Sans | Informal

Analogies *Analogies*
Analogies *Analogies*
Analogies
Analogies *Analogies*

Rotis · Sans | Semi Sans | Semi Serif | Serif

Analogies *Analogies*
Analogies *Analogies*
Analogies *Analogies*

Corporate A | Corporate S | Corporate E

Superfamily with Grotesque, Egyptian, and intermediate hybrid form

19 ▼

Analogies Analogies
Analogies Analogies
Analogies Analogies

TheSans | TheSerif | TheMix

Interpolation curve based on lightest, heaviest, and optically median font style

20 ▶

a Extra Light
a Light
a Semi Light
a Normal
a Semi Bold
a Bold
a Extra Bold
a Black

Interpolation and extrapolation: formula for the calculation of stroke weight

21 ▼

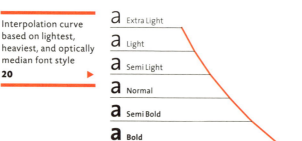

a   b   c

$b=\sqrt{ac}$ $a=b^2/c$ $c=b^2/a$

| Similar proportions, dissimilar names (above) and the opposite (below)
| 22 ▼
| Narrower – and thereby rebalanced – versions compared with the original
| 23 ▼▼

DesignFormen
DesignFormen
Frutiger – Méridien | Frutiger Serif

DesignFormen
Frutiger Next | Frutiger Serif

Multiple master

Adobe Font Creator: infinitly generating between extreme values (master)
24 ▼

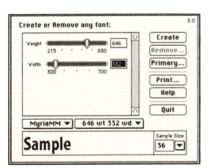

In 1994 FontShop released Thesis |19| by the Dutch type designer LUCAS DE GROOT, a superfamily made up of TheSans, TheSerif (actually a slab serif), TheMix, and later TheAntiquaB. Seven years earlier, in 1987, DE GROOT also developed his interpolation curve formula for generating optically even graduated font styles |20|21|.

Today, superfamilies are a fixture of typeface development. The combination of typefaces with and without serifs meets a need. However, it needs to be noted that not all typefaces of the same name are superfamilies. Sometimes the name is eponymous of the foundry or the designer, as in the case of the condensed Méridien that AKIRA KOBAYASHI created for Linotype in 2008 and named Frutiger Serif |22|. The typeface does not match with Frutiger itself, but it is a somewhat better fit with the likewise condensed Frutiger Next |23|.

Multiple master technology (discontinued but reintroduced as *variable fonts*) allowed users themselves to generate high-quality intermediate versions between font-style extremes. The typefaces could be interpolated along not only one but several design axes, and typefaces could be generated that exhibited both *analogy* in terms of form and *contrast* in terms of stroke terminals.

The innovative *interpolation* technology was developed in 1976 by inventor and software developer PETER KAROW at URW in Germany.[9] The interpolation method offered tremendous savings in terms of effort and cost of the production of type families. Since high-quality intermediate stages between two font styles could be generated electronically, the drawing of weights and widths could be limited to two or three masters (font-style extremes), for example light and black with the intermediate stage regular. Subsequent digitalization of the drawing process also reduced the effort involved in sampling. Improvements to the digital drawing, if required, can be carried out manually.

In 1992 Adobe Systems introduced a completely new typeface concept, the multiple master MM font format. The essential innovation here was that the generation of intermediate font styles between the predefined masters was shifted from the font producers to the font users. Fine adjustability by means of slider controls |24| made it possible to produce an almost unlimited number of intermediate stages, an aspect that can be extremely helpful when it comes to combining fonts.

Multiple master font with four masters for the width and weight design axes

25 ▼ | ▶

M	–	M	–	M
215 LT 300 CN		215 LT 600 NO		215 LT 700 SE
M	–	M	–	M
400 RG 300 CN		400 RG 600 NO		400 RG 700 SE
M	–	M	–	M
565 SB 300 CN		565 SB 600 NO		565 SB 700 SE
M	–	M	–	M
700 BD 300 CN		700 BD 600 NO		700 BD 700 SE
M	–	**M**	–	**M**
830 BL 300 CN		830 BL 600 NO		830 BL 700 SE

M	–	*M*	–	*M*
215 LT 300 CN		215 LT 600 NO		215 LT 700 SE
M	–	*M*	–	*M*
400 RG 300 CN		400 RG 600 NO		400 RG 700 SE
M	–	*M*	–	*M*
565 SB 300 CN		565 SB 600 NO		565 SB 700 SE
M	–	*M*	–	*M*
700 BD 300 CN		700 BD 600 NO		700 BD 700 SE
M	–	***M***	–	***M***
830 BL 300 CN		830 BL 600 NO		830 BL 700 SE

Myriad MM | Myriad MM Italic

At the same time, Adobe also published its first typeface especially developed for this new technology, Myriad | **25** |. The dynamic Grotesque designed by Carol Twombly and Robert Slimbach used two design axes: *weight* and *width*. Later MM faces also allowed for variations of the *optical size* and *type form*.

In the multiple master concept, the quality of the typefaces and the quality of digital typesetting found an equivalent (with some improvements) to the more than 500-year development of foundry typefaces – from the sorts in several widths in Johannes Gutenberg's perfectly justified setting of the 42-line Bible, to optical adaptations of proportion and stroke weight of the point sizes making up a typeface series, to the realization of extended type

Sidebar	Main text

Typeface family with two widths and five weights (also available as italic)
26 ▼

M Light Condensed
M Condensed
M Semibold Condensed
M Bold Condensed
M Black Condensed

M Light
M Regular
M Semibold
M Bold
M Black

Myriad

Very finely graduated weights (left); more font styles with greater differentiation (right)
27 ▼ | ▶

Light
Book
Roman
Medium
Heavy
Black

Ultra Light
Thin
Light
Regular
Medium
Demi
Bold
Heavy

Avenir | Avenir Next

Optical adjustment for reversed-out thanks to finely graduated type weights
28 ▶

Book
Book
Book
Roman

Avenir

---

families and superfamilies. Drawings of MM fonts were designed or edited to such an extent that reworking the generated font styles was not required. Typography professionals also recognized the technology's great potential, and the trade press presented the generation of intermediate weights as a success story.[10] The technology was not, however, met with the same enthusiasm in the graphic arts industry, and after seven years Adobe ceased production of further MM fonts.[11]

Although Adobe had great success with Myriad and other type families, they did not catch on in the MM version, with users preferring the older method based on a predefined selection of font styles (regular, italic, bold, bold italic, etc.) | **26** |. One reason for the rejection of the MM version was the long, seemingly cryptic, alphanumerical designations of intermediate font styles | **25** |. Another reason for the (preliminary) failure may have been the fact that the algorithmic generation of intermediate font styles was initially possible only in the separate software *Font Creator*. Although in 1997 slider controls were (finally) added to the vector graphics software *Adobe Illustrator* (from version 7 onwards), in the much more important layout software *Adobe PageMaker* and *QuarkXPress* this possibility was either not available or could only be used by means of a plug-in or XTension. The release of the layout software *Adobe InDesign* in the year 2000 and the successive replacement of PostScript Type 1 font format by the more comprehensive OpenType format ultimately marked the end of MM fonts.

Weight axis: Almost all multiple master fonts offered this design axis, which facilitated flowing transitions between light and heavy. It is an approach that was used by ADRIAN FRUTIGER in his Avenir design (1988) shortly before the development of the multiple master format | **27** |. The six very finely graded weights were designed to create an effect of a smooth gradation of typographic color.[12] Incomprehensibly, Linotype moved away from this interesting concept in the case of Avenir Next (2004), which includes two more upright font styles but uses the usual differentiated gradations | **27** |. The generation of finely graded weights is virtually predestined for the use of positive and reversed-out type. In small point sizes, a fine white typeface on a black background appears too fragile. Avenir in the next heavier font style compensates for this | **28** |. The situation is different with the reversed use of a heavier font. Because the white radiates into the black, the inverted type has to be more

Multiple master font: the style axis varies the stroke/curve terminals

29 ▼

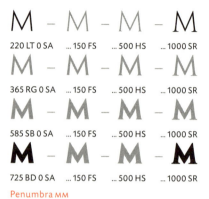

Penumbra MM

Multiple master fonts with variations in junctures (above) and in fills (below)

30 ▼ | ▼▼

Conga Brava MM | Conga Brava MM Stencil

Viva

---

finely designed and use larger letterspacing. This applies far more to signage with backlit lettering than to lettering lit from the front.[13]

Width axis: Among other things, this design axis is suited to setting titles at the same point size even if they are too long for the line. From a typographic point of view, this is usually not a good idea, because typefaces of different widths creates an unbalanced text appearance, all the more so when a subtle approach is very quickly 'sacrificed' in the name of so-called practical requirements. Good typography needs clearly graduated values, not arbitrary variability. Also required are authors who are able to write texts for newspapers and magazines using a specified character count.

However, in the search for the most appropriate type width – in the field of signage, in magazine setting with its usually narrow columns, or in combinations of two typefaces – this design axis can offer considerable advantages. Myriad MM |**25**| and other families designed by ROBERT SLIMBACH, such as Minion MM (1990/1992) and Kepler MM (1996), offer this possibility. A type that features only this axis is Motter Corpus MM by the Austrian OTHMAR MOTTER. Created in two widths for the International Typeface Corporation (ITC), it later became a multiple master font and is available today in three widths.

Form axis: This design axis can be seen as a genuine and forward-looking innovation in the field of type design. For example, it offers the possibility of nearly endless variations of stroke and curve terminals between the extremes both with and without serifs. Penumbra MM |**29**|, which was designed in 1994 by LANCE HIDY, features form and weight design axes and is an MM font whose extremes are Grotesque and Glyphic. There is no change in stroke contrast in the uppercase letters.

Changes are also possible in the fill of a typeface, as seen in the decorated face Viva (1993) by CAROL TWOMBLY, and in the junctures, as seen in Conga Brava MM Stencil (1996), a stencil-face variant of Conga Brava MM by MICHAEL HARVEY |**30**|. However, the change itself remains the same in all font styles.

Optical size axis: This design axis revives an aspect of metal faces thought to have been lost in digital typesetting: the typeface series (→*Typeface series:* p. 49). Reading comfort and aesthetic requirements make optical adaptations of the type appearance at different point sizes absolutely necessary.

When comparing common digital fonts with only one design size with fonts with optical sizes (→*Opticals:* p.78), the superiority of the opticals is clearly evident. Legibility is served, for example, by reducing the stroke contrast in small point sizes. MM typefaces with the two design axes weight and optical size include ROBERT SLIMBACH'S Adobe Jenson MM (1995) and Cronos MM (1996), and CAROL TWOMBLY'S Chaparral MM (2000). The already mentioned Minion MM and Kepler MM offer three design axes: weight, width, and optical size.

Since 2016/17, variable font technology has made a comeback. However, it had never really disappeared. Since 1999, Adobe Acrobat has used Adobe Serif MM and Adobe Sans MM as substitute fonts in order to guarantee a text version without changes to line breaks in cases where a font has not been embedded in the Portable Document Format (pdf).[14]

Variable fonts

The 'new' term variable fonts connects typeface creation to the latest technical innovation in the field of type design: *multiple master* fonts. Adjustable intermediate font styles can now be generated once again. A new aspect is that editable text can be integrated as animated type into time-based and interactive media.

The variable fonts format, the product of a collaboration between Adobe, Apple, Google, and Microsoft, has been part of the OpenType format since 2017. Adobe has developed the compact file format CFF2 for PostScript-based fonts. However, unlike the TrueType-based fonts, these will not be backwards compatible. The compactness of a single font file that contains all font-generation variables offers both a reduction of file size and better typeface integration into apps.[15]

Such fonts are especially suited for use in electronic media, which require particular flexibility in terms of formats and proportions. Variable fonts provide a prerequisite for adaptation to the modifiable window sizes and column widths of responsive websites.[16] This could finally lead to an improvement of the persistently unsatisfactory typographic quality of websites on computers, tablets, smartphones, etc. Furthermore, Cascading Style Sheets (CSS) are needed to make such design instructions for the website elements usable in browsers.

Variable fonts also offer multiple possibilities for type animations – including as a supplement to the long-established flowing transitions seen in the *morphing* of images – on websites, e-boards, animated posters, and digital postcards as well as for the design of opening credits and title sequences in film and advertising. In these instances, text can be edited at any time. Fortunately, variable fonts are also returning to the print sector, this time also by way of the layout program *Adobe InDesign*. This development increases the likelihood of these additional possibilities flowing into all areas of the design process.

Once again, it is most conspicuously Dutch designers who are bringing new innovation to type creation. As far back as 1989, ERIK VAN BLOKLAND and JUST VAN ROSSUM developed the variable RandomFont Beowolf |**31**|. The experimental quality of the typeface – in three variants with different degrees of randomness – was a response to the emerging slickness of digital type. The designers used drawings of an Antiqua of their own design as a starting point. Transcribed using the font software *IkarusM* by URW and then, as they write, "hacked into the PostScript code by hand",[17] the letterforms mutated automatically |**32**|. They were subject to ongoing change – permanent randomness. It was not possible to produce two identical laser printouts. The year 1991 saw the release of the Grotesque, BeoSans Hard and BeoSans Soft, although in this case it is not considered a superfamily.

Another noteworthy type creation by the two LettError founders is their project Twin. In 2002, the project won the competition held by the University of Minnesota Design Institute (now College of Design) for the design of a corporate type for the Twin Cities Minneapolis and St. Paul. A process involving the morphing of 800 individually drawn letterforms changes the type interactively, for instance in response to local weather data.[18] JUST VAN ROSSUM and ERIK VAN BLOKLAND, as well as the latter's brother PETR VAN BLOKLAND, describe themselves not only as type designers but also as programmers, and have not only coauthored the *IkarusM* but also created the font software *RoboFont*.

A number of variable fonts, such as Decovar |**33**| and Amstelvar by DAVID BERLOW, cofounder of the American digital type foundry The Font Bureau Inc., have existed since 2017,[19] some are currently being developed, and others will be developed in the future. Access to the diverse design parameters offered by variable fonts depends on the number and choice of slider controls that are used: weight, width, slant, height, stroke form, curve form, stroke contrast,

31 RandomFont in three variants of outlines with different degrees of randomness

32 Permanent variability and randomness on the monitor and in the printout

ABCDEFGHIJKLMNO
PQRSTUVWXYZ
abcdefghijklmnopqr
stuvwxyz
1234567890/%

ABCDEFGHIJKLMNO
PQRSTUVWXYZ
abcdefghijklmnopqr
stuvwxyz
1234567890/%

ABCDEFGHIJKLMNO
PQRSTUVWXYZ
abcdefghijklmnopqr
stuvwxyz
1234567890/%

Beowolf 21 | Beowolf 22 | Beowolf 23

Variable font *Decovar*: flowing transitions of numerous decorations and terminals

33 ▼

design and weight of stroke and curve terminals, juncture, fill, and outline. The appearance of typefaces and text can be varied at different tempos and in flowing movements simultaneously. Type undergoes change through movement; the impression made by the font is continually modified, from austere to playful, from businesslike to decorative, from noble to vulgar, from strange to broken …

Variable fonts include new typefaces specially designed to be variable as well as classics such as the two Grotesques Avenir Next by ADRIAN FRUTIGER and Meta by ERIK SPIEKERMANN.[20] The possibilities in this field seem endless. We must wait to see what the future brings – or, better still, we should work on formulating sound ideas that can guide future development. Playful, experimental, and application-oriented concepts are all required.

What should not be left out of consideration, however, is the fact that the speed of animations on websites is often much too high. Although we see the movement by way of flowing modification of type, the quality of the letterform cannot be appreciated. For sure, movement draws our attention, but the danger of permanent disturbance and annoyance should not be ignored. In addition, the manner of animation needs to be carefully considered with reference to the function of the text. Such an animation may be loud and dominant in order to attract attention – like a prominent display typeface on a static poster – or quiet and discreet in order to convey sensitive contents appropriately. It is necessary always to be aware of the danger of permanent overstimulation.

Typeface combination | Criteria

Three elements of a good typeface combination:

1.

a good idea/meaning and a coherent expression of that meaning

2.

a distinct contrast – but not necessarily a striking contrast

3.

a clear analogy/ analogies

!

*A distinct **contrast** and thus clear differentiation is a basic requirement for a good typeface combination. On the other hand, a striking contrast, that is, conspicuous differentiation, is not absolutely essential. Good quality can usually be achieved with little effort.*

*Achieving a subtle contrast usually requires a considerable investment of effort before a coherent result is attained. In this context, both **analogy** in the relationship and attention to details play a significant role. Such typeface combinations often have a more specific expressive quality and sometimes – albeit only at a second glance – a more surprising character.*

Possibilities of typeface combination

Typefaces with similar heights and proportions facilitate good typeface combinations.

1
Combining font styles within the same typeface family

Most obvious solution

Advantages
· Analogies are typical for the different font styles.
· Similarities based on type design are already present.
· Differences have been consciously formed and harmonized in the design process.

Disadvantage
· The possibilities for contrast are usually very limited.

2
Combining font styles from a superfamily

Simple solution

Advantages
· Analogies are typical for all font styles in the superfamily.
· Similarities based on type design are already present.
· Differences have been consciously formed and harmonized in the design process.

Disadvantage
· The possibilities for contrast are more varied but seldom particularly interesting.

3
Combining font styles of different typefaces

Complex solution

Advantage
· The possibilities for contrast are almost unlimited.

Disadvantages
· Analogies and similarities often require a protracted search and a complex and lengthy process of harmonization.
· Differences in terms of details can have an irritating effect and impair expressiveness.

Contrast brings tension to typeface combinations

The most popular and most often used contrast is the **bright-dark contrast** or the **light-heavy contrast**.

Advantage:
At least in the case of a pronounced difference in brightness, the result is an amplification of the active or striking effect. A distinct contrast will also drown out any dissonances in the analogies.

Disadvantage:
A brightness contrast that is too weak creates an anemic impression. As a result, more subtle statements and impressions may be concealed or suppressed.

Combining different type forms
is the most common method of typeface combination.

Such typeface combinations generally profit from obvious differences, such as those between Antiqua and Grotesque. In most cases, this type of difference is preferable.

This method makes it significantly easier to achieve a good interplay between typefaces, particularly when they have a uniform style.

Combining the same type forms
is an extremely rare and exceptional case.

Combining two Antiquas or two Grotesques, for example, is not recommended because the result is almost always clumsy or even irritating.

However, based on a sound knowledge of typefaces, a strong formal sense, and a comprehensive understanding of the expressiveness of type forms – as well as an intensive engagement with the diversity and quality of such forms – a subtle charm can nevertheless be achieved, particularly in the case of a striking title or word mark.

Analogy

The tables on pages 160–164 indicate which design features tend to require analogy and which require contrast. In many cases, the two possibilities can be seen as having equal status.

Interesting typeface combinations almost always feature a deliberately chosen difference or contrast and an interplay between this contrast and the similarity of the faces, that is, their analogous relationship. This analogous relationship forms the quieter, more subtle aspect. A love of detail combined with precision is decisive here. When combining typefaces, contrast generates vitality, while analogy generates harmony.

Along with the formation of one or more striking contrasts, high-quality typeface combinations also rely on the detection of analogies. Over time, the analysis of analogies that are either present or lacking as well as the comparative consideration of combinations – sometimes in the case of minimally different typeface variations – facilitate the development of a feel for such combinations. In successful combinations, the formal interplay between contrast and analogy results in a harmonious, mutual supplementation. And in the best cases, the expressive polyphony – based on greater diversity and simultaneous unity – conveys a visual message that supports, supplements, or extends the textual statement. Here clarity, but also ambiguity, can be the goal.

The two most important analogous relationships are those between different *curve shapes* and between different *heights*. Other analogies are almost always involved and are based on the specific requirements of the respective case. They can include relationships based on width, slant, ductus, fill and outline, style and thereby the axis of stress and proportional relationships, as well as, although rather seldom, typographic color. Finally, the details of the design of the individual letters should not be underestimated. Particularly when it comes to larger presentations such as word marks, details play a decisive role in the choice of the best type.

Given the enormous range of digital fonts now available, it should always be possible at least to find an appropriate face. However, the immense choice means that creating outstanding typeface combinations may well require as much time as it did in the predigital era. Online tools such as *Identifont, Fontjoy, Tiff (Type diff tool), FontCombinator* by Typotheque, and *FontExplorer X Pro* (from Version 7 onwards) can provide assistance in this regard, but they are no substitute for profound knowledge and certainly not for detailed engagement by means of testing, comparison, and analysis.[1]

Contrast

Creating a harmonious typeface combination – in which typefaces supplement or even amplify one another – requires much more than obvious differences in type design. An effective combination needs a formally relevant otherness that can be described as a contrast. In addition, the question of analogy needs to be considered.

In the context of typeface combination, contrast does not imply absolutely opposing designs. And it certainly does not mean that typefaces have to appear different in terms of *all* their formally relevant features. If the difference between typefaces is too great in too many aspects, they are often perceived as disharmonious. It suffices for typefaces to be clearly differentiated in terms of one or a few features. On the other hand, if the differences between the typefaces are too slight, they will not be registered at all or will be perceived as mistakes.

Insofar as the corresponding font styles are available, some contrasts can be realized within one *type family*. These obvious possibilities should always be tested first and their effect examined: *weight contrast* (→*Weight:* p.178), *width contrast* (→*Width:* p.182), and *slant contrast* (→*Slant:* p.184); for some time now, *decoration contrast* has also been increasingly utilized once again (→*Fill:* p.193).

However, typeface combination is usually understood as entailing *form contrast* (→*Type form:* p.166), that is, a combining of faces from different classification groups. The combinations easiest to realize are those between faces within a *superfamily* (→*Superfamily:* p.137), since here the heights, style, and typographic colors are unitary, meaning that significant analogies are already available. Usually more exciting and lively, although also far more time-consuming, are combinations involving different typefaces. These allow for the use of several other kinds of contrast, such as those based on *type style* (→*Type style:* p.172), *ductus* (→*Ductus:* p.186), *shaping* (→*Shaping:* p.187), *effect* (→*Effect:* p.193), and *impression* (→*Typeface character:* p.53). However, an interesting combination usually requires more than one sort of contrast.

Typographic contrasts such as *size contrast* and *color contrast* are often also utilized in the design of printed matter. Here, the amount or length of letters, words, and/or text also plays an essential role – in terms of relative proportions and positions and in terms of line measure, type area (grid), and page format.

!

Possible kinds of contrast that may help with the identification of appropriate, interesting, or surprising typeface combinations can be found in the table on the following page spread.

Varieties of contrast – a possible overview and (extendable) classification system

**Form	Style** Type form	Curve form	Type style	**Typographic color** Weight	Width	Slant	Position	Size	**Ductus** Connection	Movement	Tempo
Glyphic – … Script – … Blackletter – … Antiqua – … Egyptian – … Grotesque – … Latin – … round – broken round – angular flat – broken flat – angular inner – outer dynamic – … static – … geometric – … eccentric – …	light – heavy bright – dark linear – planar contrast – no contrast narrow – wide compressed – extended upright – inclined forward – backward above – below left – right a little – a lot short – long small – large	separated – joined passive – active still – animated calm – lively regular – irregular constant – fleeting halting – fluid jagged – flowing sedate – ebullient standing – running running – dancing dancing – leaping deliberate – hasty

Tip

Referring to such terms can help with the exact specification of the contrast that is being sought.

Shaping
Stroke form | Terminal | Juncture

waisted – parallel
waisted – bulging
parallel – conical
tapered – flared
decreasing – increasing
symmetrical – asymmetrical
straight – curved

emphasized – de-emphasized
rounded – angular
blunt – pointed
horizontal – vertical

flush – notched
open – closed

Effect | Decoration
Fill | Outline | Color | Dimension

solid – decorated
plain – embellished
austere – playful

clear – blurred
smooth – rough

full – empty
positive – reversed-out (cameo)
achromatic – colorful

flat – three-dimensional
in front – behind

Impression
Materiality | Epoch | Culture

mellow – acerbic
graceful – ungainly
smooth – coarse
soft – hard
delicate – massive
filigree – robust
fragile – stable
elegant – tacky
clean – blotchy
whole – shattered

personal – rational
organic – technical
natural – constructed
floral – technoid

classic – fashionable
traditional – modern
historical – current
old-fashioned – trendy
anachronistic – futuristic

domestic – exotic

157

Three aspects to be considered when working with contrasts:

1.

Contrasts must be concise ...

when differences in type sizes are greater.

when more than two typefaces are combined.

2.

Contrasts can be subtle ...

as type sizes increase in proportion to the format.

when typefaces are placed closer to one another.

!

*In the case of **concise** contrasts, the similarities of typefaces can be relatively slight.*

*In the case of **subtle** contrasts, the similarities of typefaces must be quite clear.*

3.

They are strengthened / weakened ...

by differences in terms of
- *color*
- *brightness*
- *texture*
- *positioning*
- *type size*
- *tracking (letterspacing)*

by interventions in the design such as
- *cutting*
- *tearing*
- *underlining*
- *strikethrough*
- *framing*
- *distorting*
  etc.

by finishing technologies such as
- *die cutting*
- *embossing*
- *varnishing*
  etc.[2]

Design features – variables in contrast and analogy

Typefaces with similar heights and proportions facilitate good typeface combinations.

1	2	3	4.1	4.2	4.3
Type form Typeface classification	**Curve form** Letter O	**Heights** Uppercase and lowercase letters	**Type style** Stress axis Counter	Curve direction Counter	Instroke Outstroke

Glyphic
 Script
 Blackletter
 Antiqua
 Egyptian
 Grotesque
 Latin
	round curve
	 · circle
	 · ellipse
	 · oval
	 flat curve
	 · superellipse
	 · stadium
	 · rounded corner
	   rectangle
	 angular form
	 · rectangle
	 · rhombus
	 mixed form
	 · ogive
		ascender
		 · towering
		 · elevated
		 · equal
		 cap height
		 small cap height
		 x-height
		 · high
		 · medium
		 · low
		 descender
		 · short
		 · medium
		 · long
			diagonal
			 · strong
			 · moderate
			 · slight
			 vertical
			 mixed
				open
				 · strong
				 · moderate
				 · slight
				 closed
				 · noticeable
				 · strong
				 · extreme
					· horizontal
					 · diagonal
					   steeply rising
					   rising
					   slightly rising
					   sloping
					 · tapered
					 · parallel
					 · broadened
					 · straight
					 · concave curve
					 · convex curve
					 · bent
					 · wavy

contrast	analogy	analogy	contrast analogy	contrast analogy	analogy

> **!** *Each of the listed, typifying formal features of letterforms points to the question of **contrast** and **analogy** in the context of typeface combination. The kind that is most common is listed at the bottom of the table.*

4.4	4.5	5.1	5.2	6	7
Rhythm Proportions	Offset Center position	**Weight** Stroke weight Downstroke	Stroke contrast Upstroke	**Width**	**Slant**

opposite
different
similar
adjusted
equal
	without
	· optical center
	with
	· upwards
	· downwards
		ultrathin
		thin
		extralight
		light
		book
		regular
		medium
		semibold / demi
		bold
		extrabold
		heavy
		black
		ultrablack
		fat
			stroke difference
			· extreme
			· high
			· distinct
			· noticeable
			· reverse-contrast
			stroke similarity
			· similar
			· optically
			  identical
			· monolinear
				extra narrow
				· compressed
				· extra condensed
				narrow
				· condensed
				normal
				wide
				· extended
				extra wide
					upright
					· roman
					· upright italic
					slanted
					· individual
					· italic
					· uniform
					· oblique
					backslanted
					  (left-leaning)

contrast analogy	analogy	contrast	contrast	contrast analogy	contrast analogy

Design features – variables in contrast and analogy

8.1	8.2	**9**.1	9.2	9.3	9.4
Ductus Connection	Movement	**Shaping** Stroke and curve	Stroke and curve terminals	Bracket Stem | Serif	Juncture Stem | Curve

separated finials
· unconnected
joined finials
· connected
	fleeting
	ebullient
	fluid
	deliberate
	leisurely
	sedate
	halting
	cramped
	jagged
		symmetrical
		· biconcave
		  (waisted)
		· parallel
		· biconvex
		  (bulging)
		asymmetrical
		· concave
		· planar
		· convex
		conical
		· tapered
		· broadened
			symmetrical
			asymmetrical
			tapered
			consistent
			broadened
			vertical
			diagonal
			horizontal
			pointed
			angular
			curved
			rounded
			concave (cupped)
			convex
				adnate
				(bracketed)
				· obtuse angle
				· right angle
				· acute angle
				abrupt
				(unbracketed)
				· obtuse angle
				· right angle
				· acute angle
				combined
					juncture type
					· angular
					· rounded
					· combined
					juncture width
					· tapered
					· broadened
					juncture depth
					· notched
					· interrupted
					curve direction
					· steep
					· oblique
					· flat

contrast	contrast	contrast analogy	contrast analogy	analogy	analogy

10.1

Letter design
a e

middle stroke
- diagonal
- horizontal
- bent

analogy

10.2

G g

cross stroke
- without
- inside
- inside/outside

juncture
- angular
- rounded

spur or chin
- without
- with

loop
- single-storey
- double-storey

analogy

10.3

i j

dot/tittle
- round
   vertical oval
   horizontal oval
- angular
   square
   tall rectangle
   wide rectangle
   rhombus
   rhomboid
- other

analogy

10.4

K k

joint
- separated
- pointed
- slightly blunt
- blunt
- offset

link
- horizontal
- diagonal

analogy

10.5

M

legs
- diagonal
- vertical

apex
- pointed
- blunt
- beveled

vertex
- aligned
- elevated

analogy

10.6 ...

W w

middle strokes
- meeting
- juncture
- overlap

analogy

Design features – variables in contrast and analogy

11.1	**11.2**	**12**	**13**	**14**
**Effect	Decoration** Fill	 Outline	**Setting length** Words	Texts	**Type size**	**Color**
solid decorated · outlined · contoured · inlined · engraved · textured · cameo · framed · 3-dimensional · beveled · shaded · embellished · illustrated	smooth rough decorated · perforated · torn · melted/ liquefied · wavy · jagged · spiky · hairy …	opposing different similar adjusted identical	opposing different similar aligned identical	opposing different similar adjusted identical
contrast analogy	contrast analogy	contrast analogy	contrast analogy	contrast analogy

Typeface combinations add flavor to typography

As a rule, letters do not touch, in either their horizontal or their vertical extension (of course there are exceptions that prove the rule).³

Words set in capitals and small caps tend to require increased tracking. They need to be letterspaced or better yet, balanced. Here, balancing is the process of creating an optically equal amount of light between all characters by manual kerning. What is required here is not mathematically identical spaces or volumes, but uniform brightness.⁴

In the case of logos, word marks, and titles or text in large point sizes, spaces between characters and words always need to be optically balanced – irrespective of what kinds of characters (uppercase letters, small caps, lowercase letters, figures, punctuation marks) are involved.

Different word lengths should not, or only to a limited extent, be adjusted to the same length.

The shortening of spaces between letters by manual kerning or decreasing tracking leads to darker word images. On the other hand, increasing tracking creates a brighter word image. And when not used properly, both can negatively impact readability and aesthetic quality.

1
Type form

The primary way of combining typefaces is based on *contrast* between type forms. Analogy should be dispenced with. The differences between typefaces with the same type form are usually too small to be perceived clearly or are too different in terms of design to generate a harmonious impression.

The addition of another type form (or, where required, more than one) brings an additional component to typography. Combining typefaces offers the possibility of an additional property, an expanded formal expressiveness, a different mood, and a more differentiated statement. On the level of type alone, the addition of another typeface can increase the degree of expressive power – without the help of other components such as gray values, colors, lines, ornaments, or images, and without a diversity of arrangement in the typographic composition.

Currently, the most popular kind of contrast between type forms is that between *Antiqua* and *Grotesque* | **01** |. This combination almost always involves a change in terms of stroke contrast (→*Stroke contrast:* p.180). The impression made by such combinations can be additionally amplified in a targeted manner by a slant contrast (→*Slant:* p.184), which sometimes involves a different proportion and ductus (→*Ductus:* p.186), or by a deliberately introduced light-heavy contrast (→*Weight:* p.178).

The period from the 1930s to the 1950s (and to some extent later) was characterized by an extensive range of typeface combinations | **02** |. Popular combinations were *Script* combined with either *Egyptian* or *Grotesque,* usually with the addition of a light-heavy contrast. Such combinations link, for example, calmness with liveliness, austerity with playfulness, and the rational with the personal. Likewise less common today are combinations of *Antiqua* or *Grotesque* with *Egyptian,* form contrasts that are also often supplemented by a light-heavy contrast. For decades now, we have also seen almost no examples of combinations with *Blackletter,* even in the German-language region. This is not due to a lack of interesting possibilities, but obviously due to the general decline in the usage of Blackletter typefaces.

Particular attention is advisable when it comes to combination with the *Glyphic* type form, since, in terms of stroke and curve terminals, it lies between *Antiqua* and *Grotesque,* and as a result there is in some cases a lack of adequate differentiation. This also applies to *Latin.* Typeface combinations between *Antiqua* and *Latin* are also only interesting in large sizes.

Most widely used combination of type forms: Antiqua and Grotesque

01 ▼

Antiqua Grotesque
Freya | Today Sans

The seven form groups offer a wide range of possibilities for typeface combinations

02 ▼

Glyphic Egyptian
Optima | Amasis

Grotesque *Script*
Kabel | Snell Roundhand

𝔅𝔩𝔞𝔠𝔨𝔩𝔢𝔱𝔱𝔢𝔯 Antiqua
Walbaum Fraktur | Ellington

Latin Grotesque
Versailles | Bau

2 Curve form
Letter O

The curve form is a decisive feature when it comes to the search for appropriate typefaces. As a general rule, the goal here is *analogy*.

The description of curve forms involves – irrespective of one's knowledge of type history and typeface classification – an important differentiating feature. Even in the case of the Grotesques with no contrast, several groups can be identified based on the diversity of basic O-forms |**03**|, with fluid transitions between the *circle* Futura, *ellipse* Frutiger, *oval* Antique Olive, *superellipse* Felbridge, *stadium* Klavika, *rounded corner rectangle* Eurostile, etc. And this list does not include all the diverse possible O-forms with corners.

Basic shapes of the O: circle, ellipse, oval, superellipse, stadium, rounded corner rectangle
03 ▶

O O O O O O

Futura | Frutiger | Antique Olive | Felbridge | Klavika | Eurostile

Only in the rarest cases is contrast based on curve form interesting. This sort of contrast needs to be quickly recognizable as the guiding idea if such a combination is to prove satisfying. If not, the result is an unpleasant tension, an expression of inherent interference. A combination of circular and oval curve forms should therefore be avoided, at least in cases where there are no additional pronounced differences.

3 Heights

Similar typeface heights facilitate combination. In the case of typeface combinations on the same line in an optically equivalent size, analogy is almost mandatory. Conversely, in the case of clearly different sizes – for example, in titles and texts – height plays a secondary role.

The letter heights of the Latin alphabets (majuscules and minuscules) can be roughly divided into four groups: cap height, ascender height, x-height, and descender height (→p.53 |**28**|). However, in reality the alphabets comprises a multiplicity of heights. For example, the stem of the lowercase t protrudes only slightly above the x-height, and the dot on the i is usually placed below the ascender height; yet other heights are introduced where accents are used. In addition, closer inspection reveals optically determined adaptations of round and pointed forms.

In the case of combinations of *uppercase typesetting,* the procedure – at least in relation to heights – is relatively simple. If letters are supposed to be of the same height, the cap heights, which are usually unequal in the different fonts, must be adjusted to the same size. Different size indications in points (pt) are normal (→*Point size:* p.70).

Generally the work here is in combining the typefaces: the search for appropriate fonts – usually faces with an analogous relationship in terms of *rhythm* (→*Rhythm:* p.176) and *letterforms* – followed by the no less difficult task of manually kerning caps with the aim of achieving optically even spacing between characters. What this amounts to, as Jost Hochuli put it so well, is achieving 'optically equal light' between characters | **04** |.⁵

DESIGNFORMEN
DESIGNFORMEN

Bodoni LT · *Book* | Glypha · *55 Roman* – each 28 pt | Glypha · *55 Roman*: 26.2 pt

Combining typefaces in *lowercase typesetting* is somewhat more complicated, since there are at least three heights to consider: ascenders, x-heights, and descenders. The most conspicuous of these is the x-height, since – due to the fact that the majority of letters are of this height – it is this particular measure that dominates the line composition. The first step therefore involves aligning the x-heights by changing the point size. The second step entails checking how similar the respective ascender and descender heights are | **05** |. If one of the heights differs too starkly for a pleasing juxtaposition, then the only solution is a change of typeface | **06** |.

hinten*vorne*
back*front*

Franklin Gothic | Adobe Garamond – each 24 pt

hinten*vorne*
back*front*

Franklin Gothic: 24 pt | Garamond: 31 pt

hinten*vorne*
back*front*

Syntax: 22.5 pt | Hollander: 23 pt

Ultimately, heights need to be selected according to their optical effect. For example, heavy typefaces – due to their smaller counters – require a somewhat larger x-height than light ones.

Combinations involving *upper- and lowercase letters* are particularly challenging – especially if the typefaces have to be used next to one another in

---

Align the heights of capitals and optically adjust the spacing between characters
04 ▶

A harmonious example with aligned x-heights in German, but not in English
05 ▼ | ▶

In both languages harmonious combination of two fonts with almost identical heights
06 ▶▶

the same size. In this case, a combination requires typefaces in which not only minuscules but also majuscules are of almost the same height. Here too, typographic quality is based on the same optical rather than numeric size | **07** |. Different point sizes are the norm.

Hagedon Hagedon

Freya | Today Sans – each 27 pt

When searching for suitable typefaces, the focus should primarily be on those exhibiting the same proportional relationship between x-height and cap height. Typefaces already exhibiting pronounced height differences in this respect are not suited to combination in the same line | **08** |. The next step is to consider the relationship between these measures and the ascender | **09** |. The length of the descender can be set aside for the moment, since it is normally related to the height of the ascender and minimally shorter than the latter in most typefaces. There are exceptions, but within the context of the immense number of typefaces these are extremely rare, one example being Bernhard Modern, which represents a radical departure from a normally balanced relationship. Here, the difference between ascender and descender lengths is unusually large | **10** |. We find a completely different situation in the case of Antique Olive by ROGER EXCOFFON, which features an extremely large x-height, resulting in an f-curve that requires a (distracting) displacement of the cross stroke | **11** |.

As discussed elsewhere in some detail (→*Font size:* p.72) there are no height norms. And as seen in the black, black condensed and Inserat font styles of Helvetica | **12** | by Linotype, even digitized fonts with the same family name – in particular, those originating from metal and wooden types – do not always feature coordinated heights.

Hirtzfelp **Hirtzfelp** Hirtzfelp

News Gothic | Antique Olive | Vectora

Hhxp Hhxp Hhxp

Helvetica · Black | Black Condensed | Helvetica Inserat · *Regular* – each 26 pt

---

The ideal case: two typefaces with almost identical heights on all levels
07 ▶

Height ratios are too different, which excludes combination on the same line
08 ▼

Ideal ratio of cap height to x-height but not to the ascender height
09 ▼▼

Adobe Garamond | Helvetica | Franklin Gothic

Hxhp Hxhp

Cartier Book | Helvetica

Hagedon

Bernhard Modern

Atypical height ratio: extremely long ascenders and short descenders
10 ▲

Extremely high x-height necessitates a downward displacement of the f-crossbar
11 ▶

Same point size, but different heights in these three font styles of *Helvetica*
12 ▶

| Typical of Lucian Bernhard's typefaces: very low x-height, long ascenders
| **13** ▶

Hagedon Hagedon Hagedon
Lucian | Bernhard Gothic | Bernhard Modern

| Grotesques (cap heights aligned) with clearly different x-heights
| **14** ▶

Hagedon Hagedon Hagedon
Akzidenz Grotesk | Futura | Kabel

Possible criteria informing the determination of heights include: planned use – for example, choosing typefaces with large x-heights for best readability in the smallest point sizes for the stock market section of a newspaper; or typefaces that belong to certain classification groups – most Grotesques have a larger x-height than Antiquas (which makes combining such typefaces difficult). Last but not least, a significant role is also played by personal, formal preferences and prevailing fashion, as shown by the examples featuring very low x-heights and very long ascenders by the graphic and type designer LUCIAN BERNHARD | **13** |. Other German designs produced between the mid-1920s and the late 1930s include PAUL RENNER's Futura and RUDOLF KOCH's Kabel | **14** |. Although the former does not exhibit such extreme height differences, it has a low x-height for a Grotesque. One model for such proportions may have been GEORGES PEIGNOT's Cochin, which was named after the French copper engraver CHARLES-NICOLAS COCHIN and produced by the Paris type foundry G. Peignot & Fils in 1912 | **15** |.

| Division into three groups of x-heights: low, medium, and high
| **15** ▶ | ▶▶

Cochin | Minion | Hollander – each 27 pt   Kabel | Today Sans | Helvetica – each 27 pt

There are thus no prescribed heights or height ratios for typefaces. Nevertheless, the *height ratios* used for lowercase letters in a large number of typefaces can be roughly divided into three or four groups: typefaces with low, medium, and high x-heights | 15 | as well as those with extremely high x-heights | 11 |.

In addition, we occasionally find typefaces with low cap heights. These are often mixed forms combining upright majuscules with inclined minuscules, for example Antiqua majuscules with Script or italic minuscules | 16 |. In 1501 ALDUS MANUTIUS set his small-format book series in this combination of roman and italic.

Hagedon Hagedon *Hagedon*

Bembo Book | Delphin | *Poetica · Chancery IV*

Low cap heights of *Delphin* and *Poetica* compared with *Bembo Book*
16 ▶

The relative heights of caps and ascenders also need to be considered. In most cases, the ascenders are somewhat higher or of the same height | 17 |.

Hh Hh Hh   Hh Hh Hh

Cartier Book | Arno | Times   Futura | Today Sans | Univers

Different ratios of cap heights to ascender heights
17 ▶ | ▶▶

It is rare these days to find typefaces with variants that differ in terms of ascender and descender dimensions. This was the case with Apollo (from 1964), Plantin, Sabon, and Times New Roman for the Monophoto phototypesetting system developed by the British Monotype Corporation.⁶ Unfortunately, the current digital fonts have not maintained these variants. Well-known examples are Trinité (released in 1982 by the Swiss phototypesetting manufacturer Bobst Graphic), which features three heights, and Lexicon, released in 1989 and featuring two heights. Both were designed by BRAM DE DOES | 18 |.⁷

Hhg Hhg

Lexicon No 1 | Lexicon No 2

A typeface in two versions with different heights
18 ▶

Typefaces with a *dynamic style* (→tables: pp. 116–129) tend to exhibit ascenders that are higher than the caps. Faces with a *static style,* particularly Egyptian and Grotesque, tend to have ascenders and caps of the same height | 19 |.

Hh Hh Hh   Hh Hh Hh

Adobe Garamond | Thesis TheSerif | Today Sans   Linotype Didot | Serifa | Univers

Higher ascenders in dynamic style (left), unlike in static style (right)
19 ▶ | ▶▶

Typefaces from different epochs to some extent reveal different approaches to heights. Nevertheless there is a tendency for the x-height to increase over the course of time. Compared to the older type form Antiqua, the younger form Grotesque therefore usually exhibits a higher middle letter band | 20 |. Typefaces from the same period tend to correspond in terms of height | 21 |, particularly when they have been designed for the same application, such as book or newspaper setting.

Hhxp Hhxp Hhxp Hhxp

Jenson | Baskerville | Didot | Bau (Schelter Grotesk)

Hhxp Hhxp Hhxp

Ionic | Modern MT | Bau (Schelter Grotesk)

This can also apply to typefaces by the same designer. However, it is impossible to generalize, since designers also take diverging approaches.

Different height concepts from the 15th to the 18th century
20 ▶

A more unified height concept in the faces of the 19th century
21 ▶

---

4 Type style

Subdivision based on type style offers a more refined classification into dynamic, static, geometric, and eccentric typefaces. Combinations can be based on both *analogy* and *contrast*. However, contrast in terms of type style alone does not suffice – it is not significant enough!

Stylistic distinctions alone obviously lack the clarity to be able to function as the basis of type contrast. Changes only to the stress axis (→*Stress axis:* p.173), counterforms, curve direction, or proportions of uppercase letters (→*Rhythm/Proportions:* p.176) do not suffice to generate an interesting tension. Moreover, a typeface is not always consistently designed in stylistic terms. A typeface combination involving a contrast in type style therefore always includes at least one further contrast – very often in terms of type form. For example, a combination of Antiqua and Grotesque may include a contrast between dynamic style and static style as well – not uncommonly augmented by a bright-dark contrast.

However, it is easier to create typeface combinations that employ stylistic analogies, since stylistically related faces tend to be more similar in terms of rhythm and – particularly important – height.

4.1
Type style
Stress axis | Counter

Typefaces with a dynamic style usually have a diagonal stress axis, and those with a static or geometric style a vertical axis. The axis does not play a fundamental role in the combination of typefaces. Both *analogy* and *contrast* are possible.

The opposing curve sections of letterforms with bowls exhibit their brightest spot at an angle of 90 degrees to their darkest spot. The stress axis defined by this relationship is very evident in the case of typefaces featuring stroke contrast; but, although less visible, it is also present in faces with no stroke contrast. The origin of this stress axis lies in the use of writing tools such as the flat brush, reed pen (calamus), broad nib pen, calligraphy pen, and calligraphy pencil. All these implements have a narrow and a broad side, and as a result, writing with them produces lines that alternate between thick and thin, or dark and bright. Based on the angle of writing, the axis of the stress in curve forms can be diagonal or vertical/horizontal | **22** |.

In the case of typefaces with a dynamic style, the extremes are usually diagonally positioned (there are exceptions for the letter O in the case of Egyptian and Grotesque), with the two brightest spots on the axis on the upper left and lower right, and the two darkest spots on the axis on the lower left and upper right. Gestalt theory teaches us that the diagonal is a fundamental feature of dynamics.

Trajan, which is based on the Capitalis monumentalis of the second century, and an Antiqua of the fifteenth-century Humanism class, such as Jenson, both have a strongly diagonal stress axis. In the Renaissance class of the sixteenth century, such as Garamond, this axis is already less diagonal but still between 10 and 20 degrees | **23** |. In the case of the transitional or Baroque class of the seventeenth and early eighteenth century, the axis begins to become more upright, approaching the vertical but remaining slightly diagonal. Typefaces such as Bell can thus also be attributed a dynamic style | **23** |. The diagonal axis is a feature of the dynamic style.

However, writing with a pen angle of almost 0 degrees generates a type appearance with vertical/horizontal axes | **22** |. In the case of the Neoclassicism class of the eighteenth century – influenced by the pointed nib pen and engraved lettering – we are referring to faces with a static style. As evident in Didot, such letters exhibit vertical/horizontal axes | **24** |. The outer form of the O is almost circular, while the elliptical form of the counter is a result of the stroke contrast | **25** |.

Nib angles:
1st century oblique,
8th century
almost horizontal
22

Capitalis Quadrata | Capitalis Rustica | Uncialis

Diagonal axes of the Capitalis monumentalis and dynamic-style Antiquas
23

Vertical-horizontal stress axes of the static-style Antiquas (Neoclassicism class)
24

Trajan | Jenson | Garamond | Bell

Didot

In the case of Antiquas: outer form of O is close to round, inner form is elliptical
25

Trajan | Jenson | Garamond | Bell | Didot

Antiqua, static style (above): basis of 19th-century type forms
26 ▼

Her
Her Her Her Her

Didot – Egyptian | Clarendon | Bau | Versailles

Representative book typeface for private press printing: Antiqua in the eccentric style
27 ▼

HOE neb

Kennerley Old Style

Dynamic Grotesque: stress axis varying from vertical to diagonal (left to right)
28 ▶

The static style is also characteristic of the new type forms of the nineteenth century. The vertical axes of the Egyptians, Grotesques, and Latins from this period point to their common origins in the neoclassical Antiqua. Even if the digital examples shown here do not correspond to the originals in every detail, the stylistic connection is still very evident | **26** |.

A return to the diagonal axis can be seen in the Antiquas that emerged from the Book Art movement and were used in its letterpress publications from the latter half of the nineteenth century onwards. Typical of the typefaces of this period is the eccentric style – a late example is Kennerley Old Style from 1911 | **27** | (→*Classification groups:* pp. 97–115). And Grotesque and Egyptian? Their development towards a dynamic style begins in the twentieth century. Still, in this case the stress axis is not consistently diagonal. The type style can therefore not be read reliably from the axis. One example of this is Gill Sans from 1927. Nevertheless, based on the proportions of the majuscules and the open curve direction, it – like the later Frutiger and Caecilia – is classed as having a dynamic style. However, the vertical axis (and the static counterforms in the Frutiger) generates a stylistic mix. This becomes evident when Gill Sans is compared with TheSans and TheSerif | **28** |. Though, in these latter cases we also find deviations from the basic circular form.

HOE neb   HOE neb   HOE neb
            HOE neb   HOE neb

Gill Sans   (Neue) Frutiger | Caecilia   TheSans | TheSerif

Other stylistic features also do not suffice as sole contrasts when it comes to typeface combinations.

4.2
Type style
Curve direction | Counter

The curve direction is related to the stress axis and thus to the type style. A distinction is made between diagonal curve direction with open apertures in the case of a dynamic style and vertical curve direction with closed apertures in the case of a static style. Typeface combinations with *analogy* **or** *contrast* **in terms of type style are possible.**

The curve direction, which should not be confused with the curve terminal (→*Stroke and curve terminals:* p.189), has long replaced the stress axis as the most important feature when it comes to the identification of style. But unfortunately, it also cannot always be unambiguously classified.

Curve direction: dynamic opening, three times geometric, static closing
29 ▼

C　C C C　C

Gill Sans | Futura | Kabel | Avant Garde | Neuzeit S

Dynamic asymmetrical counter (above), static symmetrical counter (below)
30 ▶

bp dq
bp dq

Thesis TheSans | Franklin Gothic

Hybrid letterforms: static and dynamic axes, curves, and curve directions
31 ▼

onebac onebac
onebac onebac

Rotis: Sans Serif | Semi Sans | Semi Serif | Serif

4.3
Type style
Instroke | Outstroke

A typical feature of the dynamic style is a diagonally opening curve direction, which create an open aperture. The diagonal direction guides the eye forward and creates a connection to the adjacent letter |29|. However, in the case of the static style, the curve directions are pulled into the vertical, creating an impression of self-containment. The letters appear discrete. In the case of the geometric style, the angle at which the curve form is cut determines the behavior of the curve direction. In the case of vertically and diagonally oriented cuts, the aperture appears clearly open; in the case of a horizontally oriented cut, the aperture tends to appear closed |29| (→*Stroke and curve terminals:* p.189).

There is a direct connection between the pathway of a curve (consisting of circle segments) and the counter it encloses (although the interior space is obviously shaped by the inner line, which is not necessarily identical with the outer line). In a dynamic style, the usually diagonal axis, a flatter curved lower juncture with the stem in the case of b, p, and a flatter curved upper juncture with the stem in the case of d, q results in asymmetrical counters (→*Juncture:* p.191). By comparison, in a static style, the vertical axis and rather elliptical bowl result in more symmetrical counters |30|.

There are a few exceptions – although they are increasing in number – that prove the rule of stylistic features. The most well-known example is probably the superfamily Rotis by OTL AICHER, with its hybrid qualities. Static moments can be seen in the vertical axis and the symmetrical counters in b, p, d, q, as well as the closed curve direction in the upper curve of the minuscules a and c. Dynamic moments can be seen in the diagonal axis in n, c, e and – a special feature – the extremely open apertures in c and e |31|.

Over the course of centuries and in parallel with the shift in the stress axis, the instroke of Antiqua lowercase letters changed from a dynamic diagonal to a static horizontal. In large point sizes, the emphasis should be on *analogy*.

An Antiqua with a dynamic style has a diagonal stress axis and, correspondingly, diagonal instrokes and outstrokes |32|. In the case of fifteenth-century faces heavily influenced by handwriting, such as Jenson, the serifs are also asymmetrical, exhibiting an elongated form in the direction of writing and reading. The somewhat younger Garamond, the serifs of which are symmetrically formed, already indicates a shift away from handwritten lettering

Instrokes and out-strokes: development from dynamic diagonal to static horizontal
32 ▼

A difference in angle between the instroke and the stress axis is an exception (right)
33 ▼▼

iu iu iu iu iu
Jenson | Garamond | Bell | Bodoni | Didot

lno lno
Fairfield | Breughel

4.4
Type style
Rhythm | Proportions

The straightening of the stress axis is accompanied by the change of rhythm
34 ▼

HOV ESX O
HOV ESX O
HOV ESX O
HOV ESX O
Trajan | Garamond | Bell | Didot

to drawn letterforms. Over the centuries this shift becomes increasingly pronounced. The dominance of the diagonal and thus the degree of dynamism constantly diminishes, and instrokes and outstrokes become flatter and progressively closer to horizontal, as seen in the case of Bell. This development ends in the eighteenth century with the emergence of almost static faces such as Bodoni and completely static faces such as Didot | **32** |.

Faced with the immense diversity of typefaces today, we can no longer always take as our starting point a completely consistent type style. Stylistic features are being increasingly combined. For instance, a diagonal stress axis is no longer necessarily – at least in exceptional cases – paired with diagonal instrokes and outstrokes | **33** |. Now and then we find attempts to calm the main line by drawing the instrokes at the x-height less diagonal shaped than the instrokes of the ascenders.

As the stress axis becomes more upright, the rhythm of the dynamic style is transformed into the even measure of the static style. The originally contrasting proportions of the basic shapes H, O, V and the double-storey shapes E, S, X become adjusted. In typeface combinations *analogy* **is preferable, and in uppercase word marks almost mandatory.**

In typeface combination an important role is played not only by the respective heights but also by the respective body widths of the letters. Here it is not the 'natural' body width differences that we are concerned with – for example, between I and W – but rather the rhythm as a stylistic feature of a typeface. When comparing typefaces, it is not difficult to see that capitals accord with two principles of proportion: divergent (dynamic style) and adjusted (static style) body widths.

Diversity and *asymmetry* are characteristic elements of the dynamic style. This is shown by the majuscules, the diverse letter proportions of which generate a lively rhythm. In the case of the ancient Roman capitalis monumentalis – and thus Trajan – the double-storey shapes of the letters E, S, X take up half the width in optical terms of the shapes of the circle, square, and triangle that form the basis of the letters H, O, V | **34** |. The same basic approach can still be seen in the Antiqua of the Renaissance. Over the following 300 years, the rhythm successively approximates the equal measure of the static style. In the case of the Baroque class Antiqua of the eighteenth century, this transformation is not yet complete – as clearly shown by Bell.

Square and half-width double-storey square converge to form a vertical rectangle
35 ▼

HN EFPRSX
HN EFPRSX

Garamond | Didot

In *Die Schöne Schrift* (Beautiful typefaces) František Muzika writes of a Transitional class.[8] And Hans Peter Willberg rightly attributes a dynamic style to these typefaces.[9]

Uniformity and *symmetry* are characteristic elements of the static style. This is particularly evident in the proportions of the majuscules, which are based on equal measure. In the neoclassical Antiqua, the letters H and N, which were originally based on the square, are narrowed to form a rectangle, while, compared with their Renaissance counterparts, the double-storey letters E, F, L, B, P, R, S, X, Y are widened, with the result that all the letters have similar proportions | **35** |.

Typefaces in the dynamic and geometric styles that are based on the square and the circle almost always exhibit an obvious difference in the proportions of the majuscules and therefore have a differentiating rhythm. On the contrary, typefaces in the static style that are based on the rectangle and the ellipse are characterized by adjusted proportions and an adjusted rhythm. For this reason, attention needs to be paid to rhythm particularly when it comes to large point sizes.

And when designing uppercase word marks, the mixing of different rhythms is not recommended. As with the need for correspondence between curve forms (→*Curve form:* p. 167), in the case of rhythm *analogy* is preferable.

4.5
Type style
Offset | Center position

Eccentric style (below), using an offset to replace classical centering
36 ▼

CENTRIC
ECCENTRIC

Caecilia | Belwe Mono

The majuscule forms of the Latin alphabet are based not only on basic geometric shapes; they are also based on simple ratios, mainly the ratio produced by halving letters such as H in their optical center. Typefaces in the eccentric style usually exhibit an offset here, and for this reason the emphasis should be on *analogy* in typeface combinations.

The decades around 1900 saw the development of artist-designed typefaces in the context of letterpress printing and the Art Nouveau movement. As indicated by the term, most of these type designs were created by painters, architects, etc. In doing so, these designers felt a strong need to depart from basic geometrical shapes and simple ratios. This did not necessarily lead to flowery expressiveness, however. As in the 1970s, what emerged were faces in the eccentric style in which the middle stroke is offset. When it comes to typeface combinations, analogy is important here. If both faces exhibit an offset, a combination can be interesting with offsets both above and below the center position | **36** |.

5
Weight
Typographic color

The typographic color of font styles changes primarily with the weight of the stem. In typeface combinations, *contrast* **is usually preferred, since the light-heavy contrast offers the most striking possibility and quickly leads to combinations that are at least usable. If the goal is** *analogy,* **the typefaces must exhibit an obvious, clearly different contrast.**

When it comes to the best possible degree of readability, reference is often made to an optimal or neutral typographic color. Precisely defining this quality, let alone measuring it on a numerical scale, is difficult because it is dependent on several factors operating on four different levels: the font style itself and its fitting (kerning); setting parameters such as point size, letter-spacing (tracking), word spacing and line spacing (leading); the printing ink and representational quality in print and on the screen; as well as the brightness of the printed material and the light it is viewed in.

At the level of type design, several factors also play a role in the determination of tonal value: the stroke weight of the stem (→*Stroke weight:* p.179), stroke contrast (→*Stroke contrast:* p.180), width (→*Width:* p.182), x-height and curve form, counter size and counterform, and not least the stroke terminals (→*Stroke and curve terminals:* p.189). Of course, typographic color will also change as a result of changes to the fill.

The combination of two typographic colors is the most common form of type contrast. The popularity of the light-heavy contrast lies in its directness, clarity, and simplicity. The clear difference in brightness very quickly makes a convincing impression on us as observers. And it forgives almost all formal inconsistencies, which are hardly noticeable due to the dominance of the differences in tonal value; they are quite simply drowned out by the power of the contrast. This high level of error tolerance makes the light-heavy contrast, on the one hand, highly popular and, on the other, particularly susceptible to uninspired use. Subtle differences in typeface combinations are easily overlooked. And if such differences concern qualitative aspects, these are, as it were, drowned out by the loudness.

The force of the light-heavy contrast is highly dependent on the difference in tonal value. To achieve an exciting effect, it is important that the typographic colors are not too similar |**37**|, although they do not necessarily have to represent extremes. The lightest and heaviest font styles rarely guarantee the best combination. Harmony, as it were, is found through comparison

When typographic color (gray value) is too similar, there is a lack of tension
37 ▼

Design**Formen**
Neue Helvetica · *55 Roman* | *65 Medium*

Light-heavy contrast falls apart (above) or results in a harmonic unity (below)
38 ▼

Neue Helvetica · *Ultra Light* | *Black* | *Bold*

Design**Formen**
Design**Formen**
Design**Formen**
Design**Formen**
Design**Formen**
DesignFormen

Neue Helvetica · *25 Ultra Light | 45 Light* (etc.)

When combining fonts of an extended type family, omit at least one interim weight
39 ▲

| **38** |. When applying this process to extended type families, it is necessary to skip at least one font style | **39** |.

In comparison with the use of contrasting tonal values, the use of a combination with the same tone is less noticeable or may not be noticed at all. And yet that is precisely what can lend the combination a subtle power, even if the difference between the combined typefaces only becomes evident on a closer inspection or when the text is read. This closer look can bring out the differences between the typefaces. In the silence, subtler differences are better perceived. Other qualities emerge. On the other hand, analogy based on brightness requires a much more intensive search for an appropriate and formally interesting contrast.

Analogy based on typographic color can be found, for example, in text emphasis. HANS PETER WILLBERG describes changes in slant from roman to italic that entail little or no change in brightness as integrated emphasis – a kind of emphasis that in reading texts first becomes noticeable when they are actually read and does not tempt the reader to skip ahead. He argues that unclear color differences are otherwise disturbing for the observer. He refers to the contrast created by a change in weight, for example from regular to bold, as 'active'.[10]

When searching for harmonious typeface combinations, it is worth starting with the same typographic color and then, if need be, increasing the combinatory effect by means of contrast between tonal values. Also interesting are contrasts that are formally unusual and more distinctive, even extraordinary, in terms of content. They can be very subtle, such as when the same typographic color or stroke weight is selected, so that the particular contrastive aspect only becomes evident at second glance.

5.1
Weight
Stroke weight

Because a clear difference between light and heavy, or bright and dark as discussed above, generates a strong presence, this clear *contrast* is the most readily selected. On the other hand, if the aim is *analogy* in terms of stroke weight, it is absolutely imperative that another contrasting element is very clearly established.

The terms describing the *weight* of the stem have not been standardized; they are therefore nonuniform and sometimes even misleading. Thus we find the following terms for the standard stroke weight or for the standard font style:

| Type form contrast with stroke weight analogy and stroke weight contrast
40 ▼

| Pointed-rounded contrast with stroke weight analogy and stroke weight contrast
41 ▼▼

DesignFormen
Design**Formen**
Utopia | Neue Helvetica · 55 Roman | 85 Heavy

DesignFormen
Design**Formen**
Tiepolo | Arial Rounded · Regular | Bold

5.2
Weight
Stroke contrast

Divided according to stroke contrast: none, minimal, noticeable, high (top to bottom)
42 ▶

AHOE
AHOE
AHOE
AHOE

Gill Sans | Frutiger | Mosquito | URW Imperial

regular, roman, normal, and book. Sometimes the light or medium font style is also considered the normal stroke weight.

If only *contrast* is sought in the stroke weight – for example, by combining light with heavy – the first step should always be to select this pairing from the same type family. This is not only the simplest but very often also the best approach. Then the question of which font styles relate harmoniously to one another needs to be examined in detail. In many cases, juxtaposed font styles differ too little from one another.

If the goal is *analogy* in the relationship between weights, it is still advisable to look for contrast within the type family insofar as a change in the typeface slant (roman/italic or oblique) or the typeface width (narrow/normal/wide) comes into question. Extended type families (→*Extended type family:* p.134) can provide a good solution in such cases.

However, typeface combination is usually understood as referring to something else, namely, a combination of different *type forms*. Here, an analogous relationship based on stroke weight, particularly in a display size, offers interesting and diverse possibilities | **40** | – also in terms of subtler contrasts, such as between angular and rounded or pointed and rounded, etc. | **41** |. A change in stroke weight may amplify the effect here. In this context, it is important to note that there is another factor that can affect typographic color: a possible difference in the stroke contrast.

Typographic color is influenced not only by the weight of the thicker downstroke (stem) but of course also by the thinner upstroke and cross stroke (hairline). In the case of stroke contrast, typeface combinations can be based on *analogy* or *contrast*. In this regard, they should be as similar as possible or clearly different.

The shift of Antiqua from the Renaissance class to the Neoclassicism class involves a rotation of the stress axis into vertical position and simultaneously a change in the stroke contrast – from the noticeable or distinct stroke contrast of the dynamic style to the stroke contrast of the static style, which ranges from high to extreme. In the case of Antiqua, stroke contrast is self-evident. Yet it also exists in all other type forms, although in the everyday use of Grotesque it is seen far less frequently | **42** |. On the other hand, in the case of cosmetic brands, the contrasting Grotesque is almost a standard feature of corporate design.

Hairstroke Hairstroke Hairstroke

Garamond Premier | Bell MT | Bauer Bodoni

Contrasting and no contrast Egyptian, as well as a reverse-contrast typeface
43 ▼

Historical development of stroke contrast: noticeable, distinct, extreme
44 ▶

Hairstroke
Hairstroke
Hairstroke

Excelsior | Serifa | Pareto

In terms of stroke contrast, three general groups can be distinguished from one another: contrasting, no contrast, and reverse-contrast typefaces | **43** |. The first group comprises typefaces *with* contrast – termed *stroke difference* and divided into *noticeable, distinct,* and *high* contrasting | **44** |. Humanism and Renaissance class Antiquas are noticeably contrasting, Baroque class Antiquas are distinctly contrasting, and Neoclassicism class Antiquas are highly to extremely contrasting. Typefaces with stroke difference from other classification groups can also be ordered in this way.

The second group comprises typefaces with *minimal* or *no stroke* contrast – termed *stroke similarity.* This does not mean, however, that there is no difference at all between the downstrokes and upstrokes. For optical reasons alone, the horizontal strokes in letters must be drawn more thinly because they are shorter; otherwise, they would appear too thick in relation to the longer strokes. With the exception of Antiqua, similar-stroke typefaces can be found in all classification groups. A large number of Egyptian and the majority of Grotesque typefaces belong to this group.

The third group comprises so-called *reverse-contrast* typefaces. In this case, the stroke contrast is inverted: the vertical strokes are thinner than the horizontal strokes. This principle has a special status in the history of lettering. Only the Capitalis rustica (rustic capitals) of Roman antiquity and a group of slab serif typefaces, the *Italiennes,* fall into this category. The latter are poster typefaces originating from the period of industrialization, and in recent times have enjoyed great popularity as typefaces for the film titles of Westerns. The reverse-contrast is virtually never found in text typefaces.

The less the thin strokes thicken, the more the stroke contrast increases
45 ▶

Two static Antiquas: hairlines unvarying or thickening slightly with weight
46 ▶

Today Sans | Legacy Sans

Gianotten | Fairfield

In connection with stroke contrast, it is also interesting to observe how the contrastive relationship develops across the different typeface weights. The basic rule is that the heavier the font style, the more evident the stroke contrast | **45** |. This is necessary because otherwise the counters (interior spaces) in heavy font styles would close up. The stroke-contrast relationship thus changes within the type family. There are two strategies at work here. In a number of type families the weights of both the stem and the hairline increase visibly, but differ in relation to one another |**45**|. In other type families it is only the weight of the stem that increases, whereas the weight of the hairlines in all font styles remains almost the same |**46**|. The result is a change in not only the mathematical but also the optical relationship between the stem and the hairline.

6 Width

Width can be approached from different perspectives: the width of the letters (body width), the proportions of the letters (rhythm), or, as discussed here, the overall typeface width – classified into groups. Width combination is normally oriented towards *analogy*, but a clear *contrast* can also be the goal.

Today, typeface widths are usually classified into four, sometimes five groups: *compressed, condensed,* normal, *extended* |**47**|, or also *narrow, wide,* and *extra wide.* Others also can bear the addition *extra* |**49**| or *ultra.* The normal width of a typeface is termed *regular* or *roman,* which additionally refers to both the weight and the slant. In general, a numerical width measurement is not provided. Typefaces with only one width are often labeled regular/roman even if they are narrow in terms of design. The actual widths of font styles labeled *condensed* are very diverse |**48**|. For this reason, the type appearance must always be examined. Thus, it can be stated that the designation of the font style does not always give a clear indication of the width.

Extended type family with font styles in four different widths
47 ▼

Compressed Condensed Roman Extended
Neue Helvetica · *59 Compressed* | *57 Condensed* | *55 Roman* | *53 Extended*

Three typefaces in condensed font styles with different widths
48 ▼

Condensed
Condensed
Condensed
Latin MT | Times New Roman | ITC Century

Well-developed Grotesque faces often feature two or three widths; four or even five remain an exception. The German font developer URW offers extended type families in five widths – including Antiqua and Egyptian. There is thus no unitary concept of typeface widths, and in the case of the three faces depicted here, the difference in widths in comparison with other typefaces is fairly small |**49**|. Typefaces with three or more widths for the most part fall within the static style category, which is more suited to multiple widths due to its adjusted letter widths and vertical axes (→*Rhythm:* p.176).

When speaking of typeface width, the concept behind the aforementioned Univers is particularly interesting (→*Extended type family:* p.134) because it was

Five widths of Antiqua, Egyptian, and Grotesque – a rarity
49 ▶

Hhp Hhp Hhp Hhp Hhp
URW Antiqua · *Extra Narrow* | *Narrow* | *Regular* | *Wide* | *Extra Wide*

Hhp Hhp Hhp Hhp Hhp
URW Egyptienne · *Extra Narrow* | *Narrow* | *Regular* | *Wide* | *Extra Wide*

Hhp Hhp Hhp Hhp Hhp
URW Grotesk · *Extra Narrow* | *Narrow* | *Light* | *Wide* | *Extra Wide*

Older version (above) with change in the curve form from stadium to ellipse
50 ▼

Univers LT | Univers Next

conceived from the beginning in four widths |**50**|. Neue Helvetica was subsequently also developed based on this concept |**47**|. The four typeface widths were retained in the development of Linotype Univers between 1996 and 1998 and its renaming as Univers Next in 2010. However, like all other font styles, they were subjected to a complete overhaul. A comparison of the uppercase O form shows that fundamental alterations were made – caused, on the one hand, by a changed aesthetic sensibility and, on the other, by the possibility of the computer-generated creation of font styles by means of interpolation and extrapolation. While the first digital version still features the alteration of the curve form, in the new versions the stadium form gives way to the stringency of the ellipse (→*Curve form*: p.167). The originally identical stroke thickness also gives way to an optically balanced thickness |**50**|.

Given the enormous wealth of typefaces now available, the fact that – with the exception of the Grotesques and perhaps the Egyptians – most of them offer only two widths (regular and condensed) is not necessarily a disadvantage. There is no fixed measure even for the normal width, and therefore typefaces of many different widths are available.

The computer-generated modification of typefaces – except in the case of specially designed *variable fonts* – is to be avoided as a matter of principle!

Unidirectional scaling, distortion (below) destroys the quality of the type appearance
51 ▶

Hagedon Hagedon Hagedon
Hagedon Hagedon

Trade Gothic · *Roman* | *Condensed* | *Extended* – bottom row: *Roman* scaled horizontally 74 % | 145 %

Electronic narrowing or widening alters not only the overall width of the typeface but also the stroke thickness and stroke contrast | **51** |. In the worst case, the stroke contrast is even reversed – the vertical strokes become thinner than the horizontal strokes, which leads to incorrect and very unsightly word images. Horizontal scaling or vertical scaling of type tends to be a trait of typographic unprofessionalism, and this applies to computer-generated slanting to an even greater degree | **58** | **59** |.

7
Slant

Upright (roman) and slanted (italic, oblique) typefaces feature different degrees of inclination, although cursive typefaces can actually be divided into forward-slanted, upright, and backward-slanted (the latter two being very rare). The combination of roman with italic produces a lively *contrast. Analogy* **should be confined to upright typefaces because the angles of inclination of cursives very often differ.**

Typeface slant is of course based on the angle of inclination. But what initially seems to be a simple distinction between upright and slanted turns out on closer examination to be more nuanced. There are some romans that are not really upright. These include Vendôme by FRANÇOIS GANEAU and Syntax by HANS EDUARD MEIER, which have a minimal angle of 0.5 degrees | **52** |. And in the cursive category we find a large number of different angles, on the one hand – in the case of Antiquas originally cut by hand, such as Caslon by WILLIAM CASLON I. – between the letterforms themselves | **53** | and on the other hand between different typefaces. There are versions with slight inclinations, such as Flora (3°) by GERARD UNGER, and others with much more obvious inclinations (9 to 13°), such as TheSans by LUCAS DE GROOT | **54** |. For the original Univers, ADRIAN FRUTIGER chose an angle of inclination of 16 degrees, which is at the limit of the acceptable | **55** |.[11] In his opinion, unlike in the case of an italic, the difference between an oblique and a roman version of the same letterform was not clear enough at around 11 degrees, putting the oblique at a disadvantage to the italic. Nevertheless, Linotype altered the angle in their first version, before returning to the original inclination in Linotype Univers (1996) and Univers Next (2010) | **55** |.

As already discussed in connection with type families (→*Type family:* p.132), upright and slanted typefaces differ in terms of not only inclination but also letterforms. The fact that script and italic typefaces have their origins in

---

Fonts with minimal inclination in the reading direction as an indicator of dynamism
52 ▶

Italic letters in older typefaces often exhibit different inclinations
53 ▼

Incline
Incline
Vendôme | Syntax

Inclinations
Adobe Caslon

Cursive typeface and italic font style with different angles of inclination
54 ▶

The later version of Linotype returned to the original, more pronounced inclination
55 ▼

Incline
Incline
Flora | TheSans

Roman *Oblique*
Roman *Oblique*
Univers LT | Univers Next

rapid handwriting can be seen in the different forms of the individual letters, for example a*a*, e*e*, f*f*, g*g*, and k*k*. The italic letterforms are softer and more flowing. However, every typeface must be examined in this respect, since the letterforms can vary | **56** |. In the use of italics in display sizes, this aspect generates different impressions depending on the choice of typeface. In book typography, the use of different typeface slants, normally within the same type family, is a traditional way of emphasizing text and counts among the most common sorts of combination.

Finally, as in the case of personal handwriting styles, which have a diverse range of letter inclinations, there are left-leaning or backslanted typefaces. Examples such as Kursivschrift with the font style designation backwards-lying and Venus Grotesk with the designation left-cursive | **57** | originate from the cartographic indication of waterways.

acefgknpvyz
acefgknpvyz
acefgknpvyz
acefgknpvyz

Cartier Book | Trump Mediäval

| Letterform differences, between roman and italic as well as between italics **56** ▲ | Left-leaning faces derive from cartography – rarely available as a font **57** ▶ |

back stand *slant*

Kursivschrift Rueck Liegend | Stehend | Liegend

back stand *slant*

Venus Linkskursiv | Halbfett | Halbfett · *Kursiv*

Users should be warned against computer-generated slanting, even more so than against the unidirectional scaling of height and width | **51** |. Slanting (pseudo-italic) or skewing (the term used by Adobe's InDesign) a roman font style cannot produce a well-designed oblique. Slanting destroys the quality of the curves. The stress no longer lies in the right spot and appears to sag to the left | **58** |. And this technique is certainly not capable of producing the distinctive characters of a genuine italic cut | **59** |. So stay away from pseudo-italicization!

| Computer-generated skewing of type produces inconsistencies in the curves **58** ▼ | Italics have other forms originating from a flowing handwriting style **59** ▶ |

Hagedorn *Hagedorn*
Hagedorn

Unica 77 · Regular | *Italic* – below: *Regular* electronically skewed (14°)

Hagedorn *Hagedorn*
Hagedorn

ITC Century · Book | *Book Italic* – below: *Book* electronically skewed (15.5°)

Gestalt theory teaches us that an alert person is associated with the vertical (standing), a resting person with the horizontal (lying), and a walking person with the diagonal. In the latter case, such a diagonal inclination is perhaps more evident in a figure rushing forward or sprinting, and for this reason diagonals are a fundamental feature of dynamism in design.

8.1 Ductus
Connection

Ductus of script typefaces: separated and joined finials
60 ▼

Separated finials
Joined finials

Abelina | Magneton – Kerning 0, Tracking 0

Typeface ductus is a broad term devised to provide the most comprehensive description of letterforms possible. However, in the present context, we will confine our discussion of the essential features of stroke formation to the connection of instrokes and outstrokes. A *contrast* between *separate ductus* and *connected ductus* can be interesting.

In the fields of paleography[12] and graphology,[13] ductus[14] plays an essential role in the description of forms of *handwriting*. The term is also used in the description of *setting typefaces* – in particular script typefaces. However, the ductus, or stroke characteristics, of any typeface can be described as delicate, robust, narrow, wide, upright or slanted, soft, jagged, spirited, expansive, etc. Since such formulations relating to letterform are discussed under other headings in this book, the aspect of ductus is here restricted to the possibility of designing the instrokes and outstrokes (→*Instrokes/Outstrokes:* p.175) of script faces with separated and joined finials | **60** |.

Apart from the description of letterforms, the concept of ductus is also used in connection with *typesetting*. In this case it means the tracking, that is, the size of the spaces between characters. On the one hand, tracking changes the text's appearance, which becomes darker or brighter based on the tracking configuration. However, in the process, it also causes a change in the impression made by the type appearance – and the most beautiful typeface can lose its appeal in the process. On the other hand, tracking also affects readability. Spacing that is too tight or too loose influences and may impair readability. Tracking needs to be determined in relation to the size of the counters. The lighter the type weight and thus the larger the counters, the looser the inter-letter spacing needs to be (→*Tracking:* p.68).

To ensure that the connections of finials in script faces with a connected ductus are realized in the best possible way, kerning should be changed from metrics to 0 (zero); tracking should also be set to 0.

8.2 Ductus
Movement

When formulating a description of ductus, movement plays a fundamental role. However, a *contrast* between, say, jagged and round typefaces is only discernible enough in large point sizes.

Stroke characteristics and movement influence the appearance of a typeface. Whether the movements involved make a flowing, written impression or a halting one, whether they appear ebulliently round or austerely jagged, or erratic and tremulous, is a major aspect of a typeface's presence. This applies particularly, but not exclusively, to script faces. Such movement features are generally found in typefaces, for example in the italic font styles of Antiqua | **61** |, which of course is derived from humanist cursive handwriting (→*Basic shapes:* p.57).

Movements *Movements*

Galliard | Janson Text (Kis Antiqua)

Something of the designer's preferences is probably always reflected in the design of a typeface, which may make visible a personality trait, a decade, or a writing culture. Combining typefaces can lend such a coalescence of elements a formal quality.

Similar stroke formation with pronounced difference in the kind of movement
61 ▶

9.1
Shaping
Stroke and curve

Shaping refers to the formation of important details in letterform. However, such features do not suffice for attribution to a form or stylistic group. A *contrast* between, for example, stroke and curve shapes is most likely to succeed in generating tension in display sizes. The tendency is to aim for *analogy*.

Different possibilities are available when it comes to stroke shapes. These can be categorized into four *symmetrical* main groups. Biconcave (waisted) and parallel are common, while biconvex (bulging) and conical are unusual | **64** |. There is also *asymmetrical* shaping. However, typefaces featuring uneven shaping of the left and right side of strokes, for example the concave-plano combination in Breughel | **63** |, are seldom seen.

In the case of Glyphics and older Antiquas, a majority of the downstrokes are waisted. According to ADRIAN FRUTIGER, their effect is natural or human, like a tree trunk or a well-formed human body, whereas parallel strokes suggest a technical character.[15] In fact, in the late twentieth century the formation of shapes with parallel strokes as a common feature of digital fonts had a technical background: the low resolution offered by printers and monitors made it impossible to reproduce waisted strokes adequately – a problem that is still only really solved by high-resolution imagesetter output.

In the case of curve shapes, the main difference is between orthogonal – divided into tapering and broadening – and parallel curve forms | **62** |. Even more than in the case of strokes, parallel curve forms create a technical or even lifeless impression.

Curve shaping: orthogonal, natural (left); parallel, technical (right)
62 ▶ Legacy | modified

Stroke shaping: waisted, flared stroke, parallel, bulging, tapered
63 ▶

AHES AHES AHES AHES AHES
Optima | Icone | Legacy Sans | Inagur | Green

AHES AHES AHES
Iridium | Breughel | Old Style 7

Stroke shaping: biconcave/waisted, flared stroke, parallel, biconvex, conical
64 ▶

Stroke terminal width: reduced, consistent (also asymmetrical), expanded
65 ▶

Stroke terminal cut: diagonal, horizontal, pointed/cambered, notched/cupped
66 ▶

Stroke terminal width: reduced (rounded), consistent, expanded
67 ▶

AHES AHES AHES AHES
Arial Rounded | Info | Arial | Copperplate Gothic

Stroke terminal cut: horizontal, diagonal, convex, concave
68 ▶

AHES AHES AHES AHES
Avenir | Kabel | Sauna | Nami

Stroke terminal form: serif, flared serif, end stroke
69 ▶

AHES AHES AHES
Trajan | Friz Quadrata | Copperplate Gothic

Concave serif form or flat base: rounded, angular, pointed
70 ▶

AHES AHES AHES
Bulmer | Baskerville | Versailles

Biconcave serif form: angular, rounded, decorated (Tuscan)
71 ▶

AHES AHES AHES
LinoLetter | American Typewriter | Ferrule

Serif weight: thin, normal, thick, emphasized, over-emphasized (Italianne)
72 ▶

AHES AHES AHES AHES AHES
Trajan | Adobe Garamond | Egyptian 505 | Amasis | Westside

9.2 Shaping
Stroke and curve terminals

The following closer observation of terminals is intended to supplement the previous discussion of the form and weight of stroke and curve terminals as aspects of typeface classification. In large sizes, terminals can be used to produce a precisely formed *contrast* that make for interesting and surprising combinations.

Basically, stroke and curve terminals can be divided into three categories of width: reduced, consistent, and expanded. In this context, all three can be symmetrical or asymmetrical and angular or rounded |65|.

Reduced terminals can be found in the Grotesques. Notable examples are Officina Sans and Info, both designed by ERIK SPIEKERMANN, and Arial Rounded, a variant of Arial, the version with stroke terminals of the same thickness |67|. *Consistent* terminals are also characteristic of the Grotesques. However, the majority of classification groups are defined by expanded stroke terminals, at least in the case of upright font styles. *Expanded* terminals are also a key feature of Glyphics: short serifs in the case of Trajan by CAROL TWOMBLY, flared serifs (not to be confused with flared strokes) in the case of Friz Quadrata by ERNST FRIZ, and end strokes in the case of Copperplate Gothic by FREDERIC W. GOUDY |69|. Expanded stroke terminals are exhibited particularly by the classification groups Antiqua, Egyptian, and Latin with their serifs. The great diversity of terminal forms |70|71|, weights |72|, and lengths available here is very evident. In the case of the Scripts, all kinds of stroke terminals can be found; in the case of Blackletter, expanded and consistent varieties.

Stroke terminals can vary in terms of not only width but also cut |66|. Along with diagonally and horizontally oriented cuts |68|, pointed and notched versions are also possible. The latter two are less often found and usually in the rounded version, resulting in a convex (cambered) or concave (cupped) form.

We frequently find instances of strokes and stroke terminals being shaped in ways that specifically relate to one another. Notable examples are Optima |63| designed by HERMANN ZAPF, which is popular in the cosmetics field, and Nami |68| by ADRIAN FRUTIGER, the concave-shaped forms of both are based on waisted strokes and cupped terminals. In juxtaposition, Sauna |68|, a hybrid semi serif typeface by Underware is convexly shaped and features minimally convex-plano strokes with cambered stroke and curve terminals. In display sizes, contrasts such as concave-convex and rounded-angular offer the potential for interesting combinations.

| Chronology of the curve beginning of a, from the 15th to the 20th century
73 ▼

ꝯꝯ
ꝯꝯꝯꝯꝯꝯꝯ
ꝯꝯꝯ

Terminal broadened or tapered, according to standard, axes, or writing principle
74 ▼

acs acs acs
Garamond | Freya | Dolly

Differences in the formation of curve terminals from dynamic to static
75 ▶

Curve terminal cuts of dynamic, geometric, and static Grotesques
76 ▼

Gill Sans | Avenir | Helvetica

The shaping of curve terminals basically corresponds to the possibilities discussed above. Here too we find (almost always asymmetrically) broadened as well as tapered |73|. And these can appear together, in rounded or angular versions, in different letters of a typeface, or combined in one letter |74|. In this context, beaks (half-serifs) are always constructed from a vertical and never from a horizontal approach. Diagonal end strokes, as seen in the case of Copperplate Gothic, should remain the exception |69|.

The shaping of curve terminals differs from letter to letter. It also depends on the type form and on the individual personality of the designer. At least three different categories can be identified here. A typical representative of the category defined here as the standard is Garamond. Here the *curve beginnings* are broadened, at the top of the minuscule a, at the drop-shaped beginning of the c, and at the beak of the s. The *curve ending* of the c is tapered, while the curve ending of the s is broadened and oriented to the outside |74|. Freya is distinguished by the curve beginning of the minuscule a. In keeping with the diagonal stress axis with its thin section to the upper left, the curve here also features a thin beginning. A distinguishing feature of Dolly is the orientation of the curve terminal in the case of s, which takes up the direction of writing.

CJS CJS CJS CJS CJS
acjs acjs acjs acjs acjs
Jenson | Garamond | Bell | Didot | Versailles

Epochs and type styles also affect the shape |75| and cut of curve terminals. Grotesques in the *dynamic style* feature curve terminals that are vertical or slightly angled away from the vertical |76|. The possibilities in the case of Grotesques in the *geometric style* are diverse. Along with the typically diagonal cut of curve terminals at an angle of 45 degrees, there are typefaces with vertically and horizontally cut terminals. In the case of Grotesques in the *static style,* the terminals are cut horizontally or at a slight angle from the horizontal.

9.3 Shaping Bracket

The transition between stem and serif is known as a bracket. Depending on the typeface in question, this shaping is either rounded (adnate) or angular (abrupt). Although *analogy* is rather common for typeface combinations, this aspect is at most interesting for display sizes.

The bracket usually only becomes a focus of attention when the most appropriate typeface for combination needs to be selected from two or more typefaces of similar quality. In large sizes, an adnate (bracketed) transition, for instance, increases the emphasis on analogy, while an abrupt (unbracketed) transition amplifies contrast.

There are no fixed rules for the shaping of the bracket. Although dynamic Antiquas traditionally feature adnate brackets between stem and serif, while static Antiquas feature right-angled abrupt or minimally rounded brackets, in the case of twentieth-century typefaces this aspect is no longer as clearly defined. In the case of Egyptians, bracket shape is also diverse, even though those typefaces featuring stroke contrast tend to exhibit adnate transitions and those without stroke contrast abrupt ones.

Transitions, whether adnate or abrupt, can be designed with obtuse angles, right angles, and, less commonly, acute angles. Finally, there are typefaces with combined transitions: one side abrupt, the other adnate |**77**|.

Hollander | Swift | Excelsior | Joanna | LinoLetter

Freya

Obtuse-, right-, acute-angled transitions: adnate, abrupt (above), combined (left)
77 ▲|◀

9.4 Shaping Juncture

Juncture refers to the way strokes and curves connect. Junctures can be angular or rounded, tapered or broadened, and some typefaces combine all these kinds within a single letterform. In combinations, this aspect is better suited to *analogy*.

A curve can flow *out* of a stem, for example in the case of the minuscule n, or *into* a stem, as in the case of the minuscule d. These junctures can be steep, oblique, or flat, and this has an effect on the shaping |**78**|. In the case of a steep curve, the connection tends to be rounded, while in the case of a flat curve, an angular connection tends to be the rule. The most common juncture is the oblique version, and it is associated with the greatest diversity of shapes. Whether the juncture is angular or rounded depends above all on the type designer. Even if an angular juncture emphasizes asymmetry and is therefore preferred for faces with a dynamic style, while a rounded juncture emphasizes symmetry and suits typefaces with a static style, it is not possible to derive a standard rule. There are simply too many typefaces that contradict this common tendency.

Curve direction and juncture in n: steep, oblique (rounded and angular), flat
78 ▼

EgyptienneF | Adobe Garamond | Dolly | Swift

Juncture tapered and broadened in accordance with axis and stress
79 ▶

Juncture: notch in the apex of A, ink trap, and interrupted (stencil typeface)
80 ▼

nudp
Legacy Serif

A A A
Vectora | Bell Centennial | Vida 33 Stencil

Although there are also dominant principles with regard to the width of strokes and curves at junctures, there are no rules governing the way these are shaped. One of the most important factors associated with the drawing of a text face is that there is an accumulation of black where strokes and curves connect, which leads to a blotchy type appearance. To counteract this effect, tapered or conical strokes and curves are required. And the heavier a typeface, the more attention needs to be paid to this aspect. However, there are also broadened junctures, as seen in the case of Antiquas with a dynamic style, whose curves broaden to the lower left and upper right correspondent with the diagonal axis of stress | **79** |. Tapered junctures result in an acute angle, while broadened junctures form an obtuse angle.

A notch (which in extreme cases is termed an ink trap) additionally brightens a juncture. In agate typefaces it is necessary to include notches in letters at acute-angled connections between strokes and curves. Stencil typefaces involve a special juncture shaping: the gap, which is technically required in real-world implementations | **80** |.

10 Letter design

Particularly when it comes to drafting word marks/logotypes, the design of individual letters takes on a special status. In many cases, typefaces exhibit completely different letterforms or at least different interpretations of the same form. Here, *analogy* is highly recommended.

The basic differences between the individual letterforms provide a wealth of possibilities for the design of word marks. In this context, we can utilize not only two character sets (majuscules and minuscules) whose letterforms partly differ, but also the pronounced difference between roman and italic letterforms – irrespective of the angle of inclination. In linguistic terms, an A is an a – but not in formal terms. The majuscule C and the minuscule c also do not correspond – even though their design looks much more similar. And there are two versions of majuscule M, the original diagonal and thereby dynamic form and the later vertical, static form | **81** |. In addition, in some fonts the vertex (V juncture) of the M does not reach to the baseline but is positioned above it. In the search for appropriate typeface combinations, other differences can influence the selection, for example the way in which and where the middle diagonals of the W meet each other | **81** |. Here too there are diverse variants, which include differences between the majuscule and minuscule forms.

MW variations: different angles, junctures, apex, and vertex
81 ▼

MW MW MW MW
Futura | ITC Kabel | Today Sans | Myriad

MW MW
Quire Sans | Effra

MW MW MW
Unica 77 | Brother 1816 | Gill Sans

Both font styles roman form (top left), roman and italic form (middle), both italic form (bottom right)

82 ▶|▶▶

ag *ag* ag *ag* ag *ag* ag *ag*
ag *ag* ag *ag*   ag *ag*
         ag *ag* ag *ag* ag *ag* ag *ag*

Basilia | Times | Freya | Siseriff | Glypha | StoneInformal   Syntax | TheSans | Myriad | Univers | Futura

There are also obvious differences in the case of individual letters, such as *Kk, Vv,* and *Zz*. And the originally carefully written roman form of the minuscule a is completely different from the more hurried italic *a*. The same applies to g and *g*. These differences are even more diverse in the case of other typefaces. We find a whole palette of variations, in both Antiquas and Grotesques | **82** |. These are only a few examples; there are many other letterforms with more subtle differences.

Ultimately, it is the design of the letter that perhaps marks the final step toward perfection. In the best case, for example in text setting, the difference is not noticed; in the worst case, it is disturbing.

11.1 Effect | Decoration
Fill

Typefaces that feature an effect based on their fill (decorated typefaces) offer fantastically simple and at the same time incredibly rich possibilities for typeface combinations. When used with restraint, the *contrast* between solid and decorated faces offers a variation in moods.

Decorated typefaces have been part of the standard typeface range since at least the eighteenth century. Their popularity further increased during the period of industrialization in the nineteenth century, when a large number of typefaces featuring a wide range of decorated forms and structures were developed in all classification groups, including the Grotesques. Such typefaces include what are mostly very simple graphic interventions that lend them grandeur and power, and at the same time elegance and delicacy. They have a particular aesthetic charm. Like ornaments, they exert a certain alluring effect. After a century, they offer a treasure trove that invites rediscovery | **83** |. However, to avoid the impression of gimmickry, such decorated typefaces need to be used sparingly and purposefully.

Decorated typefaces – effect of fill: variations in terms of light, sheen, and shadow

83 ▼|▶

AHOE
AHOE
AHOE

Isis | Cristal (Palace) | Augustea Open

ABCDEFGHIJKLMNOPQRSTUVWXYZ

Chevalier · Stripes Caps | Rosella · Solid | Inline | Engraved | Deco | Flourish | Hatched

Chromatic typefaces: diverse forms combined create the multicolored letters

84

A particular form of 'effect typefaces' specially designed for multicolor letterpress printing are found in the specimen books of nineteenth-century producers of wooden type, as well as in the registers of wooden letters of type foundries. All fills, outlines, and shadows have been conceived as separate 'single-color' forms that can be precisely printed over one another in multiple printings – color by color. In recent years, such multicolored (chromatic) typefaces have reemerged as a trend in the field of digital fonts | 84 |. When working with chromatic typefaces, the use of layers is helpful.

Core Circus | 3D | 3D Shadow | 2D Out | 2D Dot2 – each *Regular*

11.2
Effect | Decoration
Outline

Typefaces that fall into the effect category include examples featuring formal interventions in the typeface outline. This group comprises all typefaces that do not exhibit smooth edges. In some cases the effect is based on a combination of fill and outline. In general those decorated typefaces have limited uses, and when used in typeface combination the focus should be on *contrast*.

Perhaps the best-known outline effects are those that project materiality and traces of production and wear. Examples are the reproduction of lettering written on rough paper or the digital copy of a metal typeface already printed on a letterpress (relief printing). A contextualization is thus always inherent in these fonts. For this reason, it is important here to pay particular attention to the relationship between text and type in terms of content and form – even more so in the case of typeface combinations.

Effect of outline (and partial fill) created by abandoning smooth edges

85

written
sketched
printed

Papyrus | Fredericka the Greatest | Caslon Antique

Gill Floriated

There is space here to show only a very limited number of examples | 85 |. However, it must be acknowledged that this is somewhat fallow land in the field of type design. Diverse and surprising interventions in letterform outlines are seldom seen, despite the vast number of typefaces available.

12
Setting length
Words | Texts

Word length and text volume play a role in the context of the present discussion insofar as they are influenced by the choice of typeface. A typeface combination can be helpful as a means of generating *analogy* in the setting lengths or introducing clear length ratios to create obvious *contrast*.

The fact that different words have different lengths is of course logical. The same applies to texts. In the case of certain kinds of text, such as an article in a magazine, this natural ratio is utilized by emphasizing shorter text features such as titles, quotes, image captions, etc., in relation to the body text. Such emphasis is achieved, for instance, by making the texts bigger or bolder, or setting them in another typeface or different chromatic color. In such cases, a typeface combination can help emphasize differences in the textual hierarchy.

On the other hand, it may also be desirable to eliminate unwanted hierarchies, such as in the case of text translations into different languages. For example, a text in German is always longer than the same text in English. A typeface combination offers an opportunity to reduce this difference in length. However, it is essential that the result is not a new, unwanted hierarchy. Along with sufficient contrast, the different typefaces should therefore exhibit a high degree of similarity, for example in terms of brightness. Word marks that combine the names of business partners can also cause an unwanted hierarchy. This can already result from simply listing the names in alphabetical order. Another hierarchy can be brought on by the different lengths of the names. Here, a typeface combination can be used to generate an analogy or to counter an existing hierarchy with a formal one | **86** |.

Attempt to simultaneously create differentiation and hierarchical alignment
86 ▼

ADAM & EVE
Gill Sans · *Book* | Caslon · *Bold Italic* | Caslon Titling

13
Type size

The same optical size in typeface combinations, in particular when the typefaces are directly juxtaposed, tends to call for a lot of *analogy* and at the same time clarity of *contrast*. Different type sizes visibly reduce the demand for similarities, but stroke weight also needs to be taken into account.

Size contrast, insofar as it involves only a few, well-graduated sizes that exhibit clear ratios to one another, is one of the most powerful tools available in typography. Additional bright-dark contrast can further amplify the size contrast, but only if the larger typeface is the darker one and the smaller typeface is the brighter one. In the reverse case, the larger, brighter typeface

Darker/smaller creates more analogy; brighter/smaller creates more contrast

| 87 | ▶

**Design
Formen**

Design
Formen

Design
Formen

AG Old Face | Wilke

and the smaller, darker typeface converge in terms of typographic color. If in this case there is insufficient similarity in brightness or stroke weights, the result is an unharmonious appearance | 87 |.

An alignment of the stroke weights of two typefaces of clearly different sizes can in exceptional cases – and this needs to be emphasized – allow for the combination of two typefaces from the same classification group. In this book such a combination is achieved by using two Antiquas: Freya as a text face and Wilke, with its attractive figure forms, for the chapter numbering. While the two typefaces are stylistically related, the first has a moderately dynamic style, the second a slightly dynamic style. They also differ in terms of stroke contrast. The larger point size of Wilke has thinner hairlines, and therefore there is a similarity in the stroke weights. Such simultaneous use of display size and reading size, for example in chapter numbers and text or initial and text, can allow for a combination of a static Antiqua in a large point size with a dynamic Antiqua in a small point size. But, as stated above, only in exceptional cases.

14 Color

Finally, differences in chromatic color offer a refreshing way to enrich a typeface combination. However, it needs to be remembered in the case of such *contrast*: color dominates form. It follows that chromatic color contrast drowns out everything else, including the aesthetics of a subtly developed *analogy*.

The topic of color is too multifaceted to discuss here in even a rudimentary way. But it is self-evident that the combination of chromatic color and type increases the level of complexity, especially when different typefaces are involved. More detailed information can be acquired by studying such experimental arrangements and comparisons as well as by consulting specialist publications.[16]

According to Gestalt theory, the human eye directly associates elements of the same color with one another, even when their form is different. The connection between identical forms in this context is secondary.[17] The same color thus forges a stronger link than the same form. It follows that the use of different colors promotes separation. In the case of typeface combination, which can be understood as a change in form, a change in color introduces a further differentiating element. Color functions as a multiplier of difference between typefaces | 88 |. If the typeface combination already includes

Tonal value analogy (above); greater separation created by color change (below)

| 88 | ▼

DesignFormen
DesignFormen

Akzidenz Grotesk · *Medium* | Walbaum · *Bold*

DesignFormen
*Design*Formen
DesignFormen

Akzidenz Grotesk · *Bold* | Walbaum · *Roman*

Thinner/brighter creates more contrast; bolder/brighter creates more analogy

89

The connection based on color is clearly stronger than the one based on form

90 ▼

DesignFormen
DesignFormen

Akzidenz Grotesk · *Medium* | Walbaum · *Bold*

In thin and small typefaces, the intensity of neutral colors is reduced

91

Quire Sans · *Light* | *Bold* | *Fat*

a bright-dark contrast, the use of color can function as an augmentation – when the lighter typeface exhibits the brighter color. Conversely, a heavier typeface in a brighter color restores a sense of harmony | **89** |.

In typographic projects, the Gestalt principle referred to above should be regarded as an important aspect. In a layout involving two typefaces and two colors, a connection is established on the basis of the same color but not on the basis of the same typeface | **90** |.

Finally, it should be noted that when it comes to chromatic color, the brightness factor plays an important role. Typefaces are hardly ever really black. The interplay of black forms and white counterforms always generates a gray value. Light typefaces produce a bright tonal value, bold faces a somewhat darker value, and heavy faces a dark tonal value. The diverse range of typefaces can thus be divided, in accordance with stroke weight, into *linear, joist-like,* and *planar* type. For typefaces in chromatic color, this means that a very heavy, planar typeface will exhibit a much more saturated hue than a light, linear face. In the case of colored type, this needs to be taken into account – all the more when it comes to different sizes. The intensity of a color is reduced in light typefaces in small sizes. Indeed, their hue may become unrecognizable | **91** |. It may therefore be essential to make changes in color hue or vary saturation to produce color variations. Agate and text sizes should be set in a more robust hue than display sizes.

The combination of typefaces in interplay with color contrasts infinitely increases the design possibilities open to typography. In the case of striking applications of colored faces in particular – especially against a black background – the effect and power is amplified. And even more than in the case of bright-dark contrasts, chromatic color contrasts can almost completely cloak errors in typeface combinations – but also the appeal of more subtle details of a balanced interplay.

Typeface combination | Instructions

Three steps facilitate the process of typeface comparison:

1.

Setting word combinations / select test words

2.

Configure matrix for examining typeface combinations

3.

Configure matrix for examining combinations in the layout

!

The search for the most compatible typefaces can be laborious and time-consuming.

A correctly configured matrix, a systematic approach, and precise work facilitate the selection of the right typeface combination.

Having an intention of possible contrasts will certainly facilitate the project.

But experimenting with typeface combinations that may initially seem impossible can be just as valuable. Although time-consuming, this process is more likely to lead to surprisingly effective combinations.

Configuring a matrix for typeface combinations

Typefaces with similar heights and proportions facilitate the creation of good typeface combinations.

1.
Establishing ruler guides

Cap height	10 mm
x-height	7 mm
Baseline	

Irrespective of the typeface concerned, the guideline for the x-height can be set at a standard value of ⁷⁄₁₀ of the cap height.

Such a matrix on the one hand facilitates an efficient approach and, on the other, guarantees comparable results.

However, when the goal is to match a given typeface with a second one, it is the actual x-height that takes precedence.

2.
Setting test words

Uppercase
Upper- and lowercase
Lowercase

The word pair or two-part test word is best set in all three letter cases.

The word pair used on the example pages to create the typeface combinations is *DesignFormen*. Both words contain the lowercase letters e and n, and in text typefaces they exhibit similar word lengths.

3.
Selecting typefaces

The website identifont.com *offers functions that are very helpful when it comes to finding similar typefaces.*

If the sequence of typefaces is not predetermined, it can be worthwhile exchanging the positions of the typefaces.

The difference in the design of the letterforms of diverse typefaces often generates a qualitative distinction in the combination. Particularly in the case of special typefaces, this can lead to interesting and surprising results.

Attention should be paid to height differences (ascenders/descenders).

! *Every typeface, every font style, and every point size requires individually determined and correct tracking values:*

looser:	*tighter:*
light typefaces	*heavy typefaces*
wide typefaces	*narrow typefaces*
small sizes	*large sizes*
uppercase letters	

4.
Aligning typeface heights

Helpful tools in this context are existing scripts or XTensions and plug-ins such as TypoX *InDesign*

Since typefaces normally exhibit uneven heights, they need to be set at an optically equal height. Different point sizes (pt) are unavoidable.

Heavy typefaces require a slightly larger x-height than light typefaces. Otherwise, the smaller counters of the heavier typeface will make it appear smaller than the lighter one.

Sometimes it is necessary to align the baseline of a typeface with a baseline shift in order to achieve an optically correct result.

5.
Setting tracking values

Correct tracking values need to be established for each typeface.

Unfortunately, digital type foundries have missed the opportunity to set a tracking value of 0 (zero) for a defined point size (for example, 10 pt) as default or standard value. In principle this means that every typeface with the same point size has its own correct tracking value.

6.
Adjusting letterspaces

Whether the spaces between letters are best adjusted by means of metrics or optical kerning depends on the selected typeface.

In addition, within each typeface, some letter pairs can prove disruptive (too tight/too loose), which makes manual kerning necessary.

For optically balanced word images in logos and word marks, as well as for settings in large point sizes, spaces between characters generally require manual kerning.

ABCDEFGHIJKLM
NOPQRSTUVWXYZ
abcdefghijklm
nopqrstuvwxyz

Times Roman
Stanley Morison, Victor Lardent
1931–1932 | Monotype MT — Linotype LT
Antiqua

ABCDEFGHIJKLM
NOPQRSTUVWXYZ
abcdefghijklm
nopqrstuvwxyz

Akzidenz Grotesk Regular
unknown — Günter Gerhard Lange
1898 | H. Berthold AG — 1958 | H. Berthold AG
Grotesque

7 mm | design formen

pt | 44.7 42.6

10 mm | DESIGN FORMEN

pt | 43.1 40.4

7 mm | Design Formen

pt | 44.7 42.6

204

!

*An appropriate test word –
which can be an artificial word –
should have as many of the
following elements as possible.*

*The more corresponding forms
are involved, the more comparable
the typefaces:*
- *letters in all four heights
  (cap height, ascender height,
  x-height, descender height)
  example: |H|f|n|p|*
- *letters with verticals, horizontals,
  diagonals, and curves
  example: |n|z|v|o|*
- *letters with the basic geometrical
  shapes square, circle, and triangle,
  and the double-storey shapes
  example: |H|O|V|E|S|X|*
- *formally typical letters
  example: |G|K|M|a|e|g|*
- *formally same or similar letters
  example: |e|c|o|d|*
- *frequently occurring letters
  example: |a|e|n|*
- *typical language-relevant letters
  example: |c|k|y|*
- *letters with different body widths
  (narrow, normal, wide)
  example: |r|n|m|*

Tip

*In order to avoid an unwanted
hierarchy of test words,
they should exhibit a similar length
or a similar number of letters.*

!

*The average ratio of cap height
to x-height in today's text typefaces
is around 10:7.*

*However, since every typeface
exhibits an individual height ratio,
the same typeface can have a
different point size (pt) in all uppercase (cap height) than it does
in a mixed case or all lowercase
(x-height) setting.*

Using typeface combinations in the layout

1.
Test different sizes

Display size	>12 pt
Text size	8–12 pt
Agate size	< 8 pt

Not all typefaces function in all sizes. Some are too light, too delicate, others possibly too robust, too heavy for agate and text sizes.
In display sizes, on the other hand, some typefaces exhibit too little formal quality and lack aesthetical appeal.

2.
Defining tracking values for sizes

Tracking trend –
Tracking trend +
Tracking trend ++

Every point size has a different correct tracking value.

The larger the point size, the tighter the letterspacing needs to be. In the case of metrics kerning, typefaces in title sizes should generally be set at a minus value.
The smaller the point size, the looser the letterspacing has to be. In the case of metrics kerning, a typeface in text sizes should almost always – and in agate sizes always – be set at a plus value.

3.
Testing combinations in the layout

Ratio of typeface width to line measure, column height, and format proportions

Apply available typeface combinations to longer texts and possible layout situations.

!

The range of contrasts is enormous and is constantly increasing with the extension of the typeface repertoire. Typeface combinations offer a vast resource in terms of expressive possibilities. It is up to us to discover them.

Typeface combination | Examples

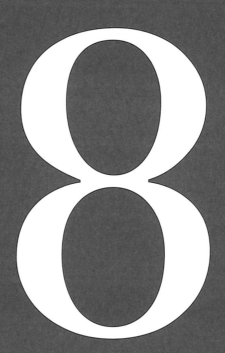

ABCDEFGHIJKLM
NOPQRSTUVWXYZ
abcdefghijklm
nopqrstuvwxyz

Palatino Roman
Hermann Zapf
1950 | D. Stempel AG / Linotype LT
Antiqua → 236/237

ABCDEFGHIJKLM
NOPQRSTUVWXYZ
abcdefghijklm
nopqrstuvwxyz

Optima Roman
Hermann Zapf
1952 | D. Stempel AG / Linotype LT
Glyphic

Sommer

104 pt

CONTRASTS
Type form

DIFFERENCES
Type style
Axis/Stress
Weight
Stroke shaping
Terminal shaping
Juncture

Letter design
|M|Q|Y|y|

ANALOGIES
Curve form
Width
Typographic color

SIMILARITIES
Heights
Curve direction
Rhythm
Stroke contrast
Slant
Ductus

Letter design
|G|J|K|R|W|
|a|f|g|j|k|w|

26.6   27.0

DESIGN FORMEN
design formen

26.5   25.6

Sommer Frische

11.0   11.0

Frische

106 pt

ABCDEFGHIJKLM
NOPQRSTUVWXYZ
abcdefghijklm
nopqrstuvwxyz

Futura Book
Paul Renner
1927 | Bauer Type Foundry — Linotype LT
Grotesque

ABCDEFGHIJKLM
NOPQRSTUVWXYZ
abcdefghijklm
nopqrstuvwxyz

Garamond Regular
Claude Garamont — Robert Slimbach
ca. 1540 | Claude Garamont — 1989 | Adobe Systems
Antiqua

ALTERNATIVE
Aldus | Hermann Zapf | 1954 | D. Stempel AG / Linotype LT

Science

100 pt

CONTRASTS
Type form

DIFFERENCES
Type style
Axis/Stress
Curve direction
Offset center position
Stroke contrast
Terminal shaping
Juncture

Letter design
|G|J|K|M|P|Q|R|W|
|a|g|j|t|

ANALOGIES
Weight
Typographic color

SIMILARITIES
Curve form
Heights
Rhythm
Width
Slant
Ductus
Stroke shaping

Letter design
|i|

24.4 27.9

DESIGN FORMEN
design formen

25.4 29.9

Science Fiction

10.8 12.8

Fiction

118 pt

ABCDEFGHIJKLM
NOPQRSTUVWXYZ
abcdefghijklm
nopqrstuvwxyz

Legacy Serif Medium
Ronald Arnholm
1982–1993 | International Typeface Corporation ITC
Antiqua

ABCDEFGHIJKLM
NOPQRSTUVWXYZ
abcdefghijklm
nopqrstuvwxyz

Legacy Sans Medium
Ronald Arnholm
1982–1993 | International Typeface Corporation ITC
Grotesque

Human

113 pt

CONTRASTS
Type form

DIFFERENCES
Stroke shaping
Terminal shaping

Letter design
|K|W|k|w|

ANALOGIES
Curve form
Heights
Type style
Axis/Stress
Curve direction
Width
Rhythm
Typographic color

SIMILARITIES
Weight
Stroke contrast
Slant
Ductus
Juncture

Letter design
|G|J|M|Q|R|
|a|e|f|g|i|j|t|y|

28.9   28.9

DESIGN FORMEN
design formen

28.4   28.4

Human Rights

12.0   12.0

113 pt

ABCDEFGHIJKLM
NOPQRSTUVWXYZ
abcdefghijklm
nopqrstuvwxyz

Freya Medium
Saku Heinänen
2010 | Incubator — Village
Antiqua

ABCDEFGHIJKLM
NOPQRSTUVWXYZ
abcdefghijklm
nopqrstuvwxyz

Today Sans Now Regular
Volker Küster
1988 | Scangraphic SG — 2014 | Elsner + Flake EF
Grotesque

ALTERNATIVE
Syntax | Hans Eduard Meier | 1968 | Linotype LT
→ 264/265

Smaragd

111 pt

CONTRASTS
Type form

DIFFERENCES
Stroke contrast
Terminal shaping

Letter design
|J|W|w|

ANALOGIES
Curve form
Heights
Type style
Rhythm
Weight
Width
Typographic color

SIMILARITIES
Axis/Stress
Curve direction
Slant
Ductus
Stroke shaping
Juncture

Letter design
|K|M|Q|
|a|g|j|k|t|y|

27.8 27.8

DESIGN FORMEN
design formen

25.7 26.7

Smaragd Edelstein

11.1 11.5

Edelstein

112 pt

217

ABCDEFGHIJKLM
NOPQRSTUVWXYZ
abcdefghijklm
nopqrstuvwxyz

Avenir Next Medium
Adrian Frutiger — Adrian Frutiger, Akira Kobayashi
Avenir | 1988 | Linotype LT — 2004 | Linotype LT
Grotesque → 236/237

ABCDEFGHIJKLM
NOPQRSTUVWXYZ
abcdefghijklm
nopqrstuvwxyz

Iridium Regular
Adrian Frutiger
1972 | D. Stempel AG / Linotype LT
Antiqua

Equator

102 pt

CONTRASTS
Type form
Stroke shaping

DIFFERENCES
Curve form
Heights
Type style
Axis/Stress
Weight
Stroke contrast
Terminal shaping
Typographic color

Letter design
|K|Q|g|k|

ANALOGIES
Width
Rhythm

SIMILARITIES
Curve direction
Slant
Ductus
Juncture

Letter design
|G|J|W|
|a|f|i|j|w|y|

26.1 26.7

DESIGN FORMEN
design formen

25.8 27.4

Equator Principles

10.8 11.4

Principles

106 pt

219

ABCDEFGHIJKLM
NOPQRSTUVWXYZ
abcdefghijklm
nopqrstuvwxyz

Univers 55 Roman
Adrian Frutiger
1954–1957 | Deberny & Peignot — 1969 | Linotype LT
Grotesque → 282/283

ALTERNATIVE
Unica 77 | Team'77 | 1980 | Haas Type Foundry — 2015 | Lineto LL
→ 226/227

ABCDEFGHIJKLM
NOPQRSTUVWXYZ
abcdefghijklm
nopqrstuvwxyz

Centennial 55 Roman
Adrian Frutiger
1985–1986 | Linotype LT
Antiqua → 226/227 → 236/237

Baldrian

100 pt

CONTRASTS
Type form

DIFFERENCES
Stroke contrast
Width
Terminal shaping

Letter design
|G|M|Q|g|i|y|

ANALOGIES
Curve form
Heights
Rhythm
Weight
Typographic color

SIMILARITIES
Type style
Axis/Stress
Curve direction
Slant
Ductus
Stroke shaping
Juncture

Letter design
|J|K|P|R|W|a|k|w|

25.6   25.8

DESIGN FORMEN
design formen

23.8   23.6

Baldrian Tropfen

10.2 10.2

Tropfen

100 pt

ABCDEFGHIJKLM
NOPQRSTUVWXYZ
abcdefghijklm
nopqrstuvwxyz

Bau Regular
unknown — Christian Schwartz
Breite Grotesque | ca. 1880 | Schelter & Giesecke — 2002 | FontFont FF Grotesque

ABCDEFGHIJKLM
NOPQRSTUVWXYZ
abcdefghijklm
nopqrstuvwxyz

Walbaum Roman
Justus Erich Walbaum
ca. 1800 | Walbaum Type Foundry — Linotype LT Antiqua → 226/227

Leipziger

101 pt

CONTRASTS
Type form
Stroke contrast

DIFFERENCES
Weight
Terminal shaping

Letter design
|G|K|Q|i|k|t|

ANALOGIES
Curve form
Type style

SIMILARITIES
Heights
Axis/Stress
Curve direction
Rhythm
Width
Slant
Ductus
Stroke shaping
Juncture
Typographic color

Letter design
|J|M|R|W|a|g|y|

24.6   25.7

DESIGN FORMEN
design formen

23.9   24.0

Leipziger Buchpreis

10.5   10.4

Buchpreis

100 pt

ABCDEFGHIJKLM
NOPQRSTUVWXYZ
abcdefghijklm
nopqrstuvwxyz

Slimbach Book
Robert Slimbach
1987 | International Typeface Corporation ITC
Antiqua

ABCDEFGHIJKLM
NOPQRSTUVWXYZ
abcdefghijklm
nopqrstuvwxyz

Armata Regular
Viktoriya Grabowska
2011 | Sorkin Type / Google Fonts
Grotesque

Eisen

106 pt

CONTRASTS
Type form

DIFFERENCES
Stroke contrast
Terminal shaping
Juncture

Letter design
|W|a|g|w|

ANALOGIES
Heights
Curve direction
Width
Typographic color

SIMILARITIES
Curve form
Weight
Type style
Axis/Stress
Rhythm
Slant
Ductus
Stroke shaping

Letter design
|G|J|K|M|Q|R|
|f|j|k|y|

27.5   24.7

DESIGN FORMEN
design formen

24.4   20.7

Eisen Oxyd

10.6 8.9

90 pt

ABCDEFGHIJKLM
NOPQRSTUVWXYZ
abcdefghijklm
nopqrstuvwxyz

AG Buch Rounded Regular
Günter Gerhard Lange
1980 | H. Berthold AG BQ
Grotesque → 204 → 250/251 → 278/279

ABCDEFGHIJKLM
NOPQRSTUVWXYZ
abcdefghijklm
nopqrstuvwxyz

Walbaum Roman
Justus Erich Walbaum
ca. 1800 | Walbaum Type Foundry — Linotype LT
Antiqua → 222/223 → below

ABCDEFGHIJKLM
NOPQRSTUVWXYZ
abcdefghijklm
nopqrstuvwxyz

Walbaum Roman
Justus Erich Walbaum
ca. 1800 | Walbaum Type Foundry — Linotype LT
Antiqua → 222/223 → above

ABCDEFGHIJKLM
NOPQRSTUVWXYZ
abcdefghijklm
nopqrstuvwxyz

Unica 77 Regular
Team '77: André Gürtler, Christian Mengelt, Erich Gschwind
Haas Unica | 1980 | Haas Type Foundry — 2015 | Lineto LL
Grotesque

ABCDEFGHIJKLM
NOPQRSTUVWXYZ
abcdefghijklm
nopqrstuvwxyz

Akkurat Regular
Laurenz Brunner
2004 | Lineto LL
Grotesque → 246/247

ABCDEFGHIJKLM
NOPQRSTUVWXYZ
abcdefghijklm
nopqrstuvwxyz

Centennial 55 Roman
Adrian Frutiger
1985–1986 | Linotype LT
Antiqua → 220/221 → 236/237

CONTRASTS
Type form
Stroke contrast

DIFFERENCES
Heights
Terminal shaping

Letter design
|G|K|Q|g|k|

ANALOGIES
Curve form
Type style
Rhythm
Weight
Width
Typographic color

SIMILARITIES
Axis/Stress
Curve direction
Slant
Stroke shaping
Juncture

Letter design
|J|M|R|W|a|i|j|t|w|y|

26.2   25.5

DESIGN FORMEN
design formen

22.7   24.3

CONTRASTS
Type form
Stroke contrast

DIFFERENCES
Terminal shaping

Letter design
|G|K|Q|a|g|i|k|

ANALOGIES
Curve form
Type style
Rhythm
Weight
Width
Typographic color

SIMILARITIES
Heights
Axis/Stress
Curve direction
Slant
Stroke shaping
Juncture

Letter design
|J|M|R|W|t|y|

25.7   25.5

DESIGN FORMEN
design formen

24.0   23.3

CONTRASTS
Type form
Stroke contrast

DIFFERENCES
Curve form
Terminal shaping

Letter design
|G|K|Q|R|i|k|

ANALOGIES
Type style
Rhythm
Weight
Width
Typographic color

SIMILARITIES
Heights
Axis/Stress
Curve direction
Slant
Stroke shaping
Juncture

Letter design
|J|M|W|a|g|t|w|y|

26.0   25.8

DESIGN FORMEN
design formen

23.5   23.6

ABCDEFGHIJKLM
NOPQRSTUVWXYZ
abcdefghijklm
nopqrstuvwxyz

Bembo Regular
Francesco Griffo — Frank Hinman Pierpont
1495 | Aldus Manutius — 1929 | Monotype MT
Antiqua

ABCDEFGHIJKLM
NOPQRSTUVWXYZ
abcdefghijklm
nopqrstuvwxyz

Gill Sans Medium
Eric Gill
1928 | Monotype MT
Grotesque →258/259

Masken

121 pt

CONTRASTS
Type form
Typographic color

DIFFERENCES
Heights
Rhythm
Stroke contrast
Stroke shaping
Terminal shaping
Juncture

Letter design
|K|M|W|f|

ANALOGIES
Curve form
Type style
Curve direction

SIMILARITIES
Axis/Stress
Weight
Width
Slant
Ductus
Juncture

Letter design
|C|G|J|Q|
|a|g|k|t|w|y|

29.6 27.5

DESIGN **FORMEN**
design **formen**

29.7 27.4

Masken **Bildner**

12.5 11.4

Bildner

109 pt

ABCDEFGHIJKLM
NOPQRSTUVWXYZ
abcdefghijklm
nopqrstuvwxyz

Semplicita Semibold
Alessandro Butti — Patrick Griffin, Bill Troop
1930 | Società Nebiolo — 2010 | Canada Type
Grotesque

ABCDEFGHIJKLM
NOPQRSTUVWXYZ
abcdefghijklm
nopqrstuvwxyz

Wilke 55 Roman
Martin Wilke
1988 | Linotype LT
Antiqua

Arabian

96 pt

CONTRASTS
Type form
Typographic color

DIFFERENCES
Curve form
Type style
Axis/Stress
Curve direction
Weight
Stroke contrast
Width
Stroke shaping
Terminal shaping

Letter design
|A|G|K|Q|R|W|
|g|k|t|u|w|y|

ANALOGIES
Heights
Rhythm

SIMILARITIES
Slant
Ductus
Juncture

Letter design
|J|M|a|j|

24.3   26.5

DESIGN FORMEN
design formen

23.7   26.3

Arabian Beauty

10.0   11.0

Beauty

107 pt

ABCDEFGHIJKLM
NOPQRSTUVWXYZ
abcdefghijklm
nopqrstuvwxyz

Aroma No.2 Extralight
Tim Ahrens
1999 / 2007 | Linotype LT
Grotesque

ABCDEFGHIJKLM
NOPQRSTUVWXYZ
abcdefghijklm
nopqrstuvwxyz

Laurentian Semibold
Rod McDonald
2003 | Monotype MT
Antiqua

108 pt

CONTRASTS
Type form
Weight
Typographic color

DIFFERENCES
Stroke contrast
Terminal shaping
Juncture

Letter design
|K|W|k|w|

ANALOGIES
Curve form
Heights
Type style
Axis/Stress
Rhythm
Curve direction

SIMILARITIES
Width
Slant
Ductus
Stroke shaping

Letter design
|G|J|M|Q|R|
|a|e|f|g|i|j|y|

27.0 28.0

DESIGN **FORMEN**
design **formen**

25.7 26.9

Flight **Board**

11.0 11.5

Board

111 pt

ABCDEFGHIJKLM
NOPQRSTUVWXYZ
abcdefghijklm
nopqrstuvwxyz

URW Antiqua Regular
Hermann Zapf
1985 | URW Type Foundry
Antiqua

ABCDEFGHIJKLM
NOPQRSTUVWXYZ
abcdefghijklm
nopqrstuvwxyz

Gotham Bold
Tobias Frere-Jones
2000 | Hoefler Type Foundry HTF
Grotesque

Sound

107 pt

CONTRASTS
Type form
Weight
Stroke contrast
Typographic color

ANALOGIES
Heights
Curve direction
Width
Juncture

DIFFERENCES
Curve form
Type style
Rhythm
Terminal shaping

SIMILARITIES
Axis/Stress
Slant
Ductus
Stroke shaping

Letter design
|J|M|Q|a|f|g|i|

Letter design
|G|K|W|k|w|y|

27.6 26.3

DESIGN **FORMEN**

design *formen*

25.5 23.6

Sound **Studio**

11.1 10.2

Studio

98 pt

ABCDEFGHIJKLM NOPQRSTUVWXYZ abcdefghijklm nopqrstuvwxyz

Palatino Black
Hermann Zapf
1950 | D. Stempel AG / Linotype LT
Antiqua → 210/211

ABCDEFGHIJKLM NOPQRSTUVWXYZ abcdefghijklm nopqrstuvwxyz

Avenir 45 Book
Adrian Frutiger
1988 | Linotype LT
Grotesque → 218/219

ABCDEFGHIJKLM NOPQRSTUVWXYZ abcdefghijklm nopqrstuvwxyz

Centennial 45 Light
Adrian Frutiger
1986 | Linotype LT
Antiqua → 220/221 → 226/227

ABCDEFGHIJKLM NOPQRSTUVWXYZ abcdefghijklm nopqrstuvwxyz

Meta Bold
Erik Spiekermann
1991–1998 | FontFont FF
Grotesque

ABCDEFGHIJKLM NOPQRSTUVWXYZ abcdefghijklm nopqrstuvwxyz

Diverda Sans Black
Daniel Lanz
2004 | Linotype LT
Grotesque

ABCDEFGHIJKLM NOPQRSTUVWXYZ abcdefghijklm nopqrstuvwxyz

Warnock Subhead
Robert Slimbach
2000 | Adobe Systems
Latin → 270/271

CONTRASTS
Type form
Weight
Typographic color

DIFFERENCES
Type style
Axis/Stress
Curve direction
Stroke contrast
Stroke shaping
Terminal shaping
Juncture

Letter design
|J|Q|Y|g|

ANALOGIES
Heights
Rhythm

SIMILARITIES
Curve form
Width
Slant
Ductus

Letter design
|K|M|W|
|a|f|i|j|k|w|y|

26.6 26.0

DESIGN FORMEN
design formen

26.5 25.5

CONTRASTS
Type form
Weight
Terminal shaping
Typographic color

DIFFERENCES
Heights
Type style
Curve direction
Stroke contrast
Stroke shaping
Juncture

Letter design
|G|J|M|R|I|

ANALOGIES
Curve form
Width

SIMILARITIES
Axis/Stress
Rhythm
Slant
Ductus

Letter design
|K|Q|W|
|a|f|g|i|j|k|t|w|y|

25.8 26.4

DESIGN **FORMEN**
design **formen**

24.0 24.3

CONTRASTS
Type form
Terminal shaping

DIFFERENCES
Weight
Stroke contrast
Stroke shaping
Typographic color

Letter design
|G|W|b|g|I|q|y|

ANALOGIES
Curve form
Heights
Width
Rhythm

SIMILARITIES
Type style
Axis/Stress
Curve direction
Slant
Ductus
Juncture

Letter design
|J|K|M|Q|R|k|w|

27.5 27.8

DESIGN FORMEN
design formen

27.0 27.3

ABCDEFGHIJKLM
NOPQRSTUVWXYZ
abcdefghijklm
nopqrstuvwxyz

Alena Thin
Roland Stieger
2017 | Nouvelle Noire NN
Grotesque

ABCDEFGHIJKLM
NOPQRSTUVWXYZ
abcdefghijklm
nopqrstuvwxyz

Albertina Bold Italic
Chris Brand — Frank E. Blokland
1966 | Monotype MT — 1996 | Monotype MT
Antiqua

Question

102 pt

CONTRASTS
Type form
Weight
Typographic color

DIFFERENCES
Type style
Axis/Stress
Stroke contrast
Width
Ductus
Terminal shaping

Letter design
|J|W|a|e|f|j|k|w|

ANALOGIES
Curve form
Heights

SIMILARITIES
Curve direction
Rhythm
Slant
Stroke shaping
Juncture

Letter design
|G|K|M|Q|R|U|
|g|y|

26.9 27.6

DESIGN *FORMEN*
design *formen*

25.1 25.4

Question *Marks*

10.7 11.1

Marks

106 pt

ABCDEFGHIJKLM
NOPQRSTUVWXYZ
abcdefghijklm
nopqrstuvwxyz

Lexicon No.1 Roman B Medium
Bram de Does
1992 | The Enschedé Font Foundry
Antiqua

ABCDEFGHIJKLM
NOPQRSTUVWXYZ
abcdefghijklm
nopqrstuvwxyz

Branding Bold Italic
Alfonso Garcia, Cesar Araya
2016–2019 | Latinotype
Grotesque

Escort

108 pt

CONTRASTS
Weight
Slant
Typographic color

DIFFERENCES
Type form
Type style
Axis/Stress
Stroke contrast
Ductus
Terminal shaping

Letter design
J	K	M	V	W
a	e	g		k	m	n	r	t
u	v	w	y	z

ANALOGIES
Curve form
Heights
Curve direction
Width

SIMILARITIES
Heights
Rhythm
Stroke shaping
Terminal shaping
Juncture

Letter design
|P|R|j|

28.2   28.8

DESIGN *FORMEN*
design *formen*

24.0   25.4

Escort *Service*

10.9   10.9

Service

108 pt

ABCDEFGHIJKLM
NOPQRSTUVWXYZ
abcdefghijklm
nopqrstuvwxyz

Origami Semibold Italic
Carl Crossgrove
1998 | Monotype MT
Latin

ABCDEFGHIJKLM
NOPQRSTUVWXYZ
abcdefghijklm
nopqrstuvwxyz

Allegra Italic
Jost Hochuli
2019 | Nouvelle Noire NN
Grotesque

Triumphal

117 pt

CONTRASTS
Type form
Weight
Typographic color
Impression

DIFFERENCES
Curve form
Heights
Type style
Axis/Stress
Rhythm
Stroke contrast
Ductus
Stroke shaping
Terminal shaping

Letter design
|K|Q|W|i|j|k|w|

ANALOGIES
Slant
Curve direction

SIMILARITIES
Width
Juncture

Letter design
|G|M|R|a|g|y|

31.8   27.8

DESIGN FORMEN
design formen

29.7   26.8

Triumphal *Symphony*

13.0   11.5

Symphony

108 pt

243

ABCDEFGHIJKLM
NOPQRSTUVWXYZ
abcdefghijklm
nopqrstuvwxyz

Goudy Sans Black Italic
Frederic William Goudy — ITC Design Staff
1929–1931 | Lanston Monotype — 1986 | ITC
Glyphic

ABCDEFGHIJKLM
NOPQRSTUVWXYZ
abcdefghijklm
nopqrstuvwxyz

Trump Mediäval Roman
Georg Trump
1954–1962 | C. E. Weber, type foundry — Linotype LT
Latin

ABCDEFGHIJKLM
NOPQRSTUVWXYZ
abcdefghijklm
nopqrstuvwxyz

Caspari Bold
Gerard Daniëls
2014 | Dutch Type Library DTL
Grotesque

ABCDEFGHIJKLM
NOPQRSTUVWXYZ
abcdefghijklm
nopqrstuvwxyz

Minion Medium Italic
Robert Slimbach
1990 | Adobe Systems
Antiqua

ABCDEFGHIJKLM
NOPQRSTUVWXYZ
abcdefghijklm
nopqrstuvwxyz

Joanna Italic
Eric Gill
1937 | Monotype MT
Egyptian

ABCDEFGHIJKLM
NOPQRSTUVWXYZ
abcdefghijklm
nopqrstuvwxyz

Myriad Bold Italic
Carol Twombly, Robert Slimbach
1992 | Adobe Systems
Grotesque   → 290/291

CONTRASTS
Weight
Slant
Ductus
Typographic color

DIFFERENCES
Type form
Curve form
Type style
Axis/Stress
Offset center position
Stroke contrast
Terminal shaping

Letter design
|A|G|M|Q|U|W|X|Y|
|a|f|v|w|x|z|

ANALOGIES
Heights
Curve direction

SIMILARITIES
Rhythm
Width
Stroke shaping
Juncture

Letter design
|J|R|g|k|y|

27.5   26.3

DESIGN FORMEN
design formen

26.3   25.2

CONTRASTS
Weight
Slant
Ductus
Typographic color

DIFFERENCES
Type form
Curve form
Stroke contrast
Width
Terminal shaping
Juncture

Letter design
|M|Q|a|f|k|p|y|

ANALOGIES
Heights
Curve direction

SIMILARITIES
Type style
Axis/Stress
Rhythm
Stroke shaping

Letter design
|G|J|K|R|W|
|g|i|j|w|

27.0   28.4

DESIGN *FORMEN*
design *formen*

25.3   27.2

CONTRASTS
Type form
Weight
Width
Terminal shaping
Typographic color

DIFFERENCES
Curve form
Heights
Stroke contrast
Slant
Juncture

Letter design
|G|J|K|M|k|y|

ANALOGIES
Curve direction
Rhythm

SIMILARITIES
Type style
Axis/Stress
Ductus
Stroke shaping

Letter design
|P|Q|R|W|
|a|e|i|j|q|w|

30.8   27.5

DESIGN **FORMEN**
design ***formen***

29.2   26.0

ABCDEFGHIJKLM
NOPQRSTUVWXYZ
abcdefghijklm
nopqrstuvwxyz

Akkurat Regular
Laurenz Brunner
2004 | Lineto LL
Grotesque →226/227

ABCDEFGHIJKLM
NOPQRSTUVWXYZ
abcdefghijklm
nopqrstuvwxyz

Egyptian F 55 Roman
Adrian Frutiger
1956–1958 | Deberny & Peignot — 1976 | Linotype LT
Egyptian

Zoological

101 pt

CONTRASTS
Type form

DIFFERENCES
Heights
Rhythm
Weight
Stroke contrast
Terminal shaping

Letter design
|G|K|M|Q|R|k|y|

ANALOGIES
Curve form
Typographic color

SIMILARITIES
Type style
Axis/Stress
Curve direction
Width
Slant
Ductus
Stroke shaping
Juncture
|g|

26.0   28.3

DESIGN FORMEN
design formen

23.6   25.0

Zoological Garden

10.1   10.6

Garden

106 pt

ABCDEFGHIJKLM
NOPQRSTUVWXYZ
abcdefghijklm
nopqrstuvwxyz

Frutiger 55 Roman
Adrian Frutiger
1974–1976 | Linotype LT
Grotesque

ALTERNATIVE
Myriad | Carol Twombly, Robert Slimbach | 1992 | Adobe Systems
→ 244/245 → 290/291

ABCDEFGHIJKLM
NOPQRSTUVWXYZ
abcdefghijklm
nopqrstuvwxyz

Caecilia 55 Roman
Peter Matthias Noordzij
1990 | Linotype LT
Egyptian → 258/259

Flughafen

100 pt

CONTRASTS
Type form

DIFFERENCES
Terminal shaping
Juncture

Letter design
|J|W|b|d|g|i|p|q|

ANALOGIES
Curve form
Heights
Width

SIMILARITIES
Type style
Axis/Stress
Curve direction
Rhythm
Weight
Stroke contrast
Slant
Ductus
Stroke shaping
Typographic color

Letter design
|G|K|M|Q|R|
|a|e|k|y|

26.4   26.4

DESIGN FORMEN
design formen

23.4   23.0

Flughafen Gebäude

10.1 10.0

Gebäude

99 pt

ABCDEFGHIJKLM
NOPQRSTUVWXYZ
abcdefghijklm
nopqrstuvwxyz

Akzidenz Grotesk Medium
unknown — Günter Gerhard Lange
1898 | H. Berthold AG — 1958 | H. Berthold AG
Grotesque   →204 →226/227 →278/279

ABCDEFGHIJKLM
NOPQRSTUVWXYZ
abcdefghijklm
nopqrstuvwxyz

Rockwell Light
Frank Hinman Pierpont
1934 | Monotype MT
Egyptian   →258/259

Geometrie

99 pt

CONTRASTS
Type form
Typographic color

DIFFERENCES
Type style
Rhythm
Weight
Terminal shaping
Juncture
Letter design
|G|J|K|Q|a|i|k|

ANALOGIES
Curve form
Heights
Curve direction

SIMILARITIES
Axis/Stress
Stroke contrast
Width
Slant
Ductus
Stroke shaping
Letter design
|M|P|R|W|e|g|y|

26.1 27.1

DESIGN FORMEN
design formen

23.8 25.2

Geometrie Dreieck

10.4 10.8

Dreieck

104 pt

251

ABCDEFGHIJKLM
NOPQRSTUVWXYZ
abcdefghijklm
nopqrstuvwxyz

Berkeley Oldstyle Book
Frederic William Goudy
1938 | University of California Press, Berkeley — 1983 | ITC
Antiqua

ABCDEFGHIJKLM
NOPQRSTUVWXYZ
abcdefghijklm
nopqrstuvwxyz

Chaparral Bold
Carol Twombly
2000 | Adobe Systems
Egyptian

Bohemian

115 pt

CONTRASTS
Weight
Typographic color

DIFFERENCES
Type form
Offset center position
Terminal shaping
Serif transition

Letter design
|J|K|W|a|e|j|k|w|

ANALOGIES
Curve form
Heights
Curve direction
Juncture

SIMILARITIES
Type style
Axis/Stress
Instroke/Outstroke
Rhythm
Stroke contrast
Width
Slant
Ductus
Stroke shaping

Letter design
|G|M|P|Q|R|S|T|
|b|g|y|

29.0 28.9

DESIGN **FORMEN**
design **formen**

27.9 28.1

Bohemian **Rhapsody**

11.9 11.8

Rhapsody

114 pt

ABCDEFGHIJKLM
NOPQRSTUVWXYZ
abcdefghijklm
nopqrstuvwxyz

Klavika Regular
Eric Olson
2004 | Process Type Foundry
Grotesque

ABCDEFGHIJKLM
NOPQRSTUVWXYZ
abcdefghijklm
nopqrstuvwxyz

Diaria Extrabold
Andriy Konstantynov
2015 | Mint Type
Egyptian

Hyazinth

107 pt

CONTRASTS
Weight
Typographic color

DIFFERENCES
Type form
Axis/Stress
Stroke contrast
Terminal shaping

Letter design
|J|K|R|X|g|i|k|x|y|

ANALOGIES
Heights
Width

SIMILARITIES
Curve form
Type style
Curve direction
Rhythm
Slant
Ductus
Stroke shaping
Juncture

Letter design
|G|M|Q|W|a|t|w|

27.8   26.3

DESIGN **FORMEN**

design **formen**

24.7   22.7

Hyazinth **Zwiebel**

10.5   9.9

Zwiebel

100 pt

ABCDEFGHIJKLM
NOPQRSTUVWXYZ
abcdefghijklm
nopqrstuvwxyz

Clarendon Medium
Hermann Eidenbenz
1953 | Haas Type Foundry — Linotype LT
Egyptian → 280/281

ABCDEFGHIJKLM
NOPQRSTUVWXYZ
abcdefghijklm
nopqrstuvwxyz

Franklin Gothic No. 2 Roman
Morris Fuller Benton
1904 | American Type Founders ATF — Linotype LT
Grotesque

Steam

109 pt

CONTRASTS
Type form
Typographic color

DIFFERENCES
Weight
Curve direction
Juncture
Terminal shaping
Letter design
|Q|R|

ANALOGIES
Curve form
Heights
Stroke contrast

SIMILARITIES
Type style
Axis/Stress
Rhythm
Width
Slant
Ductus
Stroke shaping
Letter design
|G|J|K|M|g|j|k|y|

27.7 24.4

DESIGN **FORMEN**
design **formen**

26.1 23.0

Steam **Engine**

11.2 9.6

Engine

95 pt

ABCDEFGHIJKLM
NOPQRSTUVWXYZ
abcdefghijklm
nopqrstuvwxyz

Caecilia 85 Heavy
Peter Matthias Noordzij
1990 | Linotype LT
Egyptian   → 248/249

ABCDEFGHIJKLM
NOPQRSTUVWXYZ
abcdefghijklm
nopqrstuvwxyz

Gill Sans Light
Eric Gill
1928 | Monotype MT
Grotesque   → 228/229

ABCDEFGHIJKLM
NOPQRSTUVWXYZ
abcdefghijklm
nopqrstuvwxyz

Century Gothic Regular
Sol Hess
Twentieth Century | 1936–1947 | Monotype — 1990–1995 | Monotype MT
Grotesque

ALTERNATIVE
Gotham | Tobias Frere-Jones | → 234/235

ABCDEFGHIJKLM
NOPQRSTUVWXYZ
abcdefghijklm
nopqrstuvwxyz

Rockwell Bold
Frank Hinman Pierpont
1934 | Monotype MT
Egyptian   → 250/251

ABCDEFGHIJKLM
NOPQRSTUVWXYZ
abcdefghijklm
nopqrstuvwxyz

Serifa 55 Roman
Adrian Frutiger
1963–1967 | Bauer Type Foundry — Linotype LT
Egyptian

ABCDEFGHIJKLM
NOPQRSTUVWXYZ
abcdefghijklm
nopqrstuvwxyz

Neuzeit S Book Heavy
Wilhelm Pischner
Neuzeit Grotesque | 1928 | D. Stempel AG — 1966 | Linotype LT
Grotesque

CONTRASTS
Weight
Typographic color

DIFFERENCES
Type form
Heights
Terminal shaping
Juncture

Letter design
|M|W|i|w|y|

ANALOGIES
Curve form
Curve direction

SIMILARITIES
Type style
Axis/Stress
Rhythm
Stroke contrast
Width
Slant
Ductus
Stroke shaping

Letter design
|G|J|K|Q|R|
|a|f|g|k|

26.2 26.9

DESIGN FORMEN
design formen

22.8 26.5

CONTRASTS
Type form
Weight
Typographic color

DIFFERENCES
Rhythm
Offset center position
Terminal shaping

Letter design
|A|J|M|Q|W|a|t|y|

ANALOGIES
Heights
Type style
Curve direction
Width

SIMILARITIES
Curve form
Axis/Stress
Stroke contrast
Slant
Ductus
Stroke shaping
Juncture

Letter design
|G|R|S|U|W|
|g|i|j|

25.5 27.0

DESIGN **FORMEN**
design **formen**

22.4 25.1

CONTRASTS
Type form

DIFFERENCES
Type style
Rhythm
Weight
Width
Terminal shaping
Typographic color

Letter design
|G|J|Q|i|k|y|

ANALOGIES
Heights
Curve direction
Juncture

SIMILARITIES
Curve form
Axis/Stress
Stroke contrast
Slant
Ductus
Stroke shaping

Letter design
|K|M|W|a|g|w|

28.2 24.5

DESIGN **FORMEN**
design **formen**

26.1 23.8

ABCDEFGHIJKLM
NOPQRSTUVWXYZ
abcdefghijklm
nopqrstuvwxyz

Swift Light
Gerard Unger
1995 | Dr.-Ing. Rudolf Hell GmbH — 2009 | Linotype LT
Latin

ABCDEFGHIJKLM
NOPQRSTUVWXYZ
abcdefghijklm
nopqrstuvwxyz

Vesta Regular
Gerard Unger
2001 | Linotype LT
Grotesque

Gaumen

105 pt

CONTRASTS
Type form
Terminal shaping

DIFFERENCES
Heights

ANALOGIES
Curve form
Width
Juncture

SIMILARITIES
Type style
Axis / Stress
Curve direction
Rhythm
Weight
Stroke contrast
Slant
Ductus
Stroke shaping
Typographic color

Letter design
|G|J|K|M|Q|R|W|
|a|e|g|j|k|t|w|y|

27.0   26.1

DESIGN FORMEN
design formen

24.8   23.5

Gaumen Schmaus

10.4 10.1

Schmaus

102 pt

ABCDEFGHIJKLM NOPQRSTUVWXYZ
abcdefghijklm nopqrstuvwxyz

Effra Heavy
Jonas Schudel
2008–2013 | Dalton Maag
Grotesque

ABCDEFGHIJKLM NOPQRSTUVWXYZ
abcdefghijklm nopqrstuvwxyz

Dolly Roman
Akiem Helmling, Bas Jacobs, Sami Kortemäki
2002 | Underware
Antiqua

Encoding

106 pt

CONTRASTS
Type form
Weight
Terminal shaping
Typographic color

DIFFERENCES
Curve form
Heights
Type style
Stroke contrast
Juncture
Letter design
|J|K|M|Q|g|i|k|

ANALOGIES
Curve direction

SIMILARITIES
Axis/Stress
Rhythm
Width
Slant
Ductus
Stroke shaping
Juncture
Letter design
|G|R|W|
|a|b|d|p|q|y|

27.8 28.3

DESIGN FORMEN
design formen

25.3 25.8

Encoding Numbers

11.2 11.2

Numbers

109 pt

ABCDEFGHIJKLM
NOPQRSTUVWXYZ
abcdefghijklm
nopqrstuvwxyz

Vendôme Regular
François Ganeau
1952 | Fonderie Olive — Linotype LT
Latin

ABCDEFGHIJKLM
NOPQRSTUVWXYZ
abcdefghijklm
nopqrstuvwxyz

Syntax Roman
Hans Eduard Meier
1968 | D. Stempel AG / Linotype LT
Grotesque

Reading

110 pt

CONTRASTS
Type form
Typographic color

DIFFERENCES
Stroke contrast
Terminal shaping

Letter design
|G|M|R|W|a|e|t|

ANALOGIES
Type style
Curve direction
Rhythm
Slant

SIMILARITIES
Curve form
Heights
Axis/Stress
Weight
Width
Ductus
Stroke shaping
Juncture

Letter design
|J|K|Q|g|j|k|w|y|

27.6   26.7

DESIGN **FORMEN**
design **formen**

26.5   24.0

Reading **Machine**

11.5   10.3

Machine

100 pt

265

ABCDEFGHIJKLM
NOPQRSTUVWXYZ
abcdefghijklm
nopqrstuvwxyz

Méridien Roman
Adrian Frutiger
1953–1957 | Deberny & Peignot — Linotype LT
Latin →268/269

ABCDEFGHIJKLM
NOPQRSTUVWXYZ
abcdefghijklm
nopqrstuvwxyz

Basic Sans Black
Daniel Hernández
2016 | Latinotype
Grotesque

Marketing

106 pt

CONTRASTS
Type form
Weight
Typographic color

DIFFERENCES
Stroke contrast
Terminal shaping
Juncture

Letter design
|G|K|M|R|W|k|y|

ANALOGIES
Curve form
Rhythm
Width
Stroke shaping

SIMILARITIES
Heights
Type style
Axis/Stress
Curve direction
Slant
Ductus

Letter design
|J|Q|W|a|g|j|w|

29.3 28.3

DESIGN **FORMEN**
design **formen**

26.5 26.5

Marketing **Strategy**

11.2 11.2

Strategy

106 pt

ABCDEFGHIJKLM
NOPQRSTUVWXYZ
abcdefghijklm
nopqrstuvwxyz

Méridien Roman
Adrian Frutiger
1953–1957 | Deberny & Peignot — Linotype LT
Latin →266/267

ABCDEFGHIJKLM
NOPQRSTUVWXYZ
abcdefghijklm
nopqrstuvwxyz

Mundo Sans Black
Carl Crossgrove
2002 | Monotype MT
Grotesque

Castle

109 pt

CONTRASTS
Type form
Weight
Typographic color

DIFFERENCES
Stroke contrast
Terminal shaping
Juncture

Letter design
|J|

ANALOGIES
Curve form
Rhythm
Width
Stroke shaping

SIMILARITIES
Heights
Type style
Axis/Stress
Curve direction
Slant
Ductus

Letter design
|G|K|M|Q|R|W|
|a|g|j|k|t|w|y|

29.3 27.6

DESIGN **FORMEN**
design **formen**

26.5 25.7

Castle **Garden**

11.2 10.7

Garden

102 pt

269

ABCDEFGHIJKLM
NOPQRSTUVWXYZ
abcdefghijklm
nopqrstuvwxyz

Cronos Regular
Robert Slimbach
1996 | Adobe Systems
Grotesque hybrid

ABCDEFGHIJKLM
NOPQRSTUVWXYZ
abcdefghijklm
nopqrstuvwxyz

Warnock Regular
Robert Slimbach
2000 | Adobe Systems
Latin → 236/237

Coconut

114 pt

CONTRASTS
Type form
Impression

DIFFERENCES
Stroke contrast
Stroke shaping
Terminal shaping

Letter design
|G|W|y|

ANALOGIES
Curve form
Curve direction
Rhythm
Weight
Width
Typographic color

SIMILARITIES
Heights
Type style
Axis/Stress
Slant
Ductus
Juncture

Letter design
|C|E|F|J|K|P|Q|
|a|e|f|g|j|k|w|

29.5 28.0

DESIGN FORMEN
design formen

27.5 27.5

Coconut Curry

11.8 11.4

Curry

110 pt

271

**ABCDEFGHIJKLM
NOPQRSTUVWXYZ
abcdefghijklm
nopqrstuvwxyz**

VAG Rounded Bold
Wolf Rogosky, Gerd Hiepler
VAG Rundschrift | 1979 | Volkswagen | URW Type Foundry — Linotype LT
Grotesque →314/315

ABCDEFGHIJKLM
NOPQRSTUVWXYZ
abcdefghijklm
nopqrstuvwxyz

Nikola Light
Sergio Leiva Whittle, Rodrigo López Fuentes
2017 | Untype
Latin

ALTERNATIVE
Méridien | Adrian Frutiger | 1953–1957 | Deberny & Peignot — Linotype LT
→266/267 →268/269

Nerven

98 pt

CONTRASTS
Type form
Terminal shaping
Typographic color
Impression

DIFFERENCES
Heights
Offset center position
Weight
Stroke contrast

Letter design
|G|J|K|Q|R|a|g|k|t|

ANALOGIES
Type style
Width

SIMILARITIES
Curve form
Axis/Stress
Curve direction
Rhythm
Slant
Ductus
Stroke shaping

Letter design
|M|

26.1 26.9

DESIGN FORMEN
design formen

23.0 24.6

Nerven Kitzel

9.8 10.3

Kitzel

103 pt

ABCDEFGHIJKLM
NOPQRSTUVWXYZ
abcdefghijklm
nopqrstuvwxyz

Helvetica Rounded Bold
Linotype Design Studio
1978 | Linotype LT
Grotesque →276/277 →286/287 →318/319

ABCDEFGHIJKLM
NOPQRSTUVWXYZ
abcdefghijklm
nopqrstuvwxyz

Tiepolo Book
Arthur Baker, Cynthia Hollandsworth Batty
1987 | Alpha Omega — International Typeface Corporation ITC
Glyphic

100 pt

CONTRASTS
Type form
Weight
Terminal shaping
Typographic color
Impression

DIFFERENCES
Curve form
Heights
Type style
Axis/Stress
Curve direction
Rhythm
Stroke contrast
Ductus
Stroke shaping
Juncture

Letter design
|G|J|M|Q|R|U|g|y|

ANALOGIES
Width

SIMILARITIES
Slant

Letter design
|K|W|a|f|k|t|w|

25.6 30.2

DESIGN FORMEN
design formen

23.0 26.1

Luft Schloss

9.8 11.3

Schloss

114 pt

**ABCDEFGHIJKLM
NOPQRSTUVWXYZ
abcdefghijklm
nopqrstuvwxyz**

American Typewriter Bold
Joel Kaden, Tony Stan
1974 | International Typeface Corporation ITC
Egyptian   →278/279 →300/301

ABCDEFGHIJKLM
NOPQRSTUVWXYZ
abcdefghijklm
nopqrstuvwxyz

Neue Helvetica Light
Max Miedinger, Eduard Hoffmann
1957–1966 | Haas Type Foundry / D. Stempel AG — 1983 | Linotype LT
Grotesque   →274/275 →286/287 →318/319

ALTERNATIVE
Akkurat | Laurenz Brunner | 2004 | Lineto LL
→226/227 →246/247

Dampflok

102 pt

CONTRASTS
Type form
Terminal shaping
Typographic color

DIFFERENCES
Weight
Stroke shaping

Letter design
|Q|g|i|

ANALOGIES
Curve form
Heights
Type style
Curve direction

SIMILARITIES
Axis/Stress
Rhythm
Stroke contrast
Width
Slant
Ductus

Letter design
|G|J|K|M|Q|W|
|a|k|w|y|

27.3 25.8

DESIGN FORMEN
design formen

24.0 23.4

Dampflok Kartei

10.4 10.0

Kartei

96 pt

ABCDEFGHIJKLM
NOPQRSTUVWXYZ
abcdefghijklm
nopqrstuvwxyz

AG Buch Rounded Bold
Günter Gerhard Lange
1980 | H. Berthold AG BQ
Grotesque →204 →226/227 →250/251

ABCDEFGHIJKLM
NOPQRSTUVWXYZ
abcdefghijklm
nopqrstuvwxyz

American Typewriter Bold
Joel Kaden, Tony Stan
1974 | International Typeface Corporation ITC
Egyptian →276/277 →300/301

Kolben

101 pt

CONTRASTS
Type form
Terminal shaping

DIFFERENCES
Stroke shaping

Letter design
|Q|g|

ANALOGIES
Terminal shaping
Curve form
Heights
Typographic color

SIMILARITIES
Type style
Axis/Stress
Curve direction
Rhythm
Weight
Stroke contrast
Width
Slant
Ductus

Letter design
|G|J|K|M|R|W|
|a|i|k|y|

26.3 27.3

DESIGN FORMEN
design formen

23.4 24.0

Kolben Boden

10.8 10.9

Boden

102 pt

ABCDEFGHIJKLM NOPQRSTUVWXYZ abcdefghijklm nopqrstuvwxyz

Cooper Black
Oswald Bruce Cooper
1920–1926 | Barnhart Brothers & Spindler — ITC
Egyptian   → below

ABCDEFGHIJKLM NOPQRSTUVWXYZ abcdefghijklm nopqrstuvwxyz

Versailles 55 Light
Adrian Frutiger
1984 | D. Stempel AG / Linotype LT
Latin

ABCDEFGHIJKLM NOPQRSTUVWXYZ abcdefghijklm nopqrstuvwxyz

Clarendon Medium
Hermann Eidenbenz
1953 | Haas Type Foundry — Linotype LT
Egyptian   → 256/257

ABCDEFGHIJKLM NOPQRSTUVWXYZ abcdefghijklm nopqrstuvwxyz

Cooper Black
Oswald Bruce Cooper
1920–1926 | Barnhart Brothers & Spindler — ITC
Egyptian   → above/below

ABCDEFGHIJKLM NOPQRSTUVWXYZ abcdefghijklm nopqrstuvwxyz

Cooper Black
Oswald Bruce Cooper
1920–1926 | Barnhart Brothers & Spindler — ITC
Egyptian   → above

ABCDEFGHIJKLM NOPQRSTUVWXYZ abcdefghijklm nopqrstuvwxyz

Auriol Roman
Georges Auriol — Matthew Carter
1901 | Deberny & Peignot — 1991 | Linotype LT
Script   → 304/305

CONTRASTS
Type form
Weight
Axis/Stress
Stroke shaping
Terminal shaping
Typographic color

DIFFERENCES
Curve form
Heights
Type style
Instroke/Outstroke
Width

Letter design
|G|Q|f|g|

ANALOGIES
Curve direction
Rhythm

SIMILARITIES
Stroke contrast
Slant
Ductus
Serif transition
Juncture

Letter design
|J|K|M|R|W|
|a|i|j|k|w|y|

26.4   25.9

DESIGN FORMEN
design formen

23.6   24.0

CONTRASTS
Weight
Axis/Stress
Stroke shaping
Terminal shaping
Typographic color

DIFFERENCES
Heights
Type style
Curve direction
Instroke/Outstroke
Width

Letter design
|G|K|Q|R|f|k|

ANALOGIES
Type form
Rhythm

SIMILARITIES
Curve form
Stroke contrast
Slant
Ductus
Serif transition
Juncture

Letter design
|J|M|W|
|a|g|i|j|t|w|y|

27.7   26.4

DESIGN **FORMEN**
design **formen**

26.1   23.6

CONTRASTS
Weight
Stroke shaping
Terminal shaping
Typographic color

DIFFERENCES
Type form
Heights
Juncture

Letter design
|M|V|W|Y|
|e|f|t|v|w|y|

ANALOGIES
Curve form
Axis/Stress
Rhythm

SIMILARITIES
Type style
Curve direction
Instroke/Outstroke
Stroke contrast
Width
Slant
Ductus

Letter design
|G|J|K|R|
|a|g|i|j|k|

26.4   26.6

DESIGN FORMEN
design formen

23.6   25.8

ABCDEFGHIJKLM
NOPQRSTUVWXYZ
abcdefghijklm
nopqrstuvwxyz

Eurostile Extended 2
Aldo Novarese
1962 | Società Nebiolo — Linotype LT
Grotesque

ABCDEFGHIJKLM
NOPQRSTUVWXYZ
abcdefghijklm
nopqrstuvwxyz

Univers 39 Thin Ultra Condensed
Adrian Frutiger
1954–1957 | Deberny & Peignot — 1969 | Linotype LT
Grotesque →220/221

94 pt

CONTRASTS
Width
Typographic color

DIFFERENCES
Weight

Letter design
|G|K|Q|r|t|y|

ANALOGIES
Type form
Curve form
Impression

SIMILARITIES
Heights
Type style
Axis/Stress
Curve direction
Rhythm
Stroke contrast
Slant
Ductus
Stroke shaping
Terminal shaping

Letter design
|J|R|

25.5   25.5

DESIGN FORMEN

design formen

23.4   23.8

Breit Band

10.0   10.2

Band

96 pt

ABCDEFGHIJKLM
NOPQRSTUVWXYZ
abcdefghijklm
nopqrstuvwxyz

Atomatic Regular
Johannes Plass
1997 | Linotype LT
Grotesque hybrid

ABCDEFGHIJKLM
NOPQRSTUVWXYZ
abcdefghijklm
nopqrstuvwxyz

Mekanik Regular
David Quay
1988 | International Typeface Corporation ITC
Grotesque

104 pt

CONTRASTS
Width
Slant

DIFFERENCES
Weight
Curve direction
Ductus
Terminal shaping
Typographic color

Letter design
|K|Y|a|f|k|w|

ANALOGIES
Curve form
Impression

SIMILARITIES
Type form
Heights
Type style
Axis/Stress
Rhythm
Stroke contrast
Stroke shaping
Curve shaping

Letter design
|A|M|N|S|W|y|

27.0   27.8

27.1   25.7

11.3   11.0

103 pt

ABCDEFGHIJKLM
NOPQRSTUVWXYZ
abcdefghijklm
nopqrstuvwxyz

Neue Helvetica 43 Light Extended
Max Miedinger, Eduard Hoffmann
1957–1966 | Haas Type Foundry / D. Stempel AG — 1983 | Linotype LT
Grotesque → 274/275 → 276/277 → 318/319

ABCDEFGHIJKLM
NOPQRSTUVWXYZ
abcdefghijklm
nopqrstuvwxyz

Serpentine Medium
Dick Jensen
1972 | Visual Graphics — Linotype LT
Glyphic → 294/295

97 pt

CONTRASTS
Curve form
Stroke contrast
Typographic color
Impression

DIFFERENCES
Type form
Type style
Curve direction
Weight
Terminal shaping

Letter design
|R|y|

ANALOGIES
Width

SIMILARITIES
Heights
Axis/Stress
Rhythm
Slant
Ductus
Stroke shaping

Letter design
|K|Q|k|

25.8   28.8

DESIGN **FORMEN**
design **formen**

23.4   26.0

Fire **Fighter**

10.0   10.9

106 pt

287

ABCDEFGHIJKLM
NOPQRSTUVWXYZ
abcdefghijklm
nopqrstuvwxyz

Korigan Light
Thierry Puyfoulhoux
1997 | International Typeface Corporation ITC
Script

ABCDEFGHIJKLM
NOPQRSTUVWXYZ
abcdefghijklm
nopqrstuvwxyz

Motter Sparta Regular
Othmar Motter
1997 | International Typeface Corporation ITC
Blackletter hybrid

Viking

111 pt

CONTRASTS
Weight
Typographic color

DIFFERENCES
Type form
Basic shape
Curve form
Heights
Type style
Axis/Stress
Curve direction
Stroke contrast
Stroke shaping
Terminal shaping

Letter design
E	F	J	K	M	N	S
a	d	e	f	h	m
n	s	u	w

ANALOGIES
Width
Impression

SIMILARITIES
Rhythm
Slant
Ductus

Letter design
|D|U|W|

30.7 28.0

DESIGN FORMEN

design formen

24.6 23.3

Viking **Ship**

11.0 10.3

102 pt

**ABCDEFGHIJKLM
NOPQRSTUVWXYZ
abcdefghijklm
nopqrstuvwxyz**

Myriad Bold
Carol Twombly, Robert Slimbach
1992 | Adobe Systems
Grotesque → 244/245

ALTERNATIVE
Frutiger | Adrian Frutiger | 1974–1976 | Linotype LT
→ 248/249

𝔄𝔅ℭ𝔇𝔈𝔉𝔊ℌ𝔍𝔎𝔏𝔐
𝔑𝔒𝔓𝔔ℜ𝔖𝔗𝔘𝔙𝔚𝔛𝔜𝔷
abcdefghijklm
nopqrstuvwxyz

Wittenberger Fraktur Regular
unknown
Schul-Fraktur | 1886 | Schelter & Giesecke — 1906 | Monotype MT
Blackletter

Wiener

103 pt

290

CONTRASTS
Type form
Weight
Stroke contrast
Typographic color
Impression

DIFFERENCES
Curve form
Rhythm
Width
Terminal shaping
Juncture

Letter design
A	E	F	H	J	K	M
N	P	Q	R	S	T	U
V	W	X	Y	Z	a	d
e	h	j	k	v	w	y	z

ANALOGIES
Heights
Axis/Stress
Curve direction

SIMILARITIES
Type style
Slant
Ductus
Stroke shaping

Letter design
|g|

27.3   26.9

DESIGN FORMEN
design formen

24.3   25.7

Wiener Schnitzel

10.4 10.9

Schnitzel

105 pt

ABCDEFGHIJKLM
NOPQRSTUVWXYZ

abcdefghijklm

nopqrstuvwxyz

Linotext Regular
Morris Fuller Benton
Wedding Text | 1901 | American Type Founders ATF — 1907 | Linotype LT
Blackletter

ABCDEFGHIJKLM
NOPQRSTUVWXYZ

abcdefghijklm

nopqrstuvwxyz

Didot Regular
Firmin Didot — Garrett Boge
ca. 1784 | Fonderie F. A. Didot — 1995 | LetterPerfect LP
Antiqua

ALTERNATIVE
Linotype Didot | Firmin Didot — Adrian Frutiger | 1991 | Linotype LT

123 pt

CONTRASTS
Type form
Curve form
Impression

DIFFERENCES
Type style
Instroke / Outstroke
Terminal shaping
Serif transition
Juncture

Letter design
|J|K|P|T|U|V|W|Y|Z|
|d|e|g|i|k|t|v|w|y|z|

ANALOGIES
Heights
Weight
Stroke contrast
Typographic color

SIMILARITIES
Axis / Stress
Curve direction
Rhythm
Width
Slant
Ductus
Stroke shaping

Letter design
|Q|

28.3   27.8

DESIGN FORMEN
design formen

33.0   31.0

Tages Zeitung

14.2   13.2

Zeitung

114 pt

ABCDEFGHIJKLM
NOPQRSTUVWXYZ
abcdefghijklm
nopqrstuvwxyz

Serpentine Medium
Dick Jensen
1972 | Visual Graphics — Linotype LT
Glyphic → 286/287

ABCDEFGHIJKLM
NOPQRSTUVWXYZ
abcdefghijklm
nopqrstuvwxyz

Americana Roman
Richard Isbell
1966 | American Type Founders ATF — Adobe Systems
Glyphic

ABCDEFGHIJKLM
NOPQRSTUVWXYZ
abcdefghijklm
nopqrstuvwxyz

City Medium Italic
Georg Trump
1930 | H. Berthold AG BQ
Egyptian

ABCDEFGHIJKLM
NOPQRSTUVWXYZ
abcdefghijklm
nopqrstuvwxyz

Russell Square Oblique
John Russell
1973 | Visual Graphics — Linotype LT
Grotesque → 310/311

ABCDEFGHIJKLM
NOPQRSTUVWXYZ
abcdefghijklm
nopqrstuvwxyz

Wilhelm Klingspor Gotisch Roman
Rudolf Koch
1924–1926 | Gebr. Klingspor — Linotype LT
Blackletter

ABCDEFGHIJKLM
NOPQRSTUVVXYZ
abcdefghijklm
nopqrstuvwxyz

Kharon Bold
unknown
2001 | Orgdot
Grotesque

CONTRASTS
Type form
Curve form
Typographic color
Impression

DIFFERENCES
Type style
Curve direction
Weight
Stroke shaping
Terminal shaping
Juncture

Letter design
|G|K|Q|g|i|k|y|

ANALOGIES
Heights
Width

SIMILARITIES
Axis/Stress
Rhythm
Stroke contrast
Slant
Ductus
Serif transition

Letter design
|J|M|R|W|w|

28.6   28.8

DESIGN FORMEN
design formen

25.3   23.0

CONTRASTS
Type form
Width
Terminal shaping
Typographic color
Impression

DIFFERENCES
Heights
Type style
Curve direction

Letter design
|A|K|Q|W|w|y|

ANALOGIES
Curve form
Juncture
Slant

SIMILARITIES
Axis/Stress
Rhythm
Weight
Stroke contrast
Ductus
Stroke shaping

Letter design
|G|J|M|R|V|
|a|e|g|j|k|v|

26.1   26.0

DESIGN FORMEN
design formen

25.4   23.2

CONTRASTS
Type form
Impression

DIFFERENCES
Curve form
Type style
Axis/Stress
Stroke contrast
Stroke shaping
Terminal shaping
Juncture
Effect|Decoration

Letter design
A	E	F	H	I	J	K	M	N
P	U	V	W	Y	Z
a	d	e	f	h	k	v	w	z

ANALOGIES
Weight
Typographic color

SIMILARITIES
Curve form
Heights
Curve direction
Rhythm
Width
Slant
Ductus

Letter design
|R|g|

26.1   13.3

DESIGN FORMEN
design formen

25.4   12.0

ABCDEFGHIJKLM
NOPQRSTUVWXYZ
abcdefghijklm
nopqrstuvwxyz

Tiranti Solid Regular
Tony Forster
1983 | Esselte Letraset — International Typeface Corporation ITC
Script

ABCDEFGHIJKLM
NOPQRSTUVWXYZ
abcdefghijklm
nopqrstuvwxyz

Media 77 Medium
Team'77: André Gürtler, Christian Mengelt, Erich Gschwind
Media | 1977 | Bobst Graphic / Autologic — 2015 | Optimo Type Foundry
Antiqua

129 pt

CONTRASTS
Type form
Slant
Impression

DIFFERENCES
Heights
Type style
Axis/Stress
Curve direction
Instroke/Outstroke
Width
Ductus
Terminal shaping

Letter design
|L|R|S|Y|Z|
|a|f|g|i|k|w|y|

ANALOGIES
Weight
Stroke contrast
Typographic color

SIMILARITIES
Curve form
Rhythm
Stroke shaping
Serif transition
Juncture

Letter design
|t|

28.8   26.5

*DESIGN*FORMEN
design formen

33.8   26.5

Railway Station

13.8   11.1

Station

104 pt

ABCDEFGHIJKLM
NOPQRSTUVWXYZ
abcdefghijklm
nopqrstuvwxyz

Apollo Regular
Adrian Frutiger, John Dreyfus
1960–1964 | Monotype MT
Antiqua

ABCDEFGHIJKLM
NOPQRSTUVWXYZ
abcdefghijklm
nopqrstuvwxyz

Caflisch Script Regular
Robert Slimbach (Max Caflisch)
1993–2001 | Adobe Systems
Script → 300/301

Antwort

124 pt

CONTRASTS
Type form
Slant
Impression

DIFFERENCES
Curve form
Heights
Type style
Axis/Stress
Stroke contrast
Ductus
Terminal shaping
Juncture

Letter design
|G|J|U|a|f|g|v|w|y|

ANALOGIES
Typographic color

SIMILARITIES
Curve direction
Rhythm
Weight
Width
Stroke shaping

Letter design
|K|M|Q|R|

32.0 40.8

DESIGN *FORMEN*
design *formen*

29.8 35.3

Antwort *Schreiben*

12.6 15.8

152 pt

ABCDEFGHIJKLM
NOPQRSTUVWXYZ
abcdefghijklm
nopqrstuvwxyz

American Typewriter Medium
Joel Kaden, Tony Stan
1974 | International Typeface Corporation ITC
Egyptian → 276/277 → 278/279

ABCDEFGHIJKLM
NOPQRSTUVWXYZ
abcdefghijklm
nopqrstuvwxyz

Caflisch Script Regular
Robert Slimbach (Max Caflisch)
1993–2001 | Adobe Systems
Script → 298/299

104 pt

CONTRASTS
Type form
Slant
Impression

DIFFERENCES
Curve form
Heights
Type style
Axis/Stress
Curve direction
Stroke contrast
Width
Ductus
Stroke shaping
Juncture

Letter design
|G|J|K|M|Q|R|U|
|a|f|g|v|w|y|

ANALOGIES
Typographic color

SIMILARITIES
Rhythm
Weight
Terminal shaping

27.0 40.8

DESIGN *FORMEN*
design *formen*

24.0 35.3

Type *Writer*

10.9 15.8

152 pt

301

ABCDEFGHIJKLM
NOPQRSTUVWXYZ
abcdefghijklm
nopqrstuvwxyz

Choc Regular
Roger Excoffon
1955 | Fonderie Olive — International Typeface Corporation ITC
Script

ABCDEFGHIJKLM
NOPQRSTUVWXYZ
abcdefghijklm
nopqrstuvwxyz

Arno Regular
Robert Slimbach
2007 | Adobe Systems
Antiqua

123 pt

CONTRASTS
Type form
Typographic color
Impression

DIFFERENCES
Curve form
Rhythm
Weight
Stroke contrast
Slant
Juncture

Letter design
|G|J|M|Q|R|Y|
|a|f|g|j|q|r|

ANALOGIES
Ductus

SIMILARITIES
Heights
Type style
Axis/Stress
Curve direction
Width
Stroke shaping
Terminal shaping

29.4 29.9

DESIGN FORMEN
design formen

32.4 30.3

Tusche Feder

13.0 12.8

Feder

121 pt

ABCDEFGHIJKLM
NOPQRSTUVWXYZ
abcdefghijklm
nopqrstuvwxyz

Auriol Roman
Georges Auriol — Matthew Carter
1901 | Deberny & Peignot — 1991 | Linotype LT
Script →280/281

ABCDEFGHIJKLM
NOPQRSTUVWXYZ
abcdefghijklm
nopqrstuvwxyz

Sho Roman
Karlgeorg Hoefer
1992 | Linotype LT
Script

103 pt

CONTRASTS
Weight
Width
Typographic color

DIFFERENCES
Type form
Heights
Offset center position
Terminal shaping
Juncture

Letter design
|A|E|F|M|U|W|
|a|e|g|t|v|w|y|

ANALOGIES
Juncture
Impression

SIMILARITIES
Curve form
Type style
Axis/Stress
Curve direction
Rhythm
Stroke contrast
Slant
Ductus
Stroke shaping

Letter design
|K|O|Q|V|X|Y|
|f|j|k|o|x|

26.7   38.9

DESIGN FORMEN
design formen

25.8   38.5

Pinsel **Strich**

11.2   16.3

Strich

154 pt

ABCDEFGHIJKLM
NOPQRSTUVWXYZ
abcdefghijklm
nopqrstuvwxyz

Industrial 736 Roman
Raffaello Bertieri
Torino | 1908 | Società Nebiolo — Bitstream BT
Antiqua

ABCDEFGHIJKLM
NOPQRSTUVWXYZ
abcdefghijklm
nopqrstuvwxyz

Marker Felt Wide
Pat Snyder
1992 | Apple
Script → 318/319

Dragon

105 pt

306

CONTRASTS
Type form
Typographic color
Impression

DIFFERENCES
Heights
Weight
Stroke contrast
Ductus
Terminal shaping

Letter design
|K|Q|R|g|k|t|y|

ANALOGIES
Width

SIMILARITIES
Curve form
Type style
Axis/Stress
Curve direction
Rhythm
Slant
Stroke shaping

25.8   22.6

DESIGN **FORMEN**

design **formen**

25.5   20.9

Dragon **Blood**

10.9   9.1

89 pt

ABCDEFGHIJKLM
NOPQRSTUVWXYZ
abcdefghijklm
nopqrstuvwxyz

Van Dijk Regular
Jan van Dijk
1982 | Esselte Letraset — International Typeface Corporation ITC
Script

ABCDEFGHIJKLM
NOPQRSTUVWXYZ
abcdefghijklm
nopqrstuvwxyz

Brown Bold
Aurèle Sack
2011 | Lineto LL
Grotesque

104 pt

CONTRASTS
Type form
Weight
Slant
Ductus
Typographic color
Impression

DIFFERENCES
Curve form
Type style
Axis/Stress
Curve direction
Rhythm
Width
Stroke shaping
Juncture

Letter design
|G|J|M|U|Y|f|q|y|

ANALOGIES
Heights
Offset center position

SIMILARITIES
Stroke contrast
Terminal shaping

Letter design
|K|Q|R|W|a|g|

27.0   26.4

DESIGN **FORMEN**
design **formen**

24.9   24.8

Kultur **Report**

10.8   10.6

Report

103 pt

309

ABCDEFGHIJKLM
NOPQRSTUVWXYZ
abcdefghijklm
nopqrstuvwxyz

Russell Square Oblique
John Russell
1973 | Visual Graphics — Linotype LT
Grotesque → 294/295

ABCDEFGHIJKLM
NOPQRSTUVWXYZ
abcdefghijklm
nopqrstuvwxyz

Isadora Regular
Kris Holmes
1989 | International Typeface Corporation ITC
Script

96 pt

CONTRASTS
Ductus
Type form
Curve form
Typographic color
Impression

DIFFERENCES
Heights
Type style
Axis/Stress
Curve direction
Weight
Stroke contrast
Stroke shaping
Terminal shaping
Juncture

Letter design
|A|G|J|M|Q|R|U|W|Y|
|a|f|k|v|w|

ANALOGIES
Width
Slant

SIMILARITIES
Rhythm

26.4 29.7

DESIGN *FORMEN*
design *formen*

25.3 28.4

Beton *Blume*

10.9 12.1

Blume

110 pt

ABCDEFGHIJKLM
NOPQRSTUVWXYZ
abcdefghijklm
nopqrstuvwxyz

Bauhaus Bold
Edward Benguiat, Victor Caruso
1975 | International Typeface Corporation ITC
Grotesque

ABCDEFGHIJKLM
NOPQRSTUVWXYZ
abcdefghijklm
nopqrstuvwxyz

Dot Matrix Regular
Stephan Müller, Cornel Windlin
1993 | FontFont FF
Grotesque hybrid

Computer

103 pt

CONTRASTS
Effect | Decoration
Typographic color

ANALOGIES
Type form
Impression

DIFFERENCES
Basic shape
Curve form
Type style
Axis/Stress
Rhythm
Weight
Width
Stroke shaping
Terminal shaping

SIMILARITIES
Heights
Curve direction
Stroke contrast
Slant
Ductus

Letter design
|A|E|I|J|K|M|Q|R|
|e|k|l|m|n|t|u|x|y|

26.4   22.3

DESIGN FORMEN

design formen

24.5   21.7

Computer Monitor

10.5   8.8

86 pt

ABCDEFGHIJKLM
NOPQRSTUVWXYZ
abcdefghijklm
nopqrstuvwxyz

VAG Rounded Black
Wolf Rogosky, Gerd Hiepler
VAG Rundschrift | 1979 | Volkswagen | URW Type Foundry — Linotype LT
Grotesque → 272/273

ABCDEFGHIJKLM
NOPQRSTUVWXYZ
abcdefghijklm
nopqrstuvwxyz

Russisch Brot EatOne
Markus Remscheid, Helmut Ness
1997 | Linotype LT
Grotesque

Balloon

98 pt

CONTRASTS
Effect | Decoration
Impression

DIFFERENCES
Typographic color
Width
Ductus

Letter design
|M|Q|R|

ANALOGIES
Type form

SIMILARITIES
Curve form
Heights
Type style
Axis/Stress
Curve direction
Rhythm
Weight
Stroke contrast
Slant
Stroke shaping
Terminal shaping

Letter design
|a|t|

26.1 24.3

DESIGN FORMEN
design formen

23.0 24.6

Balloon Explosion

9.8 9.7

97 pt

ABCDEFGHIJKLM
NOPQRSTUVWXYZ
abcdefghijklm
nopqrstuvwxyz

Brother 1816 Bold
Ignacio Corbo, Fernando Díaz
2016 | TipoType
Grotesque

ALTERNATIVE
Effra | Jonas Schudel | 2008–2013 | Dalton Maag
→ 262/263

ABCDEFGHIJKLM
NOPQRSTUVWXYZ
abcdefghijklm
nopqrstuvwxyz

Vegas Regular
David Quay
1984 | Esselte Letraset — International Typeface Corporation ITC
Script

Tooth

99 pt

CONTRASTS
Type form
Effect | Decoration
Impression

DIFFERENCES
Typographic color
Ductus
Terminal shaping

Letter design
|A|E|M|N|V|W|X|Y|
|a|g|k|v|w|x|y|

ANALOGIES
Weight
Stroke contrast

SIMILARITIES
Curve form
Heights
Type style
Axis/Stress
Curve direction
Rhythm
Width
Slant
Stroke shaping

25.6 30.0

DESIGN *FORMEN*
design *formen*

23.7 25.8

Tooth *Paste*

10.2 11.6

112 pt

ABCDEFGHIJKLM
NOPQRSTUVWXYZ
abcdefghijklm
nopqrstuvwxyz

Helvetica Rounded Bold Condensed
Linotype Design Studio
1978 | Linotype LT
Grotesque → 274/275 → 276/277 → 286/287

ABCDEFGHIJKLM
NOPQRSTUVWXYZ
abcdefghijklm
nopqrstuvwxyz

Aachen Bold
Colin Brignall, Alan Meeks
1969 | Esselte Letraset — Linotype LT
Egyptian

ABCDEFGHIJKLM
NOPQRSTUVWXYZ
abcdefghijklm
nopqrstuvwxyz

Tekton Regular
David Siegel (Frank Ching)
1989 | Adobe Systems
Script

ABCDEFGHIJKLM
NOPQRSTUVWXYZ
abcdefghijklm
nopqrstuvwxyz

Marker Felt Thin
Pat Snyder
1992 | Apple
Script → 306/307

ABCDEFGHIJKLM
NOPQRSTUVWXYZ
abcdefghijklm
nopqrstuvwxyz

Freddo Regular
James Montalbano
1996 | International Typeface Corporation ITC
Script

ABCDEFGHIJKLM
NOPQRSTUVWXYZ
abcdefghijklm
nopqrstuvwxyz

Humana Sans Light
Timothy Donaldson
1995 | International Typeface Corporation ITC
Script

CONTRASTS
Type form
Width
Terminal shaping
Typographic color

DIFFERENCES
Weight

Letter design
|G|J|K|Q|

ANALOGIES
Curve form
Heights

SIMILARITIES
Type style
Axis/Stress
Curve direction
Rhythm
Stroke contrast
Slant
Ductus
Stroke shaping
Juncture

Letter design
|a|g|y|

25.6   27.6

DESIGN **FORMEN**
design **formen**

22.2   24.3

CONTRASTS
Weight
Typographic color

DIFFERENCES
Curve form
Axis/Stress
Offset center position
Width
Slant
Juncture

Letter design
|A|G|U|q|t|u|y|

ANALOGIES
Impression

SIMILARITIES
Heights
Type form
Type style
Curve direction
Rhythm
Stroke contrast
Slant
Ductus
Stroke shaping
Terminal shaping

Letter design
|J|K|M|Q|R|W|
|a|g|j|k|

29.3   24.3

DESIGN **FORMEN**
design **formen**

28.2   23.1

CONTRASTS
Width
Typographic color

DIFFERENCES
Heights
Curve form
Rhythm
Weight
Stroke contrast
Stroke shaping
Terminal shaping

Letter design
|A|G|J|K|M|N|W|
|a|k|t|w|y|

ANALOGIES
Type form
Impression

SIMILARITIES
Type style
Axis/Stress
Curve direction
Slant
Ductus

Letter design
|Q|

27.3   29.2

DESIGN FORMEN
design formen

26.2   25.4

ABCDEFGHIJKLM
NOPQRSTUVWXYZ

ABCDEFGHIJKLM
NOPQRSTUVWXYZ
ABCDEFGHIJKLM
NOPQRSTUVWXYZ

Frankfurter Regular
Bob Newman, Alan Meeks, Nick Belshaw
1970–1981 | Esselte Letraset — International Typeface Corporation ITC
Grotesque → 328/329

Stenberg Regular
Tagir Safayev
1997 | International Typeface Corporation ITC
Grotesque hybrid

SCHLAUCH

101 pt

CONTRASTS
Curve form
Rhythm
Terminal shaping
Impression

DIFFERENCES
Curve direction
Weight
Width
Typographic color

Letter design
|A|K|M|Q|W|

ANALOGIES
Type form
Type style

SIMILARITIES
Axis/Stress
Stroke contrast
Slant
Ductus
Stroke shaping
Juncture

Letter design
|G|J|R|

27.6   26.3

DESIGN FORMEN

SCHLAUCH VENTIL

10.6 10.1

VENTIL

96 pt

ABCDEFGHIJKLM
NOPQRSTUVWXYZ
abcdefghijklm
nopqrstuvwxyz

Hobo Medium
Morris Fuller Benton
1910 | American Type Founders — Linotype LT
Script

ABCDEFGHIJKLM
NOPQRSTUVWXYZ

Juniper Medium
Joy Redick
1990 | Adobe Systems
Glyphic

OPEN-AIR

82 pt

CONTRASTS
Stroke shaping
Basic shape

ANALOGIES
Typographic color
Impression

DIFFERENCES
Type form
Curve form
Type style
Offset center position
Stroke contrast
Width
Slant
Terminal shaping
Juncture

Letter design
|A|M|O|V|W|

SIMILARITIES
Axis/Stress
Rhythm
Weight
Ductus

Letter design
|G|

22.2   24.6

DESIGN FORMEN

OPEN-AIR FESTIVAL

8.5   9.4

FESTIVAL

91 pt

ABCDEFGHIJKLM
NOPQRSTUVWXYZ
abcdefghijklm
nopqrstuvwxyz

Giddyup Regular
Laurie Szujewska
1974 | Adobe Systems
Script

ABCDEFGHIJKLM
NOPQRSTUVWXYZ

Cottonwood Medium
Barbara Lind, Joy Redick, Kim Buker Chansler
1989 | Adobe Systems
Tuscan

105 pt

CONTRASTS
Typographic color
Slant

DIFFERENCES
Type form
Curve form
Type style
Axis/Stress
Weight
Stroke contrast
Stroke shaping

Letter design
|G|J|M|N|W|Y|

ANALOGIES
Effect|Decoration
Impression

SIMILARITIES
Rhythm
Width
Ductus
Terminal shaping

29.0   27.4

DESIGN FORMEN

SPAGHETI WESTERN

11.3   10.5

WESTERN

97 pt

ABCDEFGHIJKLM
NOPQRSTUVWXYZ

ABCDEFGHIJKLM
NOPQRSTUVWXYZ

Castellar Regular
John Peters
1957 | Monotype MT
Latin

Charlemagne Regular
Carol Twombly
1989 | Adobe Systems
Latin

93 pt

CONTRASTS
Effect | Decoration

DIFFERENCES
Typographic color
Axis / Stress

Letter design
|A|D|M|Q|

ANALOGIES
Type form
Impression

SIMILARITIES
Curve form
Type style
Rhythm
Weight
Stroke contrast
Width
Slant
Ductus
Stroke shaping
Terminal shaping

25.6   26.3

DESIGNFORMEN

STEIG EISEN

9.9   10.1

EISEN

95 pt

ABCDEFGHIJKLM
NOPQRSTUVWXYZ
abcdefghijklm
nopqrstuvwxyz

Pump Triline Regular
Philip Kelly
1975 | International Typeface Corporation ITC — Bitstream BT
Grotesque

ABCDEFGHIJKLM
NOPQRSTUVWXYZ

Frankfurter Inline Regular
Bob Newman, Nick Belshaw, Alan Meeks
1970–1981 | Esselte Letraset — International Typeface Corporation ITC
Grotesque →320/321

102 pt

CONTRASTS
Terminal shaping
Typographic color

DIFFERENCES
Fill

Letter design
|A|C|E|F|J|K|M|N|
|S|V|W|X|Y|

ANALOGIES
Type form
Effect|Decoration
Impression

SIMILARITIES
Curve form
Type style
Axis/Stress
Rhythm
Weight
Stroke contrast
Width
Slant
Ductus
Stroke shaping

27.6   27.8

DESIGN FORMEN

GUMMI BÄREN

10.6   10.7

103 pt

ABCDEFGHIJKLM
NOPQRSTUVWXYZ
ABCDEFGHIJKLM
NOPQRSTUVWXYZ

Cancione Regular
Brenda Walton
1997 | International Typeface Corporation ITC
Script

ABCDEFGHIJKLM
NOPQRSTUVWXYZ
ABCDEFGHIJKLM
NOPQRSTUVWXYZ

Anna Regular
Daniel Pelavin
1991 | International Typeface Corporation ITC
Grotesque

KREIDE

87 pt

CONTRASTS
Effect | Decoration
Outline
Impression

DIFFERENCES
Type form
Curve form
Curve direction
Stroke contrast
Stroke shaping
Terminal shaping
Typographic color
Letter design
|A|G|M|Q|W|Y|

ANALOGIES
Offset center position
Width
Rhythm
Juncture

SIMILARITIES
Type style
Axis/Stress
Weight
Slant
Ductus
Letter design
|N|

23.3   26.2

DESIGN FORMEN

9.1 10.1

98 pt

ABCDEFGHIJKLM
NOPQRSTUVWXYZ
ABCDEFGHIJKLM
NOPQRSTUVWXYZ

Stevens Titling Boar Brush
John Stevens, Ryuichi Tateno
2011 | Linotype LT
Glyphic

ALTERNATIVE
Trajan | Carol Twombly | 1989 | Adobe Systems

ABCDEFGHIJKLM
NOPQRSTUVWXYZ

Slipstream Regular
Letraset Type Studio
1985 | Esselte Letraset — International Typeface Corporation ITC
Grotesque

FLYING

98 pt

CONTRASTS
Weight
Slant
Typographic color
Impression

DIFFERENCES
Type form
Type style
Rhythm
Axis/Stress
Stroke contrast
Stroke shaping
Terminal shaping

Letter design
|J|M|Q|Y|

ANALOGIES
Effect|Decoration

SIMILARITIES
Curve form
Curve direction
Width
Ductus
Juncture

Letter design
|G|K|P|R|W|

27.0   27.3

DESIGN *FORMEN*

FLYING *CIRCUS*

10.4 10.4

98 pt

333

Appendix

Notes

The endnotes are divided according to their respective chapters. Underscores are not part of the original cited texts but have been added to facilitate easier location of the relevant typefaces.

The book is set in Bodoni with the subheadings in City.
· See JAN TSCHICHOLD: *Typographische Gestaltung*. Benno Schwabe & Co., Basel 1935, p. 28.

Introduction →7

1. See JAN TSCHICHOLD: "Schriftmischungen" (Typeface combinations). In: *Typographische Monatsblätter (Swiss Typographic Magazine)*, no. 2, February 1935, Schweizerischer Typographenbund, Bern, pp. 33–37.
2. See JAN TSCHICHOLD: *Schriften 1925–1974*. Vol. 1. Brinkmann & Bose, Berlin 1991, pp. 169–177.
3. See TSCHICHOLD: "Schriftmischungen", p. 37. See TSCHICHOLD: *Schriften 1925–1974*. Vol. 1, p. 174.
4. In his book *Die Neue Typographie*, 1928 (*The New Typography*, 1995), Jan Tschichold formulates the goal of completely doing away with all historical letterforms and declares his support for sans serif – insofar as it was available in good quality – as the only truly contemporary letterform. He writes: "All type forms whose essence is deformed by ornaments joining the skeleton (in the case of Antiqua, hatchings [serifs], in the case of Blackletter, rhombs and trunks) are not in keeping with our aspiration to clarity and purity. Among all the available typefaces so-called Grotesque is […] the only one that is intellectually appropriate for our time." The book is set in a light Grotesque with the subheadings in the black font style.
· See JAN TSCHICHOLD: *Die Neue Typographie*. Verlag des Bildungsverbandes der Deutschen Buchdrucker, Berlin 1928, p. 75.
This statement is clearly attenuated in his book *Typographische Gestaltung* from 1935 (*Asymmetric Typography*, 1967), in which he supports a more multifaceted approach to lettering. He writes: "Since design based on contrasts is the most important tool for all new art and since over a longer period of time even sans serif tires people, a range of other typefaces are also used in the new typography. Their presence increases the effect of sans serif, which in turn makes every other typeface effective in a new way. The demand of advertising for variety therefore soon led to the use of other typefaces in different ways. It is possible to adopt the best historical forms of lettering if one follows the rules of the new typography when using them."

1
Historical considerations →11

1. See FRIEDRICH BAUER: "Vom Mischen der Schriftarten im Schriftsatz." In: *Klimschs Jahrbuch – Technische Abhandlungen und Berichte über Neuheiten auf dem Gesamtgebiete der graphischen Künste*. Vol. 24. Verlag Klimsch & Co., Frankfurt am Main 1931, pp. 30–43.
2. See https://de.wikipedia.org/wiki/Stein_von_Rosette [Feb 9, 2020].
3. See https://de.wikipedia.org/wiki/Jean-François_Champollion [Feb 9, 2020].
4. The inscription refers to a *collegium salutare*, an association of different priests and officials who, in an officially designated location, attended to matters relating to the cult of Asclepius, the emperor, and similar things. The first names in the list are those of the 'members of the board', and these are followed by those of the other association members in alphabetical order – mostly simple folk, including many house slaves (indicated by the frequent designation 'verna'). Email of February 9, 2020, from Dr. Marina Bernasconi Reusser, Research Associate, e-codices, Université de Fribourg/Switzerland.
5. The manuscript from Marmoutier Abbey in Tours (France) is known as the Grandval Bible or Moutier-Grandval Bible due to the fact that in the late sixteenth century this large-format codex belonged to Moutier-Grandval Abbey in the Bernese Jura in Switzerland. See https://de.wikipedia.org/wiki/Grandval-Bibel [Feb 9, 2020].
6. See DONALD JACKSON: *Alphabet – Die Geschichte vom Schreiben*. S. Fischer Verlag, Frankfurt am Main 1981, p. 66. (*The Story of Writing*, London 1981).
7. See https://de.wikipedia.org/wiki/Karolingische_Minuskel [Feb 9, 2020].
8. See STEPHAN FÜSSEL: *Gutenberg und seine Wirkung*. Insel Verlag, Frankfurt am Main 1999, p. 22.
9. See FRANTIŠEK MUZIKA: *Die Schöne Schrift*. Vol. 1. Verlag Werner Dausien, Hanau am Main 1965, p. 420.
10. See BAUER, "Vom Mischen der Schriftarten im Schriftsatz", p. 38.

11 Ibid., p. 32.
12 See DANIEL BERKELEY UPDIKE: *Printing Types – Their History, Forms, and Use.* Vol. 1. The Belknap Press of Harvard University Press, Cambridge, MA, 1966, image p. 266.
· See CEES W. DE JONG, ALSTON W. PURVIS, and JAN THOLENAAR: *A Visual History of Typefaces and Graphic Styles.* Vol. 1. Taschen Verlag, Cologne 2009, images pp. 85 and 88.
13 See GÜNTER SCHMITT: *Typographische Gestaltungsepochen.* Verlag Arbeitsgemeinschaft für grafische Lehrmittel, Bellach 1983.
14 See WILLIAM S. PETERSON: *William Morris – Das Ideale Buch.* Steidl Verlag, Göttingen 1986. (*The Ideal Book,* London 1986).
15 See BAUER, "Vom Mischen der Schriftarten im Schriftsatz", p. 38.
16 See [AUGUST MÜLLER?]: "Einheitliche Schriftenwahl – Ein Beitrag zur Vereinfachung des Accidenzsatzes." In: *Schweizer Graphische Mitteilungen,* no. 3, Oct 1, 1898, August Müller (ed.), St. Gallen, p. 37.
17 See "Anwendung von Zierschriften im modernen Akzidenzsatz." In: *Schweizer Graphische Mitteilungen,* no. 12, Feb 15, 1904, August Müller (ed.), St. Gallen, pp. 227–228.
18 Ibid.
19 W. STÜCKEN: "Zur Frage der Schriftenmischung." In: *Schweizer Graphische Mitteilungen,* no. 2, Sep 15, 1913, August Müller (ed.), St. Gallen, pp. 17–18.
20 "Rivoluzione tipografica. Io inizio una rivoluzione tipografica diretta contro la bestiale e nauseante concezione del libro di versi passatista e dannunziana, la carta a mano seicentesca, fregiata di galee, minerve e apolli, di iniziali rosse a ghirigori, ortaggi, mitologici nastri da messale, epigrafi e numeri romani. Il libro deve essere l'espressione futurista del nostro pensiero futurista. Non solo. La mia rivoluzione è diretta contro la così detta armonia tipografica della pagina, che è contraria al flusso e riflusso, ai sobbalzi e agli scoppi dello stile che scorre nella pagina stessa. Noi useremo perciò in una medesima pagina, *tre o quattro colori diversi d'inchiostro,* e anche 20 caratteri tipografici diversi, se occorra. Per esempio: corsivo per una serie di sensazioni simili o veloci, *grassetto tondo* per le onomatopee violente, ecc."
FILIPPO TOMMASO MARINETTI: *L'immaginazione senza fili e le Parole in Libertà. Manifesto Futurista.* Direzione del Movimento Futurista, Milan, May 11, 1913.

21 Cited from: RICHARD HUELSENBECK: "Erklärung. Vorgetragen im 'Cabaret Voltaire' im Frühjahr 1916." In: KARL RIHA and JÖRGEN SCHÄFER (eds.): *Dada total – Manifeste, Aktionen, Texte, Bilder.* Philipp Reclam jun., Stuttgart 1994, p. 33.
22 See GEORGES HUGNET and MARCEL DUCHAMP: *La septième face du dé.* Éditions Jeanne Bucher, Paris 1936. In: JAROSLAV ANDEL: *Avant-Garde Page Design 1900–1950.* Delano Greenigde Editions, New York 2002, p. 337.
23 See JUSTINIAN FRISCH: *Geist und Zweck der Schrift – Ihre Aufgaben in der Werbekunst.* C. Barth Verlag, Vienna 1927.
24 See JAN TSCHICHOLD: *Die Neue Typographie – Handbuch für zeitgemäß Schaffende.* Verlag des Bildungsverbandes der Deutschen Buchdrucker, Berlin 1928.
25 See JAN TSCHICHOLD: *Typographische Gestaltung.* Benno Schwabe & Co., Basel 1935.
26 See JAN TSCHICHOLD: "Schriftmischungen." In: *Typographische Monatsblätter (Swiss Typographic Magazine),* no. 2, Schweizerischer Typographenbund, Bern 1935, p. 35.
27 See PAUL RENNER: *Die Kunst der Typographie.* Frenzel & Engelbrecher 'Gebrauchsgraphik' Verlag, Berlin 1939.
· See PAUL RENNER: *Die Kunst der Typographie.* 3rd edition, Deutscher Verlag, Berlin 1953 (1948), p. 149.
28 See Dr. KARL KLINGSPOR: *Über Schönheit von Schrift und Druck.* Georg Kurt Schauer Verlag, Frankfurt am Main 1949, pp. 142–143.
29 See EMIL RUDER: *Typography – A Manual of Design.* Verlag Arthur Niggli, Teufen 1967.
30 See JOST HOCHULI and ROBIN KINROSS: *Bücher machen – Praxis und Theorie.* VGS Verlagsgemeinschaft St. Gallen, 1996. (*Designing Books: Practice and Theory.* London 1996)

2
A typology of type → 39
1 See www.duden.de/rechtschreibung/Schrift [Jan 22, 2020].
2 See https://de.wikipedia.org/wiki/Schrift [Jan 22, 2020].
3 See https://de.wikipedia.org/wiki/Graphem [Jan 22, 2020].
4 In specialist books from the metal typesetting era, typeface system refers to material systematized using the 'point' typographic measurement unit: typefaces in the standardized point sizes and the associated furniture.

See "Brockhaus in fünfzehn Bänden", 1998. In: JULI GUDEHUS: *Das Lesikon der visuellen Kommunikation,* 2nd ed. Verlag Hermann Schmidt, Mainz 2011 (2010), p. 637.
5 See HARALD HAARMANN: *Universalgeschichte der Schrift.* Campus Verlag, Frankfurt am Main 1991, pp. 147–149.
6 Ibid., pp. 148 and 207.
7 See RICHARD L. NIEHL: *Satztechnisches Taschen-Lexikon – mit Berücksichtigung der Schriftgießerei,* 2nd ed. Verlag Steyrermühl, Vienna 1925, pp. 822–823.
8 One example is the type specimen book of the Woellmer type foundry. The register cover sheet of the 'second section' is labeled: "Serif typefaces – text typefaces for books and newspapers." See WILHELM WOELLMER: *Schriftgiesserei Hauptprobe.* Berlin (no year, ca. 1920s), pp. 207–213.
9 See HANS PETER WILLBERG and FRIEDRICH FORSSMAN: *Lesetypographie.* Verlag Herrmann Schmidt, Mainz 1997, pp. 14 ff.
10 Based on stored coding, digital typefaces are today regarded as programs and are therefore subject to the same copyright as software. See VISCOM (ed.): *Schriftfonts.* Schweizerischer Verband für visuelle Kommunikation, Zurich 2007, p. 49.
11 For example, the Syntax typeface designed by Hans Eduard Meier has several other names: Synthesis (Autologic), Symphony (Compugraphic), Synchron (Scangraphic), and Cintal (Varityper). See LAWRENCE W. WALLIS: *Modern Encyclopedia of Typefaces 1960–90.* Lund Humphries, London 1990, p. 144.
12 Helvetica, originally produced by the Haas Type Foundry in Münchenstein near Basel, Switzerland, under the name Neue Haas Grotesk, initially provided strong competition for contemporary sans serifs such as Univers and Folio as well as the established Berthold Akzidenz Grotesk. In March 1958, with the help of director Eduard Hoffmann, Max Miedinger completed the drawings for the bold font style and went on to draw the regular, black, and italic versions. "In order to be able to satisfy the wish for other emphasis typefaces and due to a lack of time, we fell back on existing typefaces in the Haas program. First in line was the venerable Normal-Grotesk, the extended bold font style of which was quickly relabeled Helvetica extended bold … The same thing

happened with the Commercial-Grotesk series […] The semi-bold and bold font styles became medium condensed and bold condensed […] It was first with the bold italics that a 'genuine' Helvetica was created again in Münchenstein; however, it was not Miedinger to whom Hoffmann gave this task but Alfred Gerber, a young member of the type foundry staff." Parallel to these developments, the Neue Haas Grotesk in all its font styles was reworked at the D. Stempel AG type foundry in Frankfurt am Main for Linotype line casting and put on the market as Helvetica (from the Latin: 'the Swiss').
See VICTOR MALSY and LARS MÜLLER (eds.): *Helvetica forever – Geschichte einer Schrift.* Lars Müller Publishers, Baden 2008, p. 58.

- In 1909 Wagner & Schmidt in Leipzig produced a sans serif marketed by the Haas Type Foundry as Akzidenz-Grotesk. According to Indra Kupferschmid, in 1943 the Haas Type Foundry put the normal font style on the market as Normale Akzidenz-Grotesk. And in 1954, to differentiate it from the Akzidenz Grotesk produced by the H. Berthold AG type foundry in Berlin, it was dubbed Normal-Grotesk.
See https://en.wikipedia.org/wiki/Normal-Grotesk [Feb 26, 2020].

13 The following thirteen font styles are available: Venus light, bold, heavy, black, condensed light, condensed bold, condensed heavy, extended light, extended bold, extended black, light italic, bold italic, black italic. These are supplemented by three font styles of the titling typeface Aphrodite, which is based on Venus Grotesk but features right-angled stroke and curve terminals.
See BAUERSCHE GIESSEREI: *Hauptprobe in gedrängter Form.* Frankfurt am Main (no year, ca.1914), pp. 88–102.

14 Venus Grotesk extended heavy, the fourteenth font style, came out in 1927.
See "Schriftgiesserei-Neuheiten." In: AUGUST MÜLLER (ed.): *Schweizer Graphische Mitteilungen. Monatsschrift für das graphische Kunstgewerbe*, no. 7. Zollikofer & Cie., St. Gallen 1927, p. 160.

15 The overview page is titled 'The Goudy Type Family at a Glance. A Composite Picture of the complete Goudy Type Family is here shown for the first time.'
See *Specimen Book and Catalogue.* American Type Founders Company, Jersey City, NJ, 1923, p. 45.

16 See KARL FAULMANN: *Illustrirte Geschichte der Buchdruckerkunst – Mit besonderer Berücksichtigung ihrer technischen Entwicklung bis zur Gegenwart.* A. Hartlebens Verlag, Vienna 1882, p. 488.

17 See ANNA BERLINER: "'Atmosphärenwert' von Druckschriften – Ein Beitrag zur Psychologie der Reklame." In: *Zeitschrift für angewandte Psychologie*, 17, nos. 1–3. Johann Ambrosius Barth, Leipzig 1920, pp. 165–172.

18 See MICHAELA LANGEN, CARSTEN MAURISCHAT, and ANGELIKA WEBER: "Anmutungsqualitäten von Druckschriften." In: PETER KAROW: *Schrifttechnologie – Methoden und Werkzeuge.* Edition Page, Springer Verlag, Berlin 1992, pp. 405ff.

19 The semantic differential was introduced by Charles E. Osgood in 1952 and published in 1957. In 1955, Peter R. Hofstätter introduced the method to Germany in a slightly altered form known as polarity profiles.
See CHARLES E. OSGOOD, G. J. SUCI, and P. H. TANNENBAUM: *The Measurement of Meaning*, Urbana, 1957. – http://de.wikipedia.org/wiki/Semantisches_Differenzial [Mar 21, 2020].

20 In 1965, Dirk Wendt conducted research at the Psychological Institute at the University of Hamburg into the legibility of typefaces. In 1968 he tested the impressionistic quality of eighteen different typefaces.
See DIRK WENDT: *Untersuchungen zur Lesbarkeit von Druckschriften*, Report no. 2, Hamburg 1965 (duplicated manuscript);

- see DIRK WENDT: "Semantic Differentials of Typefaces as a Method of Congeniality Research." In: *The Journal of Typographic Research*, vol. II, no. 1, Cleveland 1968. – See PETER KAROW: *Schrifttechnologie. Methoden und Werkzeuge.* Berlin / Heidelberg 1992, p. 448.

- In a study at the University of Vienna, Christian Gutschi defined a polarity profile with twenty-three adjective pairs.
See CHRISTIAN GUTSCHI: "Psychologie der Schriften", in: *PAGE – Publizieren und Präsentieren mit dem Personal Computer*. Part 1: 8/1996, pp. 54ff.; part 2: 9/1996, pp. 64ff.; part 3: 10/1996, pp. 74ff.; part 4: 12/1996, pp. 66ff.; part 5: 1/1997, pp. 52ff. – See also: www.medienpsychologie.at.

**3
Basic shapes / Measurement** → 55

1 Hebrew script is referred to as a square script, as is *Capitalis quadrata*, an ancient Roman book script.

2 More information can be found in: "Die ältesten Entwicklungsphasen des phönizischen Alphabets." In: HARALD HAARMANN: *Universalgeschichte der Schrift.* Campus Verlag, Frankfurt am Main 1991, pp. 269–282.

3 Ibid., 286.

4 See FRANTIŠEK MUZIKA: *Die Schöne Schrift.* Vol. 1. Verlag Werner Dausien, Hanau am Main 1965, pp. 72–82.

5 See JOSEPH NAVEH: *Die Entstehung des Alphabets.* Benziger Verlag, Zurich 1979, pp. 87–88. (*Origins of the Alphabet,* London 1975)

6 Ibid., 86.

7 The Latin alphabet does not depict all the phonemes of a language; the available graphemes are far from sufficient for such a task. Although diacritics contribute to a better correspondence between language and writing, the use of accent marks is not consistent across languages and their number is correspondingly diverse. Moreover, (too many) accents in the text image decrease its aesthetic quality.
See PHILIPP STAMM: "Extension of the Latin alphabet for the German language." In: *Typografische Monatsblätter* (*Swiss Typographic Magazine*), TM 1, Zurich 1997, pp. 1–20.

8 See EUGEN NERDINGER: *Zeichen · Schrift und Ornament / Signs · Scripts and Ornaments / Signes · Caractères et Ornements.* Verlag Georg D. W. Callwey, Munich 1960, p. 99.

9 See ADRIAN FRUTIGER: *Der Mensch und seine Zeichen.* Vol. 2: *Die Zeichen der Sprachfixierung.* D. Stempel AG, Frankfurt am Main 1979, pp. 57–59. (*Signs and Symbols: Their Design and Meaning,* London 1989)

10 The capitalization of nouns in German may derive from the fact that in early German texts important words such as GOtt (god) and HErr (master) were written with majuscules.

11 See ANDREW ROBINSON: *Die Geschichte der Schrift. Von Keilschriften, Hieroglyphen, Alphabeten und anderen Schriftformen.* Verlag Paul Haupt, Bern 1996, pp. 182–197. (*The Story of Writing,* London 1995)

12 Ibid., 120–143.

13 See WILFRIED SEIPEL (ed.): *Der Turmbau zu Babel – Ursprung und Vielfalt von Sprache und Schrift.* Vol. 3b. Kunsthistorisches Museum Wien / Skira, Milan 2003, pp. 204, 206.

14 In principle, the fixed spaces (*White spaces* in Adobe InDesign) provide consistent divisions. However, type still exhibits differences in widths. This is even more pronounced in the case of the em and en dashes.

15 PostScript Type 1 fonts and OpenType fonts based on PostScript have an em quad of 1000×1000 units; fonts based on TrueType have an em quad of 2048×2048 units.

16 See Jost Hochuli: *Das Detail in der Typografie – Buchstabe, Buchstabenabstand, Wort, Wortabstand, Zeile, Zeilenabstand, Kolumne.* Compugraphic Corporation, Wilmington, MA, 1987, pp. 27–28. (*Detail in typography. Letters, letterspacing, words, wordspacing, lines, linespacing, columns.* Wilmington, MA, 1987).

17 Setting tight is only possible by trimming the sidebearings, which results in the width of the letters being irretrievably lost. On the other hand, setting loose, that is, widening the space between letters, can be easily achieved by inserting spacers (narrow, nonprinting lead pieces), although this is very laborious when setting longer texts.

18 The unit of measurement remains the same in the plural form, that is, 12 point rather than 12 points. In screen media the smallest unit of measurement is the pixel (or sub-pixel).

19 Deberny & Peignot's *Lumitype* was an advanced version of the phototypesetting machine manufactured by the American firm Photon and was designed for the European market. In the 1950s Adrian Frutiger defined the cap height for the machine as the standard for all typefaces and thus the visible and measurable visual size.
See Heidrun Osterer and Philipp Stamm: *Adrian Frutiger – Typefaces. The Complete Works.* Birkhäuser Verlag, Basel 2021 (2008/2014), pp. 58–59.

20 Since the launch of its version 2.0 in 1995, the Viva Press Professional layout software – now known as VivaDesigner – has enabled users to define both the point size and the cap height.

21 See Patrick Exner: "Schnelles Leben." In: *PAGE*, no. 8, MACup Verlag, Hamburg 1995, pp. 40–41.
http://www.viva.de/de/produkte/desktop-publishing/vivadesigner-desktop-version [Mar 26, 2020].
· Ralf Herrmann: "Tipp: Schriften in InDesign über x-Höhe und Versalhöhe definieren." In: http://www.typografie.info/3/page/artikel.htm/_/wissen/indesign-xhoehe [Jan 22, 2020].

22 The German standard line – defined by the Genzsch & Heyse type foundry – has been recognized and used by all German type foundries since 1905.

See Leo Davidshofer and Walter Zerbe: *Satztechnik und Gestaltung.* Bildungsverband Schweizerischer Buchdrucker. 6th edition, Zurich/Bern 1970, p. 41.

23 See Heidrun Osterer and Philipp Stamm: *Adrian Frutiger – Typefaces*, p. 32.

24 See Hans Peter Willberg and Friedrich Forssman: *Lesetypographie.* Verlag Hermann Schmidt, Mainz 1997, p. 14 ff.

25 The Scangraphic fonts can be obtained from Linotype/Monotype: www.linotype.com; Elsner+Flake: www.fonts4ever.com.

26 The digital matrix is always orthogonal, in contrast to the pebble mosaics of Greek and Roman antiquity. Although this approach was also known, the stone setting nevertheless followed the contours of the depicted forms and figures.

27 In a lecture to the General Assembly of the Association Typographique Internationale ATypI in Basel in 1980, Adrian Frutiger already expressed this sentiment when he stated: "Within the space of twenty years there have been giant steps in technical development. Without going into specific detail, one can say that in future the digitization of text typesetting will continue its journey, posing the question of whether there will be a loss of quality due to type being broken down into points or lines. However, the experience of recent years and the knowledge of what is being prepared gives us reason to be optimistic of future developments. – It is essential that the whole typesetting structure should once again receive a 'basic grid'. Type should be securely based on the digital grid, no longer floating around like in the first generation of phototypesetting. The process will be refined as the years pass. Vectors that are still somewhat disruptive today will soon be followed by curves, which the human eye desires."
See Adrian Frutiger: "Type, paper and man today." In: *Typografische Monatsblätter (Swiss Typographic Magazine)*, TM 5, St. Gallen 1980, p. 273.

28 Microsoft calls the process ClearType, Adobe calls it CoolType, and Apple calls it Quartz.

4
Typeface classification → 83

1 See Francis Thibaudeau: *La Lettre d'imprimerie.* Vol. 2. Bureau de l'Édition, Paris 1921, pp. 470 ff.

2 See Francis Thibaudeau: *Manuel français de typographie moderne.* Bureau de l'Édition, Paris 1924, pp. 108 ff.

3 See Georg Kurt Schauer: *Klassifikation · Bemühungen um eine Ordnung im Druckschriftenbestand.* Darmstadt 1975, pp. 47 ff.

4 Ibid., pp. 36 ff.

5 See Heidrun Osterer and Philipp Stamm: *Adrian Frutiger – Typefaces. The Complete Works.* Birkhäuser Verlag, Basel 2014 (2008), pp. 76 ff.

6 The decision-making ATypI committee consisted of the Frenchman Maximilien Vox, the Englishman Walter Tracy, the Dutchman Gerrit Willem Ovink, the Swiss Adrian Frutiger, the American Aaron Burns, and the German Hermann Zapf.
See Georg Kurt Schauer: *Klassifikation*, p. 15.

7 Ibid., p. 92.

8 Open to criticism is the positioning of the Blackletter faces at the end of the classification, although this group includes the oldest typefaces and should therefore be positioned at the beginning. Unfortunately, due to the classification of typefaces based on DIN 16518, the term *Venezianische Renaissance-Antiqua* became established for the first group and the term *Französische Renaissance-Antiqua* for the second group. Both terms are confusing since both groups have their origins in Venice and both refer to French type designers. In the case of the first group, the original designer was Nicolas Jenson, who practiced his trade in Venice; in the case of the second group, the Frenchman and Paris-based type designer Claude Garamont followed the model created by the Venetians Francesco Griffo and Aldus Manutius.
See Georg Kurt Schauer: *Klassifikation*, p. 112.

9 See Eugen Nerdinger: *Buchstabenbuch – Schriftentwicklung, Formbedingungen, Schrifttechnik, Schriftsammlung.* Verlag Georg D. W. Callwey, Munich 1955, p. 43.

10 See Erich Schulz-Anker: *Formanalyse und Dokumentation einer serifenlosen Linearschrift auf neuer Basis: Syntax-Antiqua.* D. Stempel AG, Frankfurt am Main 1969, pp. 8 ff.

11 Gerrit Noordzij: *Letterletter.* Hartley & Marks Publishers, Vancouver 2000;
· Gerrit Noordzij: *The Stroke – Theory of Writing.* Hyphen Press, London 2005.

12 Hans Rudolf Bosshard: *Technische Grundlagen zur Satzherstellung.* Verlag des Bildungsverbandes Schweizerischer Typografen BST, Bern 1980, pp. 69 ff.

13 See Mai-Linh Thi Truong, Jürgen Siebert, and Erik Spiekermann: *FontBook*. FontShop International, Berlin 1998.
14 See Georg Kurt Schauer: *Klassifikation · Bemühungen um eine Ordnung im Druckschriftenbestand*. Darmstadt 1975, p.45.
15 See Indra Kupferschmid: *Buchstaben kommen selten allein*. Verlag Niggli, Sulgen/Zurich 2009 (1999/2003), pp.30 ff.
16 See Hans Peter Willberg: *Wegweiser Schrift*. Verlag Hermann Schmidt, Mainz 2011 (2001), pp.48 ff.
17 See Erich Schulz-Anker: *Formanalyse und Dokumentation einer serifenlosen Linearschrift auf neuer Basis: Syntax-Antiqua*. D. Stempel AG, Frankfurt am Main 1969, pp.8 ff.
18 See František Muzika: *Die Schöne Schrift*. Vol.1. Verlag Werner Dausien, Hanau am Main 1965, pp.86 ff.
19 "Between 1933 and 1935 a series of Simplified textura was produced. They were interpretations of historical typefaces, starkly reduced in formal terms and coarsened, and referred to by typesetters disparagingly as *Schaftstiefelgrotesk* ('High Boot Grotesque'). Bearing names such as Tannenberg, National, Element and Potsdam, they were heavily promoted and also heavily used during the Third Reich." However, the range of typefaces remained diverse, producing a "highly heterogeneous text image. […] Media addressing an international audience represented an exception in this regard throughout the National Socialist regime. Such publications used internationally readable typefaces, that is, unbroken, as can be seen in the publications produced for the Olympic Games held in Berlin and Garmisch-Partenkirchen, bilingual magazines and journals, and posters designed to attract volunteers for the 'struggle against Bolshevism'. This situation led to the most dirigist and extensive intervention in typeface use during the Third Reich. On January 3, 1943, Hitler had his representative Martin Bormann issue a bulletin banning the use of broken typefaces – incorrectly and defamatorily characterized as 'Schwabacher Jewish lettering' – in official publications." The bulletin reads: "At the behest of the Führer it is to be generally observed that it is false to regard the so-called Gothic typeface as a German typeface. In reality the so-called Gothic typeface consists of Schwabacher Jewish lettering. Just as they later took possession of the newspapers, with the introduction of printing the Jews living in Germany took possession of the printing houses, which led in Germany to the heavy use of Schwabacher Jewish lettering. Today, in the course of a discussion with Reichsleiter Amman and the publisher Adolf Müller, the Führer decided that Antiqua typeface would in future be regarded as normal typeface, and that all printed materials should gradually be converted into this normal typeface. […] On behalf of the Führer, Reichsleiter Amann will first see to the conversion of newspapers and magazines that already have international circulation or are intended for international circulation to normal typeface. Signed, Bormann." See Andreas Koop: *Die Macht der Schrift*. Niggli Verlag, Sulgen/Zurich 2012, pp.191 ff.
20 The use of the term *Antiqua* to designate Serif typefaces is confusing because this letterform first emerged in the Renaissance, and Glyphic faces (and, depending on usage, Grotesque faces) are the letterform of antiquity. *Typica* could be an alternative term for Serif typefaces. However, since *Antiqua* is the established term in German-language textbooks, it has been retained here.
21 See Nicolete Gray: *Nineteenth Century Ornamented Typefaces*. Faber and Faber, London 1976 (1938/1951).
22 See https://en.wikipedia.org/wiki/French_frigate_Égyptienne_(1799) [Jan 22, 2020].
23 The flat curve design was used from the beginning for narrow Egyptian typefaces and was typical for narrow faces well into the second half of the twentieth century. Worthy of mention here is the type designer Georg Trump, who designed several faces in this class, including City (1930), a narrow Egyptian without stroke contrast, and Schadow, a normal-width typeface family with stroke contrast. Hermann Zapf continued the class in 1952 with Melior.
24 See Nicolete Gray: *Nineteenth Century Ornamented Typefaces*, pp.38 ff.
25 See Emil Ruder: "Univers, eine Grotesk von Adrian Frutiger." In: *Typographische Monatsblätter (Swiss Typographic Magazine)*, no.5, St.Gallen 1957, p.362.
26 See Nicolete Gray: *Nineteenth Century Ornamented Typefaces*, p.78.
· Charles Mazé claims the year was 1852; see https://www.abyme.net/revue/berthe/ [Sep 12, 2019].
· *The Handbook of Type Classes* shows a Schmale Renaissance from the inventory of the type foundry J.G. Schelter & Giesecke, Leipzig. See Albrecht Seemann: *Handbuch der Schriftarten*. Albrecht Seeman Verlag, Leipzig 1926, p.139.
· The face is included in the type specimen book by the foundry in 1912; see *Hauptprobe J.G. Schelter & Giesecke*. Vol.1. Leipzig 1912, p.G3.
· However, Seemann attributes this typeface to the Berlin foundry W. Woellmer and dates it to 1830 – both of which are questionable. Although the latter's main sample contains several examples of Renaissance and Etienne, this type is not included. See *Wilhelm Woellmer's Schriftgiesserei Hauptprobe*. Berlin (undated, ca.1920s), pp.207–213.
27 The register section 'Les Latines' covers a total of 48 pages. See *Spécimen général*. Vol.2. Fonderies Deberny & Peignot, Paris 1926.
28 In France, Elzévir is a common group designation for serif faces with a dynamic style. The name refers to the printing and publishing family Elzevier, which was active in the Netherlands from the later sixteenth century onwards.
29 See *Printing Types*. Stephenson, Blake & Co., Sheffield 1924, pp.331–341.
30 It is possible that Etienne refers to the Frenchman Robert Estienne (Latinized: Robertus Stephanus; Robert Étienne), who in the first half of the sixteenth century – and thus the Rennaisance – was a very important printer and publisher.
31 See Heidrun Osterer and Philipp Stamm: *Adrian Frutiger – Typefaces*, pp.41 ff. The digital font available from the free-font provider FontsGeek, which has a rather questionable assortment, is called Palace Regular.

5
Typeface concepts → 131

1 What was actually a five-digit numbering system – the last two digits provided an unambiguous, internationally comprehensible designation of the font style – was originally created as a classification system for metal typefaces. The 26-year-old Adrian Frutiger described his numbering system in a concept paper dated 1954, which was connected with the development and subsequent Europe-wide marketing of the Lumitype phototypesetting machine at Deberny & Peignot in Paris.

See Heidrun Osterer and Philipp Stamm: *Adrian Frutiger – Typefaces. The Complete Works.* Birkhäuser Verlag, Basel 2014 (2008), p.76.

2 Ibid., p. 95.

3 Andreas Maxbauer writes: "The first step in the search for combinable typeface families is the identification of connecting and separating elements – to an equal degree. On the one hand, the difference between the typefaces must be immediately evident so that a contrast emerges, while, on the other, the laws of harmony demand a consonance. Both are most readily achieved by the designer when he or she uses the different typefaces of one type designer. Like all artists, type designers have stylistic idiosyncrasies that run like a common thread through their entire oeuvre."
See Andreas Maxbauer: "Die Mischung macht's." Part 1 in: *PAGE – Publizieren und Präsentieren mit dem Personal Computer*, no. 10, 10.1995, MACup Verlag GmbH, Hamburg, pp. 72–73.

4 Hans Peter Willberg comments rather caustically on this subject: "In the TGM Werkstattbrief (2), Philipp Luidl writes '… Typefaces by the same type designer and those from the same period can be combined without any problem …' The *Werkstattbrief* series produced by the Typographische Gesellschaft München is a commendable source of basic knowledge. The series is addressed to beginners, and consequently such a statement runs the risk of being taken literally. Let's test this thesis using typefaces by Adrian Frutiger. Surely it is far from 'unproblematic' to mix Univers with Vectora or Frutiger with Avenir! — Now we will surely hear the argument that sans serif typefaces should not be combined anyway. So let's try Breughel with Centennial, or Versailles with Serifa. Also impossible! Next attempt: Centennial with Frutiger, or Vectora with Glypha. The results are again not good, indeed cannot be good. – So what typefaces designed by Frutiger do fit together? Centennial and Univers, or Apollo and Frutiger: not because they have been produced by the same designer, but because they share the same spirit. The pairs are stylistically related, they have a common ancestry. – The reason for this confusion is that the second clause in Luidl's claim contradicts the first. Adrian Frutiger deliberately designed typefaces that refer to different typeface periods and that cannot 'be combined without any problem'. Bodoni and Gill can tolerate one another just as little as can the 'neoclassical' Centennial and the 'Renaissance' Frutiger. It is about questions of style, not a type designer's signature. — Of course, one can find 'incorrect' typeface combinations that are nevertheless compelling. But in the case of Luidl it concerns basic knowledge, not daredevil typographic acrobatics. — However, the actual message is quite different. It relates to schools of thought and specialist literature. That message is: Don't believe a word; always check that what is being claimed is also correct."
See Hans Peter Willberg: *Typolemik – Typophilie.* Verlag Hermann Schmidt, Mainz 2000, pp. 82 ff.

5 See Adrian Frutiger: *Type Sign Symbol.* ABC Verlag, Zurich 1980, p. 64.

6 "The best typographic effect is achieved with extended families such as Lucida, which contains both Antiqua and Grotesque, or ITC Stone, which along with a Sans and a Serif includes an Informal. […] It is far more courageous to invite in members of other typeface families, thereby ensuring variety and even excitement. Nothing can really go wrong if one mixes typefaces by the same designer (Erik Gill's Joanna combines well with Gill Sans, and all typefaces by Adrian Frutiger are able to tolerate one another). But this also applies to typefaces from the same time and even to typefaces from quite different periods. There is no patent solution, just good taste. The text typefaces in this book are a good example: Minion for the body text, Myriad – bold without serifs – for the marginalia and in a somewhat lighter font style for the image captions."
See Erik Spiekermann: *Über Schrift.* Verlag Hermann Schmidt, Mainz 2004, p. 109.

7 See John Dreyfus: *The Work of J. Van Krimpen.* Sylvan Press, London 1952, pp. 36–46.

8 In a conversation with Yvonne Schwemer-Scheddin in 1990 about his typeface trilogy, Kurt Weidemann said: "Today you can no longer think simply, you have to differentiate. Using the same Helvetica for a wreath ribbon, a ceremonial address, and a book about spare parts isn't possible anymore."
See Yvonne Schwemer-Scheddin: "Die Ästhetik der Technik." In: Manfred Klein, Yvonne Schwemer-Scheddin, and Erik Spiekermann: *Typen & Typografen.* Edition Stemmle, Schaffhausen 1991, p. 204.

9 See Peter Karow: *Schrifttechnologie – Methoden und Werkzeuge.* Springer Verlag, Berlin 1992, p. 7.

10 From the German computer and design magazine *PAGE*: 'Adobe's multiple master technology and the sans serif typeface Myriad have been inseparably connected since their creation. The typeface was developed by Adobe primarily to demonstrate the new font technology – now it is in second position on the Adobe hit parade and, with the exception of Futura, has left all other sans serifs behind. Helmut Kraus looked behind the scenes of this typographic success story.'
See Helmut Kraus: "Milliarden von Myriaden." In: *PAGE* 1/1996. MACup Verlag, Hamburg 1996, p. 60.

11 See Thomas Phinney: "FAQ: Multiple master fonts on OS X." February 26, 2002; https://forums.adobe.com/thread/395592 [Jan 23, 2020].

12 Well aware of prevailing typographic trends – and against convention – Adrian Frutiger designed his sans serif Avenir in six very finely graduated weights. He thereby anticipated a possibility later offered by multiple master technology.
See Heidrun Osterer and Philipp Stamm: *Adrian Frutiger – Typefaces*, p. 337.

13 In 1997, MetaDesign created FF Transit, an exemplary signage typeface based on Frutiger. It features the font styles normal, italic, bold, bold italic, and black as well as Front Negativ, Front Positiv, Back Negativ, and Back Positiv, each in normal, italic, and bold versions.
See www.fontshop.com/families/ff-transit [Jan 23, 2020].

14 https://helpx.adobe.com/ch_de/acrobat/using/pdf-fonts.html [Jan 23, 2020].

15 See Ralf Herrmann: "OpenType 1.8 – die Rückkehr der Multiple-Master-Schriften." Sep 14, 2016; www.typografie.info/3/artikel.htm/n/t/opentype18-font-variations/ [Jan 23, 2020].

· See Antje Dohmann: "Das sind die ersten verfügbaren Variable Fonts." May 19, 2017; https://page-online.de/typografie/variable-fonts-das-muessen-sie-wissen/ [Jan 23, 2020].

16 See https://de.wikipedia.org/wiki/Responsive_Webdesign [Jan 23, 2020].

17 See Manfred Klein: "Keine Werbung für den FontShop? Die Beowolf und ihre Zeitgenossen." In: Klein, Schwemer-Scheddin, and Spiekermann: *Typen & Typografen*, p. 30 (fig. 'AntwortFax').

18 See Bruce Willen and Nolen Strals: *Lettering & Type – Creating Letters and Designing Typefaces*. Princeton Architectural Press, New York 2009, p. 98.
19 See "A Multistyle Decorative Variable Font by David Berlow for Google." 2017. www.typenetwork.com/brochure/decovar-a-decorative-variable-font-by-david-berlow [Jan 23, 2020].
20 See www.monotype.com/de/node/1486; www.monotype.com/fonts/variable-fonts [Jan 23, 2020].

6
Typeface combination | Criteria → 149

1 The unprofessional appearance of the web tool Identifont may be discouraging, but the tool is in fact very useful.
www.identifont.com
https://fontjoy.com
https://tiff.herokuapp.com
www.typotheque.com/fonts/combinator/latin
www.fontexplorerx.com
[Jan 25, 2020].
2 Karl Gerstner provides an interesting compilation of possibilities in his highly readable book: Karl Gerstner: *Kompendium für Alphabeten – Systematik der Schrift*. Verlag Arthur Niggli, Heiden 1990.
3 On this subject, Erik Spiekermann writes: "There is a rule that says that descender and ascender may never touch. There is an exception to this rule that states touching is allowed if it looks better." See Erik Spiekermann: *Ursache & Wirkung: ein typografischer Roman*. Context GmbH, Erlangen 1982, p. 44.
4 This aspect is particularly clearly described and shown in: Jost Hochuli: *Das Detail in der Typografie*. Compugraphic Corporation, Wilmington, MA, 1987, pp. 25–28. (*Detail in Typography. Letters, letterspacing, words, wordspacing, lines, linespacing, columns*. Wilmington, MA, 1987).
5 Ibid.
6 These typefaces were available as phototypesetting faces in two variants: with normal and shortened descenders. See "List of Monophoto Faces" available. In: *Specimen Book of "Monophoto" Filmsetter Faces*. The Monotype Corporation, Salfords, no date; see Heidrun Osterer and Philipp Stamm: *Adrian Frutiger – Typefaces. The Complete Works*. Birkhäuser Verlag, Basel 2021 (2008), p. 140.
7 Comprehensive articles on numerous typefaces, including the two referred to here, were written by Max Caflisch. First printed in the Swiss trade journal *Typografische Monatsblätter (Swiss Typographic Magazine)*, they were later collected and republished in two volumes. Max Caflisch: "Von der analogen zur digitalen Trinité." In: *Schriftanalysen*. Vol. 2. Typotron, St. Gallen 2003, pp. 173–182. And: "Lexicon, eine umfassende, viel versprechende Schriftfamilie." Ibid., pp. 183–195.
8 See František Muzika: *Die Schöne Schrift*. Vol. 2. Verlag Werner Dausien, Hanau am Main 1965, p. 186 ff.
9 See Hans Peter Willberg: *Wegweiser Schrift*. Verlag Hermann Schmidt, Mainz 2011 (2001), p. 50.
10 See Hans Peter Willberg and Friedrich Forssman: *Lesetypographie*. Verlag Herrmann Schmidt, Mainz 1997, pp. 122 ff.
11 See Heidrun Osterer and Philipp Stamm: *Adrian Frutiger – Typefaces*, pp. 102 ff.
12 Paleography (Old Greek παλαιός *palaiós*, 'old' and Greek -γραφή *-graphē* / -γραφία *-graphia*, originating from the verb γράφειν *gráphein*, 'to write, to draw'). See https://en.wikipedia.org/wiki/Palaeography; https://en.wikipedia.org/wiki/-graphy. An ancillary historical discipline involving systematic research into writing systems (calligraphy) and the history of lettering from antiquity to the Renaissance, that is, up to the beginnings of proto-typography or typography. Paleography also involves the classification of all types of lettering based on their graphic features and the dating, deciphering, and transcription of manuscripts. See www.typolexikon.de/palaeografie/ [Jan 25, 2020].
13 The science of the interpretation of handwriting, particularly as an expression of character. See www.merriam-webster.com/dictionary/graphology [Jan 25, 2020].
14 The terminology in *Wörterbuch des Buches* (Book dictionary) includes the following terms: *Schriftart* (type class): differentiation based on intended use; *Schriftbild* (type appearance): appearance of the printed reproduction of a letter; *Schriftcharakter* (typeface character): the impression made by a typeface – mental connection; *Schriftduktus* (typeface ductus): stroke characteristics of a typeface; *Schriftfamilie* (type family): totality of font styles that are grouped under one name; *Schriftform* (type form): appearance of a particular typeface; *Schriftgarnitur* (typeface series): all point sizes of a typeface; *Schriftgattung* (typeface genre): a group of typefaces that can be differentiated in formal and cultural-historical terms.
See Helmut Hiller and Stephan Füssel: *Wörterbuch des Buches*. 7th edition. Vittorio Klostermann, Frankfurt am Main 2006, pp. 292 ff.
15 See Adrian Frutiger: *Der Mensch und seine Zeichen*. Vol. 2: *Die Zeichen der Sprachfixierung*. D. Stempel AG, Frankfurt am Main 1979, pp. 68–72. (*Signs and Symbols: Their Design and Meaning*, London 1989)
16 The following book is recommended, in spite of the topic of color playing a relatively minor role in the text: Moritz Zwimpfer: *2d Visuelle Wahrnehmung / 2d Visual Perception*. Verlag Niggli, Sulgen / Zurich 1994.
17 Ibid., p. 5.6.

Index

Names

A
Adobe Systems Inc.   67 71 78 80 81 140 141 142 143 145 146 185 212 236 244 248 252 270 290 294 298 300 302 318 322 324 326 332 338 339 341
Agfa Type   46
Ahrens, Tim   232
Aicher, Otl   84 140 175
Alpha Omega   274
American Type Founders   47 112 138 256 292 294 322
Apple Inc.   80 139 145 306 318 339
Arabena, Yani   101
Araya, Cesar   240
Arnholm, Ronald   214
Arts and Crafts Exhibition Society   23 105
Association Typographique Internationale ATypI   87 88 89 90 91 93 94 339
Auriol, Georges   280 304
Austin, Richard   23 107
Autologic   296 337

B
Baker, Arthur   99 274
Ball, Hugo   28 33
Barnhart Brothers & Spindler, type foundry   280
Baskerville, John   107
Bauer, Friedrich   12 19 47
Bauer Type Foundry   47 212 258
Bauhaus   112 113
Bell, John   107
Belshaw, Nick   320 328
Bembo, Pietro   105
Benguiat, Edward   115 138 312
Berliner, Anna   53
Berlow, David   147
Bernasconi Reusser, Marina   336
Bernhard, Lucian   170
H. Berthold AG, type foundry   46 76 112 204 226 250 278 294 337 338 357
Bertieri, Raffaello   306
Bigelow, Charles   101 139
Bitstream   46 306 328
Blokland, Frank E.   238
Blokland, Erik van   146
Blokland, Petr van   146
Bobst Graphic   171 296
Bodoni, Giambattista   23 107
Boge, Garrett   292

Bonaparte, Napoléon   13
Bormann, Martin   340
Bosshard, Hans Rudolf   90
Boton, Albert   99
Benton, Linn Boyd   76 138
Brand, Chris   238
Brignall, Colin   318
British Museum   13
Brunner, Laurenz   226 246 276
Buker Chansler, Kim   324
Bulmer, William   107
Burke, Jackson   43
Burns, Aaron   339
Butti, Alessandro   114 230

C
Cabaret Voltaire   32 337
Caflisch, Max   298 300 342
Canada Type   230
Carter, Matthew   43 44 99 101 280 304
Caruso, Victor   312
Caslon, William I.   107 184
Caslon, William IV.   112 113
Champollion, Jean-François   13
Charlemagne (Charles the Great)   13
Ching, Frank   318
Chiswick Press   107
Cobden-Sanderson, Thomas J.   23
Cochin, Charles-Nicolas   170
Compugraphic   337
Cooper, Oswald Bruce   280
Corbo, Ignacio   316
Crane, Walter   23
Crossgrove, Carl   242 268

D
Daimler-Benz AG   140
Dalton Maag   262 316
Daniëls, Gerard   244
Díaz, Fernando   316
Didot, Firmin   23 69 107 108 292
Didot, François Ambroise   69 107
Dijck, Christoffel van   107
Dijk, Jan van   308
Does, Bram de   171 240
Donaldson, Timothy   318
Doves Press   23
Dr.-Ing. Rudolf Hell GmbH   260
Dreyfus, John   298
Dürckheim, Karlfried von   53
Dutch Type Library   46 244

E
Eidenbenz, Hermann   111 256 280
Elsner + Flake   46 216 339
Elzevier   340

Emigre   79
Erbar, Jakob   113
Esselte Letraset   46 296 308 316 318 320 328 332
Estienne, Robert   340
Eusebius   105
Excoffon, Roger   43 101 169 302

F
Faccio, Giovanni de   132
Farey, David   113
Figgins, Vincent   110 112
Fleckhaus, Willy   34 37
Fleischmann, Johann Michael   107
Fonderie F. A. Didot   292
Fonderie Olive   114 264 302
Fonderie G. Peignot & Fils   170
Fonderies Deberny & Peignot   48 71 114 134 220 246 266 268 272 280 282 304 339 340
Fonderies Laurent & Deberny   114
FontFont   46 222 236 312
FontsGeek   340
FontShop   44 91 141
Fontspring   44
Forster, Tony   296
Fournier, Pierre-Simon   19 24
Frankfurter Allgemeine Zeitung   103
Freitez, Alejandro   115
Frere-Jones, Tobias   135 234 258
Frisch, Justinian   33
Friz, Ernst   99 189
Frutiger, Adrian   43 48 60 71 79 88 99 100 111 113 114 115 134 135 136 143 147 184 187 189 218 220 226 236 246 248 258 266 268 272 280 282 290 292 298 339 341 359
Fuller Benton, Morris   43 111 112 138 256 292 322

G
Ganeau, François   114 184 264
Garamont, Claude   106 212 339
Garcia, Alfonso   240
Genzsch & Heyse, type foundry   47 339
Gerber, Alfred   338
Gerstner, Karl   342
Gill, Eric   111 113 135 228 244 258 341
Girard, Alexander   34 37
Google   41 145 224 342
Goudy, Frederic William   47 99 109 189 244 252
Grabowska, Viktoriya   224

343

Grandjean, Philippe   107
Gray, Nicolete   110 114
Griffin, Patrick   230
Griffo, Francesco   105 132 228 339
Groot, Luc(as) de   141 184
Gschwind, Erich   226 296
Gürtler, André   226 296
Gutenberg, Johannes
   15 63 88 101 102 142
Gutschi, Christian   338
H
Haas Type Foundry   111 220 226
   256 276 280 286 337 338
Hagmann, Sibylle   111
Hammer, Victor   100
Harling, Robert   29
Harvey, Michael   99 144
Heinänen, Saku   216
Helmling, Akiem   262
Hernández, Daniel   266
Hess, Sol   258
Hidy, Lance   144
Hiepler, Gerd   272 314
Hillman, David   36 37
Hochuli, Jost   36 37 168 242
Hoefer, Karlgeorg   304
Hoefler, Jonathan   135
Hoefler Type Foundry   46 234
Hoffmann, Eduard   276 286 337 338
Hofstätter, Peter R.   53 338
Hollandsworth Batty, Cynthia   274
Holmes, Kris   101 139 310
Huelsenbeck, Richard   32
Hugnet, Georges   29 33
Hunter Middleton, Robert   99
Huot-Marchand, Thomas   43
I
Identifont   154 202 342
Incubator   216
International Typeface Corporation
   46 77 144 214 224 274 276 278
   284 288 296 300 302 308 310 312
   316 318 320 328 330 332
Isbell, Richard   294
ITC Design Staff   244
J
Jackson, Donald   13 14
Jacobs, Bas   262
Jannon, Jean   106
Jensen, Dick   286 294
Jenson, Nicolas   23 63 105 339
Johnston, Edward   113
K
Kaden, Joel   276 278 300
Karner, Lui   132

Karow, Peter   141
Kelly, Philip   328
Kelmscott Press   105
Gebr. Klingspor, type foundry
   37 294
Klingspor, Karl   32 37
Kobayashi, Akira   141 218
Koch, Rudolf   170 294
Konstantynov, Andriy   254
Kortemäki, Sami   262
Kraus, Helmut   341
Krimpen, Jan van   138
Kupferschmid, Indra   92 338
Küster, Volker   216
L
Lange, Günter Gerhard
   204 226 250 278 357
Lanston Monotype   244
Lanz, Daniel   236
Lardent, Victor   107 204
Latinotype   240 266
Le Monde   103
Leipzig Typographic Society   23
Letraset Type Studio   332
LetterPerfect   46 292
LettError   146
Ličko, Zuzana   79
Lind, Barbara   324
Lineto   220 226 246 276 308
Linotype   46 47 80 100 135 141 143
   169 184 204 210 212 216 218 220
   222 226 230 232 236 244 246 248
   256 258 260 264 266 268 272 274
   276 280 282 284 286 290 292 294
   304 310 314 318 322 332 338
Linotype Design Studio   274 318
Linotype-Hell   46
Lipton, Richard   98 101
London Underground   113
López Fuentes, Rodrigo   272
LucasFonts   46
Luidl, Philipp   341
Lumitype   71 339
M
Manutius, Aldus
   105 106 132 171 228 339
Marinetti, Filippo Tommaso
   28 32
Marmoutier Abbey   336
Maxbauer, Andreas   341
McDonald, Rod   232
Meeks, Alan   318 320 328
Meier, Hans Eduard
   89 113 184 216 264 337
Melvas, Mika   101

Mendelsund, Peter   37
Mengelt, Christian   226 296
MetaDesign   341
Microsoft   46 80 81 145 339
Miedinger, Max
   113 276 286 337 338
Minnesota College of Design   146
Mint Type   254
Möllenstädt, Bernd   99
Monotype   46 47 107 113 171 204
   228 232 238 242 244 250 258 268
   290 298 326
Montalbano, James   318
Morison, Stanley   107 204
Morris, William   23 105
Motter, Othmar   144 288
Moutier-Grandval Abbey   336
Müller, Stephan   312
Muzika, František   177
MyFonts   44
N
Nazi government   103
Nerdinger, Eugen   89
Ness, Helmut   314
Neue Zürcher Zeitung   103
Newman, Bob   320 328
Noordzij, Gerrit   90 91
Noordzij, Peter Matthias
   111 248 258
Norton, Robert   111
Nouvelle Noire   238 242
Novarese, Aldo   86 88 113 114 282
O
Olson, Eric   113 254
Optimo Type Foundry   296
Orgdot   294
Osgood, Charles E.   53 338
Ovink, Gerrit Willem   114 339
P
PAGE, Magazine   341
Paratype   46
Peignot, Georges   170
Peignot, Rémy   115
Pelavin, Daniel   330
Peters, John   98 326
Photon   71 339
Pierpont, Frank Hinman
   228 250 258
Pischner, Wilhelm   258
Plass, Johannes   284
Poppl, Friedrich   99
Pott, Gottfried   100
Process Type Foundry   254
Ptolemy V   13
Puyfoulhoux, Thierry   288

Q
Quay, David   284 316
R
Redick, Joy   322 324
Reid, Jamie   35 37
Reiner, Imre   101
Remscheid, Markus   314
Renner, Paul   31 37 113 170 212
Rogosky, Wolf   272 314
Rossum, Just van   146
Ruder, Emil   37 359
Russell, John   294 310
S
Sack, Aurèle   113 308
Safayev, Tagir   320
Scangraphic   46 76 77 216 337 339
Schauer, Georg Kurt   91
Schelter & Giesecke, type foundry
   112 222 290 340
Schneider, Werner   101
Schudel, Jonas   113 262 316
Schulz-Anker, Erich   89 93
Schwartz, Christian   112 222
Schweizer Graphische Mitteilungen
   24
Schwemer-Scheddin, Yvonne   341
Seemann, Albrecht   340
Sex Pistols   35
Siegel, David   318
Slimbach, Robert   78 101 132 135
   142 144 145 212 224 236 244 248
   270 290 298 300 302
Società Nebiolo, Fonderia di
   caratteri   230 282 306
Sorkin Type   224
Snyder, Pat   306 318
Spiekermann, Erik   147 189 236 342
Stan, Tony   276 278 300
D. Stempel AG, type foundry
   93 210 212 218 236 258 264 276
   280 286 338
Stephenson, Blake & Co.,
   Letter Foundry   114
Stevens, John   98 332
Stieger, Roland   238
Stone, Sumner   140
Szujewska, Laurie   324
T
Tateno, Ryuichi   98 332
Team'77   220 226 296
The Enschedé Font Foundry   240
The Font Bureau Inc.   146
The Guardian   37
The New York Times   103
The Telegraph   103

344

The Washington Post   103
Thibaudeau, Francis   85 114
Thorowgood, William   112
TipoType   316
Tracy, Walter   339
Troop, Bill   230
Trump, Georg
   100 101 132 244 294 340
Tschichold, Jan   7 8 33 336
twen   34 37
Twombly, Carol   98 142 144 145
   189 244 248 252 290 326 332
Type Directors Club   43
Typographische Gesellschaft
   München TGM   341
Swiss Typographic Magazine   7 33
Typotheque   154
Tzara, Tristan   28
U
Underware   79 189 262
Unger, Gerard   43 135 139 184 260
Unger, Johann Friedrich   15
University of Hamburg   338
University of Vienna   338
Université de Fribourg   336
University of California Press   252
University of Minnesota   146
Untype   272
URW, type foundry
   46 137 141 146 182 234 272 314
V
VanderLans, Rudy   79
Varityper   337
Village   216
Visual Graphics   286 294 310
Viva Designer   339
Vizzari, Guille   101
Vox, Maximilien
   86 88 93 98 100 339
W
Wagner & Schmidt, type foundry
   338
Walbaum, Justus Erich
   23 107 222 226
Walbaum, type foundry   222 226
Walker, Emery   23
Walton, Brenda   330
Warnock, John   80
C. E. Weber, type foundry   244
Weidemann, Kurt   140 241
Wilhelm Woellmer, type foundry
   337 340
Wendt, Dirk   53 338
Whittle, Sergio Leiva   272
Wilke, Martin   230

Willberg, Hans Peter
   92 177 179 341
Windlin, Cornel   312
Wolf, Rudolf   111
Wolpe, Berthold   99
X
Xerox   80
Z
Zapf, Hermann   99 101 109 111 135
   136 189 210 212 234 236 339 340
Zdanévitch, Ilja   28

Typefaces

A
Aachen   318
Abelina   101 186
Adobe Caslon   106 184
Adobe Garamond
   44 105 106 168 169 171 188 191 212
Adobe Jenson   52 105
Adobe Jenson MM   145
Adobe Sans MM   145
Adobe Serif MM   145
AG Buch Rounded   226 278
AG Old Face   113 126 196
Akkurat   226 246 276
Akzidenz Grotesk   46 47 52 75 90
   112 170 196 197 204 250 337 338
Akzidenz-Grotesk   338
Albertina   238
Albertus   88 99
Aldus   42 46 106 137 212
Alena   238
Allegra   242
Alte Schwabacher   103 120
Amasis   42 124 166 188
American Typewriter
   188 276 278 300
Americana   294
Amstelvar   146
Andron   41
Anna   330
Antique No. 3 (Egyptian 710)   174
Antique Olive   43 167 169
Aphrodite   338
Apollo   136 171 298 341
Arial   41 113 188 189
Arial Rounded   180 188 189
Armata   224
Arnhem   107
Arno   42 78 106 171 302
Aroma No. 2   232
Arrus   98
Arsis   3
Askan   125
Atomatic   284
Augustea Open   114 193
Auriol   280 304
Avant Garde Gothic   175
Avenir   46 53 113 136 143 188 190
   218 236 341
Avenir Next   143 147 218
B
B42-Type   15 63 102
Baker Signet   117
Barcelona   115 128

Basic Commercial   46
Basic Sans   266
Basilia   46 48 108 193
Baskerville   46 88 107 172 188
Baskerville, New   68
Bau   112 113 166 172 174 222
Bauer Bodoni   42 77 181
Bauhaus   312
Bell   107 122 173 176 177 181 190
Bell Centennial   43 44 192
Belwe Mono   111 124 177
Bembo   105 106 132 228
Bembo Book   171
Benguiat   138
Benguiat Gothic   126 138
Beowolf   146
Berkeley Oldstyle   46 252
Bernhard Gothic   170
Bernhard Modern   169 170
Bickham Script   101
Blackhaus (Kursachsen)   103 121
Blado Italic   132
Bodoni   46 76 108 176 336 341
Bodoni LT   77 168
Bodoni, Bauer   42 77 181
Bodoni, ITC   77 108
Boscribe   119
Bradley Hand   118
Bramley   111
Branding   240
Breughel   176 187 188 341
Brewery   117
Brioso   78
Brother 1816   192 316
Brown   113 308
Bulmer   42 108 188
C
Caecilia
   46 110 111 132 174 177 248 258
Caflisch Script   119 298 300
Caledonia, New   108
Calicanto   115 129
Calluna   105
Calluna Sans   126
Cancellaresca Bastarda   138
Cancione   330
Capita   125
Carolina   100
Carter Sans   117
Cartesius   117
Cartier Book   169 171 185
Caslon   46 107 184 195
Caslon Antique   194
Caslon Gotisch   103 121
Caslon Titling   195

Caslon, Adobe   106 184
Caspari   244
Castellar   98 326
Celeste   115
Centaur   88 105
Centennial LT
   136 220 226 236 341
Century Gothic   258
Century Old Style   138
Century, ITC   182 185
Chaparral   110 124 252
Chaparral MM   145
Charlemagne   326
Chevalier   193
Choc   101 302
Cholla Slab   111
City   42 125 294 336 340
Clarendon   111 124 174 256 280
Clearface   138
Clearface Gothic   77 138
Cochin   52 73 170
Codex   100
Commercial-Grotesk   338
Condor   127
Conga Brava MM   144
Conga Brava MM Stencil   144
Cooper   280
Copperplate Gothic
   98 99 188 189 190
Core Circus   194
Corporate A   140
Corporate E   140
Corporate S   140
Cottonwood   324
Courier   66 111
Cristal   114 115 193
Cronos   78 270
Cronos MM   145
D
Decovar   146 147
Delphin   132 171
Demos   138 139
Deutschmeister   121
Diaria   254
Didot   76 88 108 122 172 173 174
   176 177 190
Didot HTF   108
Didot LP   292
Didot LT   171 292
Diverda Sans   236
Dolly   106 190 191 262
Dot Matrix   312
E
Eckmann   103 120
Edwardian   109 122

Effra   113 192 262 316
Egyptian 505   188
Egyptian 710 (Antique No. 3)   174
Egyptienne F   111 136
Elan   98 99
Element   340
Ellington   42 166
Emigre 15   79
Emperor 15   79
Erbar   113
Eurostile   113 127 167 282
Excelsior   124 181 191
F
Fairfield   176 181
Fedra   41
Felbridge   167
Ferrule   188
Fette Gotisch   44
Finnegan   84
Flora   118 138 139 184
Formata   99
Frankfurter   320
Frankfurter Inline   328
Franklin Gothic ATF   43 112
Franklin Gothic LT   256
Franklin Gothic, ITC
   43 52 168 169 175
Freddo   48 318
Fredericka the Greatest   194
Freight   107
Freya   3 66 72 80 106 166 169 190
   191 193 196 216
Freytag   3
Friz Quadrata   99 117 188 189
Frutiger   46 48 112 113 126 136 137
   141 167 174 180 248 290 341
Frutiger Capitalis   100
Frutiger Next   141
Frutiger Serif   141
Frutiger, Neue   48 174
Futura   46 88 90 113 126 134 137
   167 170 171 175 192 193 212 341
G
Galliard   187
Garamond
   46 88 122 168 173 175 176 177 190
Garamond Premier   52 78 181
Garamond, Adobe
   44 105 106 168 169 171 188 191 212
Garamond, Simoncini   105 106
Garamond, Stempel   106
Genzsch-Antiqua   47
Gianotten   181
Giddyup   324
Gilgamesh   84

Gill Floriated   194
Gill Sans   46 90 112 113 126 134 137
   174 175 180 190 192 195 228 258 341
Glypha   132 136 168 193 341
Golden Cockerel   41
Gotham   234 258
Gothic 725 (Akzidenz Grotesk)   46
Goudy Catalogue   47
Goudy Handtooled   47
Goudy Old Style   47 48
Goudy Sans   99 244
Green   188
Grotesque   113
Gulliver   43
H
Haas Grotesk, Neue   113 337 338
Haas Unica   226
Hammer Unziale, Neue   100
Helvetica   46 47 89 90 113 137 169
   170 190 337 338 341
Helvetica (Swiss 721)   46
Helvetica Inserat   169
Helvetica Rounded   274 318
Helvetica, Neue   48 68 178 179 180
   182 183 276 286
Herculanum   100
Hobo   322
Hollander   43 73 168 170 191
Horley Old Style   109
House Sans   127
Humana Sans   318
Humana Script   53
I
Icone   53 188
Impressum   49
Inagur   188
Industrial 736 (Torino)   306
Info   188 189
Ionic   88 111 172
Iridium   108 188 218
Isadora   310
Isis   193
J
Jaguar   45 53 101
Janson Text   187
Jenson
   63 105 106 122 172 173 175 176 190
Jenson, Adobe   52 105
Jenson, Adobe MM   145
Joanna   110 111 191 244 341
Johnston   112 113
Juniper   322
K
Kabel   44 65 113 166 170 175 188
Kabel, ITC   192

Kaliber   127
Kallos   84
Kennerley Old Style   109 174
Kepler   78
Kepler MM   144 145
Kharon   294
Klavika   113 167 254
Klepto   118
Knockout   135
Korigan   288
Korinna   117
Krete   129
Kulukundis   119
Kursachsen (Blackhaus)   103 121
Kursivschrift   185
L
Latin   42 114 182
Latin Wide   114
Laudatio   99 116
Laurentian   232
Legacy Sans   52 126 181 187 188 214
Legacy Serif   51 52 105 192 214
Lexicon   46 106 171 240
Lightline Gothic   112
Linex Sans   126
LinoLetter   110 188 191
Linotext   292
Linotype Didot   171 292
Linotype Univers   135 183 184
Lithos   58 116
Lovato   128
Lucian   170
Lucida Calligraphy   101 118
Lucida Fax   110
Lucida Handwriting   119
Lucida   113 341
Lucida Sans   139
Luna   126
Luthersche Fraktur   103
Lydian   116
M
Madison   89 90
Magneton   101 186
Marconi   109
Marker Felt   306 318
Media   108 296
Mekanik   284
Melior   111 135 137 340
Memo   99 117
Memphis   111
Mendoza   124
Mentor Sans   99 116
Méridien   114 115 128 141 266 268 272
Meta   74 147 236
Minion   70 73 78 106 170 244 341

346

Minion MM 144 145
Minuscule 43
Mistral 88 101 119
Modern 172
Monoline Script 119
Mosquito 180
Motter Corpus MM 144
Motter Sparta 288
Mrs Eaves 107
Mundo Sans 268
Myriad 68 142 143 192 193 244 248 290 341
Myriad MM 142 144

N
Nami 188 189
National 340
Neue Frutiger 48
Neue Haas Grotesk 113 337 338
Neue Hammer Unziale 100
Neue Helvetica 48 68 178 179 180 182 183 276 286
Neuzeit Grotesk 258
Neuzeit S 175 258
New Baskerville 68
New Caledonia 108
News Gothic 43 112 113 138 169
Nikola 272
Nimbus 41
Normal-Grotesk 337
Normale Akzidenz-Grotesk 338
Noto Sans 41

O
Oakland 79
Odense 116
Officina Sans 189
Old Style 7 188
Optima 99 116 135 166 188 189 210
Oranda 110
Origami 129 242

P
Palatino 135 210 236
Palatino Sans 116
Panache 126
Papyrus 118 194
Pareto 181
Pensum 125
Penumbra MM 144
Pepita 101
Phoebus 114
Photina 108
Plantin 171
Playbill 29
Poetica 132 171
Poliphili-Type 132
Poliphilus 132

Pompei 117
Pompeijana 100
Potsdam 340
Praxis 138 139
Président 42 73 114 128
Prillwitz 109
Pump Triline 328

Q
Quire Sans 192 197

R
Raleigh 110 111 125
Redonda 118
Reliq 118
Rialto 132
Rockwell 66 111 124 250 258
Romain du Roi 107
Romulus 138
Romulus Greek 138
Romulus Sans Serifs 138
Rosella 193
Rotis Sans 140 175
Rotis Semi Sans 140 175
Rotis Semi Serif 84 140 175
Rotis Serif 140 175
Russell Square 294 310
Russisch Brot 314
Rusticana 58 98 99
Rutherford 125

S
Sabon 46 89 90 106 171
San Marco 103 120
Sanvito 78 100 101 118
Sassoon Infant 84
Sauna 188 189
Scarlet 127
Schadow 340
Scherzo 125
Schmale Renaissance 340
Schul-Fraktur (Wittenberger Fraktur) 44 290
Semplicita 230
Serif Gothic 117
Serifa 72 111 124 135 136 171 181 258 341
Serpentine 286 294
Shannon 116
Shelley Script 42
Sho 304
Simoncini Garamond 105 106
Siro 127
Siseriff 193
Skia 99
Slimbach 123 224
Slipstream 332
Snell Roundhand 101 119 166

Sophia 98 99
Stellar 99
Stempel Garamond 106
Stenberg 320
Stevens Titling 98 332
Stone Informal 140 193 341
Stone Sans 126 140 341
Stone Serif 140 341
Stylus 118
Stymie 111
Sunetta 101 118
Swift 42 43 46 115 128 191 260
Swiss 721 (Helvetica) 46
Syntax 61 89 90 112 113 168 184 193 216 264 337
Syntax Lapidar 58
Syntax Lapidar Serif 58

T
Tannenberg 44 340
Teknik 3
Tekton 318
Thesis TheAntiquaB 141
Thesis TheMix 140 141
Thesis TheSans 140 141 174 175 184 193
Thesis TheSerif 124 140 141 171 174
Tiemann 108
Tiepolo 99 117 180 274
Times LT 204
Times New Roman 107 140 171 182
Times Ten 193
Tiranti Solid 296
Today Sans 3 112 166 169 170 171 181 192 216
Torino (Industrial 736) 306
Trade Gothic 43 183
Trajan 58 59 98 173 176 188 189 332
Transit 341
Trinité 46 171
Trump Mediäval 115 185 244
Twentieth Century 258
Twin 146

U
Unger Fraktur 121
Unibody 8 79
Unica 185 192 220 226
Univers 48 113 134 135 136 137 140 171 182 184 193 220 282 337 341
Univers (Zurich) 46
Univers Next 135 183 184
Univers, Linotype 135 183 184
Universal 79
URW Antiqua 182 234
URW Egyptienne 183

URW Grotesk 137 183
URW Imperial 113 126 180
Utopia 94 107 180

V
VAG Rounded 272 314
VAG R§schrift 272 314
Van Dijck 106
Van Dijk 308
Vectora 43 169 192 341
Vegas 316
Veljovic 115
Vendôme 52 114 115 128 184 264
Venn 127
Venus Egyptienne 111
Venus Grotesk 47 113 134 137 185 338
Venus Linkskursiv 185
Verdana 43
Versailles 115 128 135 166 174 188 190 280 341
Vesta 260
Vida 33 Stencil 192
Vista Slab 125
Viva 43 94 144

W
Walbaum LT 46 108 109 196 197 222 226
Walbaum MT 108
Walbaum Fraktur 121 166
Warnock 45 78 115 236 270
Westside 188
Wilhelm Klingspor Gotisch 76 294
Wilke 52 107 196 230
Wittenberger Fraktur 44 290

Z
Zapf Book 109 123
Zapf Dingbats 150 158 200
Zapf International 137
Zapfino 101
Zemestro 112 113 127
Zurich (Univers) 46

Bibliography

A

Otl Aicher: *typographie*. Ernst+Sohn, Lüdenscheid 1989. (German/English edition)

American Type Founders Company: *Specimen Book and Catalogue 1923*. Jersey City 1923.

Jaroslav Andel: *Avant-Garde Page Design 1900–1950*. Delano Greenigde Editions, New York 2002.

Kathryn A. Atkins: *Masters of the Italic Letter – Twenty-two Exemplars from the Sixteenth Century*. David R. Godine, Publisher, Inc., Boston 1988.

[Alois Auer]: *Die Buchschriften des Mittelalters mit besonderer Berücksichtigung der deutschen, und zwar vom sechsten Jahrhundert bis zur Erfindung der Buchdruckerkunst*. K.K.Hof- und Staatsdruckerei, Vienna 1852.

B

Peter Bain and Paul Shaw: *Blackletter: Type and National Identity*. Princeton Architectural Press, New York 1998.

Phil Baines and Andrew Haslam: *Type and Typography*. Laurence King Publishing, London 2005 (2002).

A. Baldegger: "Vom Schriftmischen." In: *Schweizer Graphische Mitteilungen*, no. 8, August Müller (ed.), St.Gallen 1938.

Reinhold Bammes: *Der Titelsatz, seine Entwicklung und seine Grundsätze*. Verlag des Deutschen Buchgewerbevereins, Leipzig 1911.

Reinhold Bammes: "Neue Wege der Typographie." In: *Schweizer Graphische Mitteilungen*, no. 6, August Müller (ed.), St.Gallen 1922.

Hermann Barge: *Geschichte der Buchdruckerkunst von ihren Anfängen bis zur Gegenwart*. Verlag Philipp Reclam jun., Leipzig 1940.

Gustav Barthel: *Konnte Adam schreiben? Weltgeschichte der Schrift*. DuMont, Cologne 1972.

Fernand Baudin and Netty Hoeflake (ed.): *The Type Specimen of J.F.Rosart, Brussels 1768*. Van Gendt&Co, Amsterdam 1973.

Friedrich Bauer: *Handbuch für Schriftsetzer*. Verlag Klimsch&Co., Frankfurt am Main 1904; 9. revised edition. Verlag Klimsch&Co., Frankfurt am Main 1938.

Friedrich Bauer: *Anfangsgründe für Schriftsetzer-Lehrlinge*. Klimsch&Co., Frankfurt am Main 1918.

Friedrich Bauer: "Vom Mischen der Schriftarten im Schriftsatz." In: *Klimschs Jahrbuch – Technische Abhandlungen und Berichte über Neuheiten auf dem Gesamtgebiete der graphischen Künste*. Vol. 24. Verlag Klimsch&Co., Frankfurt am Main 1931.

Konrad F. Bauer: *Aventur und Kunst – Eine Chronik des Buchdruckgewerbes*. Bauersche Gießerei, Frankfurt am Main 1940.

Bauer&Co. Schriftgiesserei und Messinglinienfabrik: *Hauptprobe unser Schriftgießerei- und Messing-Erzeugnisse*. Stuttgart/Berlin n.d. (nach 1907).

Bauersche Giesserei: *Hauptprobe in gedrängter Form*. Frankfurt am Main n.d. (ca.1914).

Paul Beaujon (actually: Beatrice Warde): "Pièrre Simon Fournier and XVIIIth century French typography." In: *The Monotype Recorder*, March–April, May–June, London 1926.

Anna Berliner: "'Atmosphärenwert' von Druckschriften – Ein Beitrag zur Psychologie der Reklame." In: *Zeitschrift für angewandte Psychologie*, 17, Heft 1–3, Johann Ambrosius Barth, Leipzig 1920.

Philipp Bertheau, Eva Hanebutt-Benz and Hans Reichart: *Buchdruckschriften im 20.Jahrhundert. Atlas zur Geschichte der Schrift*. Technische Hochschule Darmstadt, 1995.

H. Berthold AG: *Exportprobe unserer Schriftgießerei- und Messing-Erzeugnisse*. Berlin/St.Petersburg n.d. (ca. 1913).

H. Berthold AG: *Deutschland: Die neue deutsche Schrift*. Berlin n.d. (ca.1934).

Lewis Blackwell: *20th century type [remix]*. Gingko Press, Corte Madera, CA/Hamburg 1998.

Hans H.Bockwitz: *Beiträge zur Kulturgeschichte des Buches – Ausgewählte Aufsätze*. VEB Otto Harrassowitz, Leipzig 1956.

Gustav Bohadti: *Die Buchdruckletter – Ein Handbuch für das Schriftgießerei- und Buchgewerbe*. Ullstein, Berlin 1954.

Max Bollwage: "Formen und Strukturen – Gedanken über eine moderne Klassifikation der Druckschriften." In: Stephan Füssel (ed.): *Gutenberg-Jahrbuch 2000*. Gutenberg-Gesellschaft, Mainz 2000.

Hans Rudolf Bosshard: *Technische Grundlagen zur Satzherstellung*. Verlag des Bildungsverbandes Schweizerischer Typographen, Bern 1980.

Hans Rudolf Bosshard: *Mathematische Grundlagen zur Satzherstellung*. Verlag des Bildungsverbandes Schweizerischer Typographen, Bern 1985.

Hans Rudolf Bosshard: *Typografie Schrift Lesbarkeit*. Niggli Verlag, Sulgen 1996.

Christian Brändle, Karin Gimmi, Barbara Junod, Christina Reble and Bettina Richter (eds.): *100 Years of Swiss Graphic Design*. Lars Müller Publishers, Zurich 2014.

W. Breuninger: "Nochmals zur Frage der Schriftenmischung." In: *Schweizer Graphische Mitteilungen*, no. 3, August Müller (ed.), St. Gallen 1913.

Robert Bringhurst: *The Elements of Typographic Style*. Version 4.2, Hartley & Marks Publishers, Vancouver 2016.

Erich Buchholz: *Schriftgeschichte als Kulturgeschichte*. Verlag des Instituts für Geosoziologie und Politik, Bellnhausen 1965.

C

Max Caflisch: *William Morris – Der Erneuerer der Buchkunst*. The Monotype Corporation, Bern 1959.

Max Caflisch: *Schriftanalysen*. Vol. 1+2. Typotron, St. Gallen 2003.

Harry Carter (ed.): *The House of Enschedé: 1703–1953*. Joh. Enschedé en Zonen, Haarlem 1953.

Rob Carter, Philip B. Meggs, Ben Day, Sandra Maxa and Mark Sanders: *Typographic Design – Form and Communication*. John Wiley & Sons., Hoboken 2015.

Sebastian Carter: *Twentieth century type designers*. Trefoil Publications, London 1987.

David Chambers (ed.): *Specimen of Modern Printing Types by Edmund Fry 1828*. Printing Historical Society, London 1986.

Karen Cheng: *Designing Type*. Laurence King Publishing, London 2006.

Stephen Coles: *The Geometry of Type – The Anatomy of 100 Essential Typefaces*. Thames & Hudson, London 2014.

Antonia M. Cornelius: *Buchstaben im Kopf*. Verlag Hermann Schmidt, Mainz 2017.

D

Leo Davidshofer and Walter Zerbe: *Satztechnik und Gestaltung*. Bildungsverband Schweizerischer Buchdrucker, Bern 1970.

Fonderies Deberny & Peignot: *Spécimen Général*. Tome II. Paris 1926.

Hermann Degering: *Die Schrift – Atlas der Schriftformen des Abendlandes vom Altertum bis zum Ausgang des 18. Jahrhunderts*. Verlag Ernst Wasmuth, Berlin 1929.

Ernestus Diehl: *Inscriptiones latinae*. Tabulae in usum scholarum. Vol. 4. A. Marcus et E. Weber, Bonn 1912.

John Dreyfus: *The Work of Jan Van Krimpen*. Sylvan Press, London 1952.

E

E.: "Anwendung von Zierschriften im modernen Akzidenzsatz." In: *Schweizer Graphische Mitteilungen*, No. 12, August Müller (ed.), St. Gallen 1904.

Fritz Helmuth Ehmcke: *Schrift – Ihre Gestaltung & Entwicklung in neuerer Zeit*. Günther Wagner, Hannover 1925.

Fritz Helmuth Ehmcke: *Die Historische Entwicklung der Abendländischen Schriftformen*. Otto Maier Verlag, Ravensburg 1927.

Fritz Helmuth Ehmcke: *Wandlung des Schriftgefühls*. Ludwig Wagner type foundry, Leipzig 1958.

Franciscus Ehrle and Paulus Liebhaert: *Specimina codicum latinorum vaticanorum*. Tabulae in usum scholarum. Vol. 3. Walter de Gruyter, Berlin/Leipzig 1927.

Petra Eisele and Isabel Naegele: *Texte zur Typografie – Positionen zur Schrift*. Niggli Verlag, Sulgen/Zurich 2012.

Petra Eisele, Isabel Naegele and Michael Lailach (eds.): *Moholy-Nagy and the New Typography. A–Z*. Verlag Kettler, Bönen 2019.

Patrick Exner: "Schnelles Leben." In: *PAGE*, Nr. 8, macup Verlag, Hamburg 1995.

F

Karl Faulmann: *Illustrirte Geschichte der Buchdruckerkunst*. A. Hartleben's Verlag, Vienna 1882.

Martina Fineder, Eva Kraus and Andreas Pawlik (ed.): *postscript – Zur Form von Schrift heute*. Hatje Cantz Verlag, Ostfildern 2004.

Alfred Finsterer (ed.): *Hoffmanns Schriftatlas*. Verlag Julius Hoffmann, Stuttgart 1952.

Gerda Finsterer-Stuber (ed.): *Geistige Väter des Abendlandes – Eine Sammlung von hundert Buchtiteln antiker Autoren*. Chr. Belser Verlag, Stuttgart 1960.

Heinrich Fischer: *Anleitung zum Accidenzsatz*. 2nd revised and extended edition. Verlag C. G. Naumann, Leipzig 1893.

Schriftgiesserei Flinsch: *[Type specimen book]*. Frankfurt am Main n.d.

Károly Földes-Papp: *Vom Felsbild zum Alphabet*. Chr. Belser Verlag, Stuttgart 1966.

Justinian Frisch: *Geist und Zweck der Schrift – Ihre Aufgaben in der Werbekunst*. C. Barth Verlag, Vienna 1927.

Carl August Franke: *Handbuch der Buchdruckerkunst. Nach ihrem neuesten Standpunkte in Deutschland*. Verlag Bernhard Friedrich Voigt, Weimar 1855.

Friedrich Friedl, Nicolaus Ott and Bernard Stein: *Typography – when who how*. Könemann, Cologne 1998.

Friedrich Friedl: "Zwischen Tradition und Experiment. Aspekte typografischen Formwillens im 20. Jahrhundert." In: Stephan Füssel (ed.): *Gutenberg-Jahrbuch 2000*. Gutenberg-Gesellschaft, Mainz 2000.

Adrian Frutiger and Alfred Willimann: *Schrift Ecriture Lettering*. Bildungsverband Schweizerischer Buchdrucker, Zurich 1951.

Adrian Frutiger: *Signs and Symbols: Their Design and Meaning*, Van Nostrand Reinhold, London 1989.

Adrian Frutiger: *Type Sign Symbol*. ABC Verlag, Zurich 1980.

Adrian Frutiger: "Schrift und Papier – der Mensch heute / La typographie et le papier – l'homme aujourd'hui / Type, paper and man today." Special print of *Typografische Monatsblätter*, St. Gallen 1980.

Stephan Füssel: *Gutenberg und seine Wirkung*. Insel Verlag, Frankfurt am Main 1999.

G

Elisabeth Geck: *Das Wort der Meister*. Mergenthaler-Verlag Linotype GmbH, Berlin/Frankfurt am Main 1966.

Genzsch & Heyse, Schriftgiesserei AG: *Proben von Schriften und Initialen – Handprobe*. Hamburg/Munich n.d. (ca. 1910).

Karl Gerstner and Markus Kutter: *die neue Graphik / the new graphic art / le nouvel art graphique*. Verlag Arthur Niggli, Teufen 1959.

Karl Gerstner: *Designing Programmes*. Verlag Arthur Niggli, Teufen 1968.

Karl Gerstner: *Kompendium für Alphabeten – Systematik der Schrift*. 3rd edition, Verlag Arthur Niggli, Heiden 1990.

Rudolf Paulus Gorbach: *Typografie professionell*. 2nd edition, Galileo Press, Bonn 2002.

Frederic W. Goudy: *Goudy's Type Designs [Complete] – His Story and his Specimens*. The Myriade Press, New Rochelle, NY, 1978.

M. Gr.: "Eine fachliche Plauderstunde." In: *Schweizer Graphische Mitteilungen*, no. 2, August Müller (ed.), St. Gallen 1933.

Nicolete Gray: *Lettering on Buildings*. The Architectural Press, London 1960.

Nicolete Gray: *Nineteenth Century Ornamented Typefaces*. Faber and Faber, London 1976.

Nicolete Gray: *A History of Lettering*. Phaidon Press Limited, Oxford 1986.

Marie-Rose Guarniéri (ed.): *L'Éloge des Cent Papiers*. Librairie des Abbesses, Paris 2011.

Juli Gudehus: *Das Lesikon der visuellen Kommunikation*. Verlag Hermann Schmidt, Mainz 2011.

André Gürtler: "Die Entwicklung der lateinischen Schrift / L'évolution de l'écriture latine / The development of the Roman Alphabet." Schweizerischer Typographenbund zur Förderung der Berufsbildung, special print *Typografische Monatsblätter, TM 11*, St. Gallen 1969.

ANDRÉ GÜRTLER: *Schrift und Kalligrafie im Experiment / Experiments with Letterform and Calligraphy*. Niggli Verlag, Sulgen 1997.
CHRISTIAN GUTSCHI: "Psychologie der Schriften." Part 1 in: *PAGE* 8/1996; part 2 in: 9/1996; part 3 in: 10/1996; part 4 in: 12/1996; part 5 in: 1/1997; MACup Verlag, Hamburg.

H

HARALD HAARMANN: *Universalgeschichte der Schrift*. Campus Verlag, Frankfurt am Main 1991.
ALLAN HALEY: *Type: Hot designers make cool fonts*. Rockport Publishers, Gloucester, MA, 1998.
WILLEM HASPER: *Kurzes practisches Handbuch der Buchdruckerkunst in Frankreich*. Verlag D. R. Marx'sche Buchhandlung, Carlsruhe/Baden 1828.
STEVEN HELLER: *Merz to Emigre and Beyond: Avant-Garde Magazine Design of the Twentieth Century*. Phaidon Press Limited, London 2003.
STEVEN HELLER and GAIL ANDERSON: *New Vintage Type – Classic Fonts for the Digital Age*. Thames & Hudson, London 2007.
FRANK HIERONYMUS: *1488 Petri – Schwabe 1988. Eine traditionsreiche Basler Offizin im Spiegel ihrer frühen Drucke*. Vol. 1+2. Schwabe & Co. Verlag, Basel 1997.
HELMUT HILLER and STEPHAN FÜSSEL: *Wörterbuch des Buches*. 7th edition. Vittorio Klostermann, Frankfurt am Main 2006.
STANLEY C. HLASTA: *Printing Types & how to use them*. Carnegie Press, Carnegie Institute of Technology, Pittsburgh 1950.
JOST HOCHULI: *Detail in Typography*. Compugraphic Corp., Wilmington, MA, 1987.
JOST HOCHULI: *Kleine Geschichte der geschriebenen Schrift*. Verlag Typophil, St. Gallen 1991.
JOST HOCHULI and ROBIN KINROSS: *Designing Books: Practice and Theory*. Hyphen Press, London 1996.
WIEBKE HÖLJES: *Dreiklänge – Schriftmischmusterbuch*. Verlag Hermann Schmidt, Mainz 2000.
BERND HOLTHUSEN: *Digital Design*. Econ Verlag, Dusseldorf 1988.
RUDOLF HOSTETTLER: *Technical terms of the printing industry / Fachwörter der graphischen Industrie*. 3rd edition, St. Gallen / London 1959.
H-x.: "Satztechnische Kleinigkeiten?" In: *Schweizer Graphische Mitteilungen*, no. 8, August Müller (ed.), St. Gallen 1935.

J

DONALD JACKSON: *The story of writing*. Shuckburgh Reynolds, London 1981.
W. PINCUS JASPERT, W. TURNER BERRY and A. F. JOHNSON: *Encyclopaedia of Type Faces*. Blandford Press, London 1970.
HANS JENSEN: *Die Schrift in Vergangenheit und Gegenwart*. VEB Deutscher Verlag der Wissenschaften, Berlin 1969.
CEES W. DE JONG, ALSTON W. PURVIS and JAN THOLENAAR: *Type – A Visual History of Typefaces and Graphic Styles*.
Vol. 1. Taschen, Cologne 2009.
Vol. 2. Taschen, Cologne 2010.
STEPHANIE DE JONG and RALF DE JONG: *Schriftwechsel – Schrift sehen, verstehen, wählen und vermitteln*. Verlag Hermann Schmidt, Mainz 2008.
ROXANE JUBERT: *Typography and Graphic Design*. Flammarion, Paris 2006.

K

WALTER KÄCH: *Schriften Lettering Ecritures*. Verlag Otto Walter, Olten 1949.
WALTER KÄCH: *Rhythmus und Proportion in der Schrift / Rhythm and Proportion in Lettering*. Walter-Verlag, Olten/Freiburg im Breisgau 1956.
ALBERT KAPR: *Deutsche Schriftkunst*. VEB Verlag der Kunst, Dresden 1955.
ALBERT KAPR: *Schriftkunst – Geschichte, Anatomie und Schönheit der lateinischen Buchstaben*. VEB Verlag der Kunst, Dresden 1971.
ALBERT KAPR: *Fraktur – Form und Geschichte der gebrochenen Schriften*. Verlag Hermann Schmidt, Mainz 1993.
ALBERT KAPR and WALTER SCHILLER: "Vom Schriftmischen." In: *Gestalt und Funktion der Typografie*. 3rd edition, VEB Fachbuchverlag, Leipzig 1983.
PETER KAROW: *Font Technology – Methods and Tools*. Edition Page, Springer Verlag, Berlin/Heidelberg 1994.
PETER KAROW: *Digital Typefaces – Description and Formats*. Springer-Verlag, Berlin/Heidelberg 1994.
OTTO KERN: *Inscriptiones graecae*. Tabulae in usum scholarum. Vol. 7. A. Marcus et E. Weber, Bonn 1913.
ROBERT KLANTEN, MIKA MISCHLER, SILJA BILZ and NIK THOENEN: *Type One – discipline and progress in typography*. Die Gestalten Verlag, Berlin 2004.
MANFRED KLEIN, YVONNE SCHWEMER-SCHEDDIN and ERIK SPIEKERMANN: *Type & Typographers*. V+K Publishing, Laren 1991.
GEBR. KLINGSPOR SCHRIFTGIESSEREI: *Vierte Abteilung: Antiqua-Schriften – Ältere Brot- und Titelschriften*. Offenbach am Main n.d.

KARL KLINGSPOR: *Über Schönheit von Schrift und Druck – Erfahrungen aus fünfzigjähriger Arbeit*. Georg Kurt Schauer, Frankfurt am Main 1949.
SCHRIFTGIESSEREI JULIUS KLINKHARDT: *Gesamt-Probe*. Leipzig/Vienna 1883.
OTTO KLUG: "Die Auszeichnungsarten im Werksatz." In: *Schweizer Graphische Mitteilungen*, No. 10, August Müller (ed.), St. Gallen 1942.
MICHAEL KOETZLE (ed.): *twen – Revision einer Legende*. Klinkhardt & Biermann, Munich/Berlin 1995.
HANS-MICHAEL KOETZLE and CARSTEN WOLFF: *Fleckhaus – Design, Revolte, Regenbogen / Design, Revolt, Rainbow*. Museum für Angewandte Kunst, Cologne 2016.
ANDREAS KOOP: *NSCI – Das visuelle Erscheinungsbild der Nationalsozialisten 1920–1945*. Verlag Hermann Schmidt, Mainz 2008.
ANDREAS KOOP: *Die Macht der Schrift*. Niggli Verlag, Sulgen/Zurich 2012.
HILDEGARD KORGER: *Schrift und Schreiben*. Fachbuchverlag, Leipzig 1991.
HELMUT KRAUS: "Milliarden von Myriaden." In: *PAGE*, no. 1. MACup Verlag, Hamburg 1996.
MATEO KRIES, JOCHEN EISENBRAND (ed.): *Alexander Girard – A Designer's Universe*. Vitra Design Museum, Weil am Rhein 2016.
MARTIN KUCKENBURG: *Die Entstehung von Sprache und Schrift*. DuMont, Cologne 1989.
ANITA KÜHNEL (ed.): *Welt aus Schrift – Das 20. Jahrhundert in Europa und den USA*. Verlag der Buchhandlung Walther König, Cologne 2010.
INDRA KUPFERSCHMID: *Buchstaben kommen selten allein – Ein typografisches Handbuch*. 2nd edition, Niggli Verlag, Sulgen/Zurich 2009.

L

HANS LEHNACKER (ed.): *Vita Activa – Georg Trump: Bilder, Schriften & Schriftbilder*. Typographische Gesellschaft München, Munich 1967.
JOHN LEWIS: *Printed Ephemera – The changing uses of type and letterforms in English and American printing*. W. S. Cowell, Ipswich 1962.
CHARLOTTE VAN LINGEN (ed.): *Charles Nypels Prijs Award 1998: Zuzana Licko, Rudy vanderLans – Emigre*. Charles Nypels Stichting/Drukkerij Rosbeek, Antwerpen/Nuth 1998.
MATHIEU LOMMEN (ed.): *Bram de Does: letterontwerper & typograaf / typographer & type designer*. Uitgeverij De Buitenkant Publishers, Amsterdam 2003.

CARL B. LORCK: *Handbuch der Geschichte der Buchdruckerkunst.* J. J. Weber, Leipzig 1882.
PHILIPP LUIDL: *Typografie – Herkunft Aufbau Anwendung.* Schlütersche Verlagsanstalt, Hannover 1984.
PHILIPP LUIDL: *Schrift – die Zerstörung der Nacht.* Typographische Gesellschaft München, Munich 1993.
PHILIPP LUIDL: *Typografie – Basiswissen.* Deutscher Drucker, Ostfildern (Ruit) 1996.
ELLEN LUPTON: *Thinking with type.* Princeton Architectural Press, New York 2004.

M
NEIL MACMILLAN: *An A–Z of Type Designers.* Laurence King Publishing, London 2006.
VICTOR MALSY and LARS MÜLLER (eds.): *Helvetica forever – Story of a typeface.* Lars Müller Publishers, Baden 2009.
AUGUST MARAHRENS (ed.): *Vollständiges theoretisch-praktisches Handbuch der Typographie nach ihrem heutigen Standpunkt.* Vol. 1 + 2. Verlag der Vereinsbuchdruckerei, Leipzig 1870.
ANDREAS MAXBAUER: ‹Typografische Tendenzen." In: *PAGE – Publizieren und Präsentieren mit dem Personal Computer,* no. 7, MACUP Verlag, Hamburg 1995.
ANDREAS MAXBAUER: "Die Mischung macht's." In: *PAGE – Publizieren und Präsentieren mit dem Personal Computer,* Teil 1: no. 10; Teil 2: no. 11, MACUP Verlag GmbH, Hamburg 1995.
ANDREAS MAXBAUER and REGINA MAXBAUER: *Praxishandbuch Gestaltungsraster – Ordnung ist das halbe Lesen.* Hermann Schmidt Verlag, Mainz 2002.
OTTO MAZAL: *Paläographie und Paläotypie.* Anton Hiersemann Verlag, Stuttgart 1984.
PAUL MCNEIL: *The Visual History of Type.* Laurence King Publishing, London 2019.
PHILIP B. MEGGS: *A History of Graphic Design.* Van Nostrand Reinhold Company, New York 1983.
HANS EDUARD MEIER: *Die Schriftentwicklung / The Development of Writing / Le developpement de l'écriture.* Graphis Press, Zurich 1958.
MERGENTHALER LINOTYPE COMPANY: *Specimen Book Linotype Faces.* Brooklyn, NY, n.d. (ca. 1933)
FRANCIS MEYNELL: *The Typography of Newspaper Advertisements.* Ernest Benn Limited, Edinburgh 1929.
JAN MIDDENDORP: *Dutch Type.* 010 publishers, Rotterdam 2004.
JAN MIDDENDORP, TWOPOINTS.NET: *Type Navigator – The Independent Foundries Handbook.* Die Gestalten Verlag, Berlin 2011.
JAN MIDDENDORP: *Shaping Text.* BIS Publishers, Amsterdam 2012.
ELMAR MITTLER (ed.): *Bibliotheca Palatina.* Edition Braus, Heidelberg 1986.
STANLEY MORISON: *The Art of the Printer.* Ernest Benn Limited, London 1925.
STANLEY MORISON: *Type Designs of the Past and Present.* The Fleuron, London 1926.
STANLEY MORISON: *The Art of Printing.* British Academy, London 1937.
STANLEY MORISON: *Four Centuries of Fine Printing.* Ernest Benn Limited, London 1949.
JAMES MOSLEY (ed.): *S. & C. Stephenson – A Specimen of Printing Types & Various Ornaments 1796–1797.* The Printing Historical Society – St Bride Institute, London 1990.
AUGUST MÜLLER: *Lehrbuch der Buchdruckerkunst.* 9. revised and extended edition. Verlagsbuchhandlung J. J. Weber, Leipzig 1913.
JENS MÜLLER and JULIUS WIEDEMANN (eds.): *The History of Graphic Design.* Vol. 1: 1890–1959. Taschen, Cologne 2017; Vol. 2: 1960–Today. Taschen, Cologne 2018.
JOSEF MÜLLER-BROCKMANN: *Geschichte der visuellen Kommunikation / A History of Visual Communication.* Verlag Arthur Niggli, Niederteufen 1986.
JOSEF MÜLLER-BROCKMANN: *Gestaltungsprobleme des Grafikers / The Graphic Designer and His Design Problems / Les problèmes d'un graphiste.* Niggli Verlag, Sulgen 2003
FRANTIŠEK MUZIKA: *Die Schöne Schrift.* Vol. 1 + 2. Verlag Werner Dausien, Hanau am Main 1965.

N
JOSEPH NAVEH: *Origins of the Alphabet.* Cassell's Introducing Archaeology Series, book 6, London 1975.
ISABEL NAEGELE, PETRA EISELE and ANNETTE LUDWIG (eds.): *New Typefaces. Positions and Perspectives.* Niggli Verlag, Sulgen 2013.
EUGEN NERDINGER: *Buchstabenbuch – Schriftentwicklung, Formbedingungen, Schrifttechnik, Schriftsammlung.* Verlag Georg D. W. Callwey, Munich 1955.
EUGEN NERDINGER: *Zeichen · Schrift und Ornament / Signs · Scripts and Ornaments / Signes · Caractères et Ornements.* Verlag Georg D. W. Callwey, Munich 1960.
LEOPOLD NETTELHORST: *Schrift muss passen. Schriftwahl und Schriftausdruck in der Werbung – Handbuch für die Gestaltungsarbeit an Werbemitteln.* Wirtschaft und Werbung Verlagsgesellschaft, Essen 1959.
QUENTIN NEWARK: *What is Graphic Design?* RotoVision, Mies 2002.

RICHARD L. NIEHL: *Satztechnisches Taschen-Lexikon – mit Berücksichtigung der Schriftgießerei.* 2nd edition, Verlag Steyermühl, Vienna 1925.
GERRIT NOORDZIJ: *Letterletter.* Hartley & Marks Publishers, Vancouver, BC, 2000.
GERRIT NOORDZIJ: *The Stroke – Theory of Writing.* Hyphen Press, London 2005.

O
CHARLES E. OSGOOD, G. J. SUCI and P. H. TANNENBAUM: *The Measurement of Meaning.* Urbana 1957.
HEIDRUN OSTERER and PHILIPP STAMM: *Adrian Frutiger – Typefaces. The Complete Works.* Birkhäuser Verlag, Basel 2021 (2008/2014).

P
FONDERIE G. PEIGNOT & FILS: *Spécimen Géneral.* Vol. I. Paris 1900.
WILLIAM S. PETERSON: *The Ideal Book – Essays and Lectures on the Art of the Book by William Morris.* University of California Press, Berkeley, CA, 1982.
JOEP POHLEN: *Letter Fountain (on Printing Types).* Taschen, Cologne 2011.
RICK POYNOR: *No more Rules. Graphic Design and Postmodernism.* Laurence King Publishing, London 2003.

R
RR: "Londoner Drucksachen." In: *Typographische Monatsblätter, TM 7,* Schweizerischer Typographenbund, Bern 1939.
KARL RAHN: "Vom Schriftmischen." In: *Typographische Monatsblätter, TM 9,* Schweizerischer Typographenbund, Bern 1944.
VOLKER RATTEMEYER and DIETRICH HELMS: *Typographie kann unter Umständen Kunst sein: Kurt Schwitters – Typographie und Werbegestaltung.* Museum Wiesbaden, 1990.
MARGARET RE: *Typographically Speaking – The Art of Matthew Carter.* Princeton Architectural Press, New York 2004.
PAUL RENNER: *Typografie als Kunst.* Verlag Georg Müller, Munich 1922.
PAUL RENNER: *Mechanisierte Grafik – Schrift, Typo, Foto, Film, Farbe.* Verlag Hermann Reckendorf, Berlin 1931.
PAUL RENNER: *Die Kunst der Typographie.* Frenzel & Engelbrecher Verlag, Berlin 1939. Newly edited by Georg Schautz. 3rd edition. Deutscher Verlag/Ullstein AG, Berlin 1953.
PAUL RENNER: *Das moderne Buch.* Jan Thorbecke Verlag, Lindau 1946.
PAUL RENNER: *Der Künstler in der mechanisierten Welt.* Akademie für das Grafische Gewerbe, Munich 1977.

Karl Riha and Jörgen Schäfer (eds.):
Dada total – Manifeste, Aktionen, Texte, Bilder.
Philipp Reclam jun., Stuttgart 1994.
Caroline Roberts: *graphic design visionaries.*
Laurence King Publishing, London 2015.
Andrew Robinson: *The Story of Writing.*
Alphabets, Hieroglyphs and Pictograms.
Thames & Hudson, London 1995.
Stefan Rögener, Albert-Jan Pool and
Ursula Packhäuser: *Typen machen Marken mächtig.* AdFinder GmbH, Hamburg 1995.
Peter Rück (ed.): *Historische Hilfswissenschaften. Vol. 4: Methoden der Schriftbeschreibung.*
Jan Thorbecke Verlag, Stuttgart 1999.
Emil Ruder: "Univers, eine Grotesk von Adrian Frutiger." In: *Typographische Monatsblätter, TM 5,* Schweizerischer Typographenbund, Bern 1957.
Emil Ruder: "Die Univers in der Typographie."
In: *Typographische Monatsblätter. Sondernummer Univers. TM 1,* Schweizerischer Typographenbund, Bern 1961.
Emil Ruder: *Typographie – Ein Gestaltungslehrbuch / Typography – A Manual of Design / Typographie – Un Manuel du Création.*
Verlag Arthur Niggli, Teufen 1967.
Ruedi Rüegg and Godi Fröhlich:
Typografische Grundlagen – Handbuch für Technik und Gestaltung / Bases Typographiques – Manuel pour technique et conception / Basic Typography – Handbook of technique and design.
ABC Verlag, Zurich 1972.

S

H.S.: "Aus der Praxis – für die Praxis.
Zur Frage der Schriftenmischung." In:
Schweizer Graphische Mitteilungen, no. 11,
August Müller (ed.), St. Gallen 1918.
Ina Saltz: *Typografie – 100 Prinzipien für die Arbeit mit Schrift.* Stiebner Verlag,
Munich 2010.
Georg Kurt Schauer: *Klassifikation · Bemühungen um eine Ordnung im Druckschriftenbestand.* Darmstadt 1975.
J.G. Schelter & Giesecke: *Hauptprobe – 1. Band Schriften, Messinglinien usw.* Leipzig 1912.
Günter Schmitt: *Typographische Gestaltungsepochen.* Verlag Arbeitsgemeinschaft für grafische Lehrmittel, Bellach 1983.
Günter Schmitt: *Schriftkunde – Herkunft, Entstehung und Entwicklung unserer Schrift.*
Verlag Schweizerische Typographische Vereinigung, St. Gallen 1994.
Beat Schneider: *Design – Eine Einführung. Entwurf im sozialen, kulturellen und wirtschaftlichen Kontext.* Birkhäuser Verlag, Basel 2005.

Ulrich Johannes Schneider (ed.):
Textkünste – Buchrevolution um 1500.
Philipp von Zabern Verlag, Darmstadt 2016.
Wilhelm Schubart: *Papyri graecae berolinenses.*
Tabulae in usum scholarum. Vol. 2.
A. Marcus e E. Weber, Bonn 1911.
Erich Schulz-Anker: *Formanalyse und Dokumentation einer serifenlosen Linearschrift auf neuer Basis: Syntax-Antiqua.* D. Stempel AG, Frankfurt am Main 1969.
Albrecht Seemann: *Handbuch der Schriftarten.*
Albrecht Seeman Verlag, Leipzig 1926.
Tony Seddon: *Perfect Typeface Combinations.*
Thames & Hudson, London 2015.
Tony Seddon: *Let's talk type – an essential lexicon of type terms.* Thames & Hudson, London 2016.
Wilfried Seipel (ed.): *Der Turmbau zu Babel – Ursprung und Vielfalt von Sprache und Schrift.*
Kunsthistorisches Museum Wien /
Skira editore, Milan 2003.
Paul Shaw (ed.): *The Eternal Letter –
Two Millenia of the Classical Roman Capital.*
MIT Press, Cambridge, MA, 2015.
Paul Shaw: *Revival Type – Digital typefaces inspired by the past.* Yale University Press, New Haven 2017.
Richard von Sichowsky and Hermann Tiemann: *Typographie und Bibliophilie – Aufsätze und Vorträge über die Kunst des Buchdrucks aus zwei Jahrhunderten.*
Maximilian-Gesellschaft, Hamburg 1971.
Manfred Simoneit: *Typographisches Gestalten – Regeln und Tips für die richtige Gestaltung von Drucksachen.* Polygraph Verlag, Frankfurt am Main 1989.
Slanted (ed.): *Year Book of Type.*
Vol. 1. Niggli Verlag, Sulgen 2013.
Vol. 2. Niggli Verlag, Zurich 2015.
Herbert Spencer: *Pioneers of modern typography.* Lund Humphries, London 1969.
Erik Spiekermann: *Ursache & Wirkung:
ein typografischer Roman.* Context GmbH, Erlangen 1982.
Erik Spiekermann: *ÜberSchrift.*
Verlag Hermann Schmidt, Mainz 2004.
Erik Spiekermann and E. M. Ginger:
Stop Stealing Sheep & find out how type works.
Adobe Press, Mountain View 1993.
Philipp Stamm: "Extension of the Latin alphabet for the German language." In: *Typografische Monatsblätter, TM 1,* Zurich 1997.
Philipp Stamm: "Pop is Round · Pop is Colorful."
In: Madeleine Schuppli u.a.: *Swiss Pop Art.*
Scheidegger & Spiess, Zurich 1997.

Gregor Stawinski: *Retrofonts.*
Verlag Hermann Schmidt, Mainz 2009.
Stephenson, Blake & Co. Ltd: *Printing Types – Borders, Initials, Electros, Brass Rules, Spacing Material, Ornaments.* Sheffield 1924.
Stephenson, Blake & Co. Ltd: *Printing Types – Borders, Initials, Electros, Brass Rules, Spacing Material.* Sheffield 1934.
Stephenson, Blake & Co. Ltd: *Specimens of Woodletter, Borders, Ornaments &c.* 3rd edition. Sheffield 1936.
D. Stempel AG: *Altmeister der Druckschrift.*
Frankfurt am Main 1940.
Gustav Stresow: *Die Kursiv – Vierhundert Jahre Formwandel einer Druckschrift.* Technische Universität Darmstadt, Darmstadt 2001.
W. Stücken: "Zur Frage der Schriftenmischung."
In: *Schweizer Graphische Mitteilungen,* No. 2, August Müller (ed.), St. Gallen 1913.
W. Stücken: "Typographische Zeit- und Streitfragen." In: *Schweizer Graphische Mitteilungen,* No. 1, August Müller (ed.), St. Gallen 1923.
James Sutton and Alan Bartram: *An atlas of typeforms.* Hastings House Publishers, New York 1968.

T

Francis Thibaudeau: *La Lettre d'Imprimerie.*
Vol. 1 + 2. Bureau de l'Édition, Paris 1921.
Francis Thibaudeau: *Manuel Français de Typographie Moderne.* Bureau de l'Édition, Paris 1924.
Mai-Linh Thi Truong, Jürgen Siebert and
Erik Spiekermann: *FontBook.* FontShop International, Berlin 1998.
Jan Tschichold: *sonderheft elementare typographie.* Typographische Mitteilungen –
Zeitschrift des Bildungsverbandes der deutschen Buchdrucker, Leipzig 1925. Reprint:
Verlag H. Schmidt, Mainz 1986.
Jan Tschichold: *The New Typography –
A Handbook for Modern Designers.*
University of California Press, Berkeley 1995.
Jan Tschichold: "Schriftmischungen."
In: *Typographische Monatsblätter, TM 2,*
Schweizerischer Typographenbund, Bern 1935.
Jan Tschichold: *asymmetric typography.*
Faber and Faber Ltd., London 1967.
Jan Tschichold: *Was jedermann vom Buchdruck wissen sollte.* Verlag Birkhäuser, Basel 1949.
Jan Tschichold: *Treasury of Alphabets and Lettering. A handbook of type and lettering.*
Norton Books, New York 1992.
Jan Tschichold: *Erfreuliche Drucksachen durch gute Typographie – Eine Fibel für jedermann.*
MaroVerlag, Augsburg 1992 (Ravensburg 1960).

Jan Tschichold: *Schriften 1925–1974.* Vol. 1+2. Brinkmann & Bose, Berlin 1991.

La Fonderie Typographique Française: *Catalogue général.* Paris 1927.

U

Gerard Unger: *While You're Reading.* Mark Batty Publisher, New York 2006.

Gerard Unger: *Theory of type design.* nai010, Rotterdam 2018.

Daniel Berkeley Updike: *Printing Types – Their History, Forms, and Use.* Vol. 1+2. The Belknap Press of Harvard University Press, Cambridge, MA, 1966.

V

viscom (ed.): *Schriftfonts.* Schweizerischer Verband für visuelle Kommunikation, Zurich 2007.

Ulysses Voelker: *Read+Play – Einführung in die Typografie.* Verlag Hermann Schmidt, Mainz 2015.

Karl Vöhringer: *Druckschriften – kennenlernen, unterscheiden, anwenden.* Verlag Form und Technik, Stuttgart 1989.

W

Alexander Waldow: *Illustrierte Encyklopädie der graphischen Künste und der verwandten Zweige.* Verlag Alexander Waldow, Leipzig 1884.

Alexander Waldow: *Lehrbuch für Schriftsetzer.* Verlag Alexander Waldow, Leipzig 1888.

Alexander Waldow (ed.), Friedrich Bauer: *Die Lehre vom Accidenzsatz.* Verlag Alexander Waldow, Leipzig 1892.

Lawrence W. Wallis: *Modern Encyclopedia of Typefaces 1960–90.* Lund Humphries, London 1990.

Hendrik Weber: *Italic – What gives Typography its emphasis.* Niggli Verlag, Salenstein 2021.

Kurt Weidemann: *Wo der Buchstabe das Wort führt.* Cantz Verlag, Ostfildern 1994.

Wolfgang Weingart: *Typography. My Way to Typography / Wege zur Typographie.* Verlag Lars Müller, Baden 2000.

Dirk Wendt: *Untersuchungen zur Lesbarkeit von Druckschriften.* Report no. 2 (duplicated manuscript), Hamburg 1965.

Dirk Wendt: "Semantic Differentials of Typefaces as a Method of Congeniality Research." In: *The Journal of Typographic Research.* Vol. 2, Cleveland 1/1968.

Emil Wetzig: *Ausgewählte Druckschriften.* Verein Leipziger Buchdruckerei Besitzer, Leipzig 1925.

F. J. M. Wijnekus: *Elsevier's Dictionary of the Printing and Allied Industries.* Elsevier Publishing Company, Amsterdam 1967.

Walter Wilkes: *Atlas zur Geschichte der Schrift.* 2nd edition – Vol. 1–7. Technische Universität, Darmstadt 2001.

Hans Peter Willberg and Friedrich Forssman: *Lesetypographie.* Verlag Hermann Schmidt, Mainz 1997.

Hans Peter Willberg: *Typolemik – Typophilie.* Verlag Hermann Schmidt, Mainz 2000.

Hans Peter Willberg: "Schrift und Typographie im 20. Jahrhundert." In: Stephan Füssel (ed.): *Gutenberg-Jahrbuch 2000.* Gutenberg-Gesellschaft, Mainz 2000.

Hans Peter Willberg: *Wegweiser Schrift.* Verlag Hermann Schmidt, Mainz 2001.

Bruce Willen and Nolen Strals: *Lettering & Type – Creating Letters and Designing Typefaces.* Princeton Architectural Press, New York 2009.

Wilhelm Woellmer: *Schriftgießerei Hauptprobe.* Berlin n.d. (ca. 1920er-Jahre).

Berthold Wolpe (ed.): *Vincent Figgins – Type Specimens 1801 and 1815.* Printing Historical Society, London 1967.

Z

Hermann Zapf: *William Morris. Sein Leben und Werk in der Geschichte der Buch- und Schriftkunst.* Monographien Künstlerischer Schrift, Vol. 11. Klaus Blanckertz Verlag, Scharbeutz/Lubeck 1949.

Hermann Zapf: *Über Alphabete. Gedanken und Anmerkungen beim Schriftentwerfen.* Verlagsbuchhandlung Georg Kurt Schauer, Frankfurt am Main 1960.

Hermann Zapf: ‹Vom Stempelschnitt zur Digitalisierung von Schriftzeichen. Die technischen Veränderungen der Schriftherstellung." In: Stephan Füssel (ed.): *Gutenberg-Jahrbuch 2000.* Gutenberg-Gesellschaft, Mainz 2000.

Ursula Zeller (ed.): *Lucian Bernhard – Werbung und Design im Aufbruch des 20. Jahrhunderts.* Institut für Auslandsbeziehungen e.V., Stuttgart 1999.

Moritz Zwimpfer: *2d Visual Perception.* Niggli Verlag, Sulgen/Zurich 1994.

Unknown

o.V.: "Einheitliche Schriftenwahl – Ein Beitrag zur Vereinfachung des Accidenzsatzes." In: August Müller (ed.): *Schweizer Graphische Mitteilungen,* no. 3, St. Gallen 1898.

o.V.: "Ein typographisches Experiment." In: August Müller (ed.): *Schweizer Graphische Mitteilungen,* no. 13, St. Gallen 1910.

o.V.: "Schriftenmischung." In: August Müller (ed.): *Schweizer Graphische Mitteilungen,* no. 23/24, St. Gallen 1913.

o.V.: "Rationelle und geschmackvolle Inseraten-Ausstattung." In: August Müller (ed.): *Schweizer Graphische Mitteilungen,* no. 5, St. Gallen 1916.

o.V.: "Die Schriftmischung." In: August Müller (ed.): *Schweizer Graphische Mitteilungen,* no. 4, St. Gallen 1924.

o.V.: "Schriftgiesserei-Neuheiten." In: August Müller (ed.): *Schweizer Graphische Mitteilungen.* no. 7, Zollikofer & Cie., St. Gallen 1927.

Websites

www.abcdinamo.com
www.adobe.com
www.archiviotipografico.it
www.bridgemanimages.de
www.digitale-sammlungen.de
www.duden.de
www.e-codices.ch
www.e-rara.ch
www.fontexplorerx.com
https://fontjoy.com
www.fonts4ever.com
www.fonts.com
www.fontshop.com
https://fontsinuse.com
www.fontspring.com
https://forums.adobe.com
www.identifont.com
https://lineto.com
https://linotype.com
www.mengelt-blauen.ch
www.monotype.com
www.myfonts.com
www.optimo.ch
https://tiff.herokuapp.com
www.typenetwork.com
https://typofonderie.com
www.typografie.info
www.typolexikon.de
www.typotheque.com
www.viva.de
https://de.wikipedia.org
https://en.wikipedia.org

Illustrations

The author extends his thanks to the responsible lenders and licensers for granting the relevant printing rights. All image rights remain with the lenders and licensers. Images not included in the following list were produced by the author.

1
Historical considerations →11

|01| Rosetta Stone, trilingual inscription of a decree by King Ptolemy V: Old Egyptian using hieroglyphic script (above), Late Egyptian in Demotic script (middle), Ancient Greek in Greek script (below); Egypt, 196 BCE, British Museum, London, England, www.britishmuseum.org © The Trustees of the British Museum. All rights reserved.

|02| Latin dedicatory inscription, marble inscription in Capitalis quadrata, list of members in Capitalis rustica; Italy, early second century. See FRANZ STEFFENS: *Lateinische Paläographie*. Berlin and Leipzig 1929. © University of Fribourg, Switzerland, www.paleography.unifr.ch/steffens/tafeln_frm.htm / www.e-codices.ch

|03| Grandval Bible or Moutier-Grandval Bible, Carolingian illuminated manuscript in Capitalis quadrata, Uncial and Carolingian miniscule; Tours, France, circa 840. British Library, London, England, www.bl.uk © Bridgeman Images, Berlin, Germany, www.bridgemanimages.de

|04| Pericope book from St. Erentrud in Salzburg – Evangelia in missa legi solita, praecedente capitulari evangeliorum. Parchment manuscript, text in Carolingian miniscule (late form), colored text and initials in Capitalis quadrata combined with Uncial (rounded forms of the E and H), decorative initial I; Salzburg, Austria, circa 1140. © Bayerische Staatsbibliothek, Munich, Germany, www.bsb-muenchen.de / www.digitale-sammlungen.de

|05| JOHANNES GUTENBERG, papal indulgence, very early letterpress print, text in Bastarda, highlighting in Textura; Mainz before April 5, 1455. © Herzog August Bibliothek Wolfenbüttel: Ältere Einblattdrucke, Wolfenbüttel, Germany, www.hab.de

|06| CHARLES ESTIENNE: *De dissectione partium corporis humani libri tres*. Text in Antiqua roman, marginalia in italics with roman capitals; Simon de Colines, Paris 1545. © Bibliothèque publique et universitaire Neuchâtel, Switzerland, www.bpun.unine.ch / www.e-rara.ch

|07| HIERONYMUS CARDANUS: *Hieronymi Cardani mediolanensis medici, de rerum varietate libri XVII*. Text pages in Antiqua italic with roman marginalia; Heinrich Petri, Basel 1557. © Kantonsbibliothek Vadiana, St. Gallen, Switzerland, www.kb.sg.ch

|08| QUEEN ELISABETH I.: *By the Queene. A proclamation for bringing into the Realme of unlawfull and seditious bookes*. Text in Textura, framed initial letter as incised, title in Antiqua Roman, subtitle in Italic; Christopher Baker, London 1568. © Folger Shakespeare Library, Washington DC, USA, www.folger.edu

|09| JOHANN ANDREAS STISSER: *Botanica Curiosa Oder Nützliche Anmerckungen*. Title page set in Fraktur, Latin terms in Antiqua; Georg Wolfgang Hamm, Helmstedt 1697. © Zentralbibliothek Zurich, Switzerland, www.zb.uzh.ch / www.e-rara.ch

|10| PIERRE-SIMON FOURNIER: *Manuel Typographique*, Première Partie. Text in Antiqua Roman, title in decorative variant, subtitles in italic; Paris 1764. © Bibliothèque nationale de France, Paris, France, www.bnf.fr

|11| *Proef van letteren, welke gegooten worden in de nieuwe Haarlemsche lettergieterij van J. Enschedé*. Type specimen book, title page set in Antiqua roman and italic with decorative variants; Johan Enschede, Haarlem 1768. © Erfgoedbibliotheek Hendrik Conscience, Antwerp, Belgium, www.consciencebibliotheek.be

|12| *Specimen of Printing Types, by Vincent Figgins, Letter-Founder*. Type specimen book, title page set in Antiqua roman, decorative variant, italic and Textura; London, 1815. In: BERTHOLD WOLPE (ed.): *Vincent Figgins Type Specimens 1801 and 1815*. Printing Historical Society, St Bride Institute, London 1967, p. 47.

|13| "Portable Hall of Varieties", event information, set in a wide range of typefaces, including Antiqua, heavy Antiqua, Egyptienne, Italienne, Tuscan, Grotesque and Latin; Brighton, nineteenth century. British Library, London, England, www.bl.uk © Bridgeman Images, Berlin, Germany, www.bridgemanimages.de

|14| M. DE MONTREL: *Vida del duque de Reichstadt, hijo de Napoléon*. Title page set in diverse decorative typefaces (including Antiqua, Italienne and Textura) Script, Antiqua roman and italic; Imprenta de Cabrerizo, Valencia 1836.

|15| KARL FAULMANN: *Illustrirte Geschichte der Buchdruckerkunst, ihrer Erfindung durch Johann Gutenberg und ihrer technischen Entwicklung bis zur Gegenwart*. Title page with a range of typefaces: ornamental variant of a Grotesque, Antiqua, narrow Grotesque, Latin, Egyptienne; A. Hartleben's Verlag, Vienna, Pest, Leipzig 1882.

|16| Filippo Tommaso Marinetti: *Zang Tumb Tumb*. Book cover with typographic onomatopoeia set in Grotesque with and without stroke contrast; Edizioni Futuriste di 'Poesia', Milan 1914. © Obelisk Art History Project, www.arthistoryproject.com

|17| Hugo Ball: *Karawane*. Sound poem set in different typefaces. In: Richard Huelsenbeck (ed.): *Dada Almanach*. Erich Reuss Verlag, Berlin 1920, p.53.
© International Dada Archive, Special Collections, University of Iowa Libraries, www.uiowa.edu

|18| Tristan Tzara / Ilja Zdanévitch (?): *Le cœur à barbe*. Dada-Zeitschrift, Umschlag Nr.1, Paris 1922. Picture rights: Marie-Thérèse Tzara, Paris, France. © International Dada Archive, Special Collections, University of Iowa Libraries, www.uiowa.edu

|19| Georges Hugnet: *La septième face du dé*. Éditions Jeanne Bucher, Paris 1936 – poémes, découpages: Georges Hugnet; couverture: Marcel Duchamp. © Kunsthaus Zurich, library, signature: GB163, www.kunsthaus.ch

|20| Robert Harling: *Home: A Victorian Vignette*. Book jacket, set in Italienne and Antiqua italic; Constable, London 1938.

|21| Jan Tschichold: *Typografische Gestaltung*. Title page set in Script, Egyptienne, and Antiqua; Benno Schwabe & Co., Basel 1935.

|22| "Injecting life into Grotesque typesetting …" Advertisement in Fraktur and Grotesque; Ludwig & Mayer Type Foundry, Frankfurt am Main. In: *Typographische Monatsblätter, TM 4*, Schweizerischer Typographenbund, Bern 1934, p.U3.

|23| "A resounding advertising impact through emphasized contrasts", advertisement set in Script and Egyptienne; Ludwig & Mayer Type Foundry, Frankfurt am Main. In: *Schweizer Graphische Mitteilungen*, no.8, St.Gallen 1936, p.32.

|24| Paul Renner: *Die Kunst der Typographie*. 3rd edition. Deutscher Verlag / Ullstein AG, Berlin 1953, p.149.

|25| Karl Klingspor: *Über Schönheit von Schrift und Druck – Erfahrungen aus fünfzigjähriger Arbeit*. Exemplary contrast between multiplicity and unity. Georg Kurt Schauer, Frankfurt am Main 1949, pp.142 f.

|26| "Textiles & Objects", Advertising poster for Herman Miller Inc., 1961 by Alexander Girard, in a diverse range of typefaces. In: Mateo Kries and Jochen Eisenbrand (ed.): *Alexander Girard – A Designer's Universe*. Vitra Design Museum GmbH, Weil am Rhein 2016, p.433. © Vitra Design Museum, Nachlass Alexander Girard, Weil am Rhein, Germany, www.design-museum.de

|27| *twen* magazine, double-page spread set in Grotesque and Antiqua, design concept by Willy Fleckhaus; *twen*, no.9, Verlag Theodor Martens & Co., Munich 1962, pp.72 f. © Münchner Stadtmuseum, Sammlung Fotografie, Munich, Germany, www.muenchner-stadtmuseum.de

|28| Sex Pistols: *Never Mind the Bollocks – Here's the Sex Pistols*, record cover designed by Jamie Reid, Virgin Records Ltd., London, England, 1977.

|29| *The Guardian*. Title page of the newspaper with its new masthead in Antiqua italic and Grotesque, design concept by David Hillman; London and Manchester, 12.02.1988. © Ancestry Ireland Unlimited Company, Dublin, Ireland, www.newspapers.com

|30| Jost Hochuli and Robin Kinross: *Bücher machen – Praxis und Theorie*. Book jacket set in Grotesque and Antiqua; Verlagsgemeinschaft St.Gallen, 1996.

|31| Solomon Volkov: *Shostakovich and Stalin*. Book jacket with diverse typefaces by Peter Mendelsund; Alfred A. Knopf, New York 2004. In: Steven Heller and Gail Anderson: *New Vintage Type – Classic Fonts for the Digital Age*. Watson-Guptill, New York 2007, p.146.

2
A typology of type → 39

|22| Type specimens of *Impressum* light by Fundición Tipografica Neufville, S.A., Barcelona, Spain. In: *bg-schriften*, Neotype bg-schriften, Frankfurt am Main, Germany, undatet, p.15.

3
Basic shapes | Measurements → 55

|01| See https://de.wikipedia.org/wiki/Phönizische_Schrift [Aug 25, 2017].

|02| Rounded basalt stele bearing an inscription in the name of King Meša (Mesha) made up of 34 lines of Old Phoenician script with a right-to-left reading direction (segment); Dhiban, 842 BCE. Agence photographique de la RMN-GP, Paris, France, www.photo.rmn.fr © RMN-Grand Palais (Musée du Louvre, Paris, www.louvre.fr), photograph: Mathieu Rabeau.

|03| Idameneus inscription (rear side), boustrophedonic writing; Rhodes, early 6th century BCE; Staatliche Museen zu Berlin, Antikensammlung, Berlin, Germany. In: Wilfried Seipel (Hg.): *Der Turmbau zu Babel*. Kunsthistorisches Museum Wien / Skira editore, Milan 2003, p.204.

|04| Decree of Canopus, Greek lapidary script, trilingual inscription (segment), Canopos, Egypt, 238 BCE; Egyptian Museum, Cairo. In: Wilfried Seipel (ed.): *Der Turmbau zu Babel*. Kunsthistorisches Museum Wien / Skira editore, Milan 2003, p.133.

|06| Inscription in Capitalis monumentalis in the name of the emperor Caesar Nerva Trajanus Augustus on the base of Trajan's column (replica), Rome, Italy 113 CE. © Victoria and Albert Museum, London, England, www.vam.ac.uk

|08| *Left*: Capitalis quadrata, Vergilius Sangallensis, Virgil transcription, 4th to 5th century — *middle*: Roman uncial, Gospels, Italy, 5th century — *right*: Roman half-uncial, parchment, 5th to 6th century. See André Gürtler: "The development of the Roman Alphabet." Special print, *Typografische Monatsblätter, TM 11*, St.Gallen 1969, pp.31–42. © Kantonsbibliothek Vadiana, Sammlung André Gürtler, St.Gallen, Switzerland, www.sg.ch/kultur/kantonsbibliothek-vadiana

|09| *Right*: Roman majuscule italic, sales contract for a slave, 166 CE — *far right*: Roman minuscule italic, papyrus scroll, act of purchase, Ravenna, Italy, 572. See André Gürtler: "The development of the Roman Alphabet." *TM 11*, St.Gallen 1969, pp.28–38.

|11| Irish-Anglo-Saxon half-uncial, Book of Kells, Ireland, circa 800.

|12| *Left*: Carolingian miniscule, Folchart Psalter, circa 860, St.Gallen, Switzerland. — *Right*: humanist miniscule, first half of the 16th century. See André Gürtler: "The development of the Roman Alphabet." *TM 11*, St.Gallen 1969, pp.55 f. and 79 ff.

|13| Humanist cursive, letter, 1517. See André Gürtler: "The development of the Roman Alphabet." *TM 11*, St.Gallen 1969, pp.84 f.

|16| *Far left*: Giant Bible of Mainz, manuscript, first page of Genesis (segment), Mainz (or in the vicinity), Germany, 1452. © The Library of Congress, Washington DC, USA, www.loc.gov — *Left*: Gutenberg Bible B42, incunable (segment), the first book in the Western world to be typeset with movable lead letters, Textura with a total of 290 letter variations by Johannes Gensfleisch, known as Gutenberg, Mainz, Germany, circa 1454. Georg-August-Universität Göttingen © Niedersächsische Staats- und Universitätsbibliothek, SUB Göttingen, Germany, www.sub.uni-goettingen.de

|18| Eusebius Caesariensis: *De evangelica praeparatione.* Text in Antiqua by Nicolas Jenson, Venice, Italy, 1470. © Bridwell Library Special Collections, Dallas TX, USA, www.smu.edu/bridwell

|19| Decree authorizing the construction of the Athena-Nike-Tempel, inscription in Greek lapidary script (segment), stoichedon text style; Athens, Greece, circa 448 BCE © OhioLINK Digital Recource Commons, www.drc.ohiolink.edu

|20| Qingshan, inscription (replica), China, 219 BCE. https://commons.wikimedia.org/wiki/File:Yishankeshi.jpg

|21| Hunminjeongeum Haerye (explanations and examples of Hunminjeongeum, the original promulgation of the Korean script Hangul) by King Sejong. Kansong Art Museum, Seoul, South Korea.

|22| Stone relief-plinth featuring a Mayan inscription, Pre-Columbian Maya civilization, Yucatan, Central America. https://stock.adobe.com/photograph: bennnn [Jun 10, 2020].

|35| In: Ruedi Rüegg and Godi Fröhlich: *Basic Typography – Handbook of technique and design.* ABC Verlag, Zurich 1972, p.15.

|39|40| In: Friedrich Bauer: *Handbuch für Schriftsetzer.* Verlag Klimsch & Co., Frankfurt am Main 1904, p.235.

|42| In: Heidrun Osterer and Philipp Stamm: *Adrian Frutiger – Typefaces. The Complete Works.* Birkhäuser Verlag, Basel 2008, p.32.

|45| In: Hans Rudolf Bosshard: *Technische Grundlagen zur Satzherstellung.* Verlag des Bildungsverbandes Schweizerischer Typographen, Bern 1980, pp.24 f.

|47| In: Karl Klingspor: *Über Schönheit von Schrift und Druck – Erfahrungen aus fünfzigjähriger Arbeit.* Exemplary juxtapostion of multiplicity and unity. Georg Kurt Schauer, Frankfurt am Main 1949, p.24.

|49| In: Bernd Holthusen: *Digital Design.* Econ Verlag, Dusseldorf 1988, p.13.

|58| Font software Glyphs – screenshot of outline depiction.

4
Typeface classification →83

|03| In: Francis Thibaudeau: *Manuel Français de Typographie Moderne.* Bureau de l'Édition, Paris 1924, pp.108 f.

|04| In: Friedrich Friedl, Nicolaus Ott and Bernard Stein: *Typography – when who how.* Könemann, Cologne 1998, p.536.

|05| https://typofonderie.com/gazette/post/maximilien-vox-typographer-etc [Jun 2, 2020].

|06| In: Georg Kurt Schauer: *Klassifikation · Bemühungen um eine Ordnung im Druckschriftenbestand.* Technische Hochschule Darmstadt, 1975, pp.36 f.

|09|10|11| See Erich Schulz-Anker: *Formanalyse und Dokumentation einer serifenlosen Linearschrift auf neuer Basis: Syntax-Antiqua.* D. Stempel AG, Frankfurt am Main 1969, p.8.

|12| In: Gerrit Noordzij: *The Stroke – Theory of Writing.* Hyphen Press, London 2005, p.U1.

|13| See Indra Kupferschmid: *Buchstaben kommen selten allein – Ein typografisches Handbuch.* Niggli Verlag, Sulgen / Zurich 2009, p.32.

|14| See Hans Peter Willberg: *Wegweiser Schrift.* Verlag Hermann Schmidt, Mainz 2001, p.49.

5
Typeface concepts →131

|05| *Left:* In: Heidrun Osterer and Philipp Stamm: *Adrian Frutiger – Typefaces. The Complete Works.* Birkhäuser Verlag, Basel 2008, p.89. — *Right:* In: Emil Ruder: "Univers, eine Grotesk von Adrian Frutiger." In: *Typographische Monatsblätter, TM 5,* Schweizerischer Typographenbund, Bern 1957.

|08| In: Heidrun Osterer and Philipp Stamm: *Adrian Frutiger – Typefaces. The Complete Works.* Birkhäuser Verlag, Basel 2008, p.409.

|15| *Above right:* In: John Dreyfus: *The Work of Jan Van Krimpen.* Sylvan Press, London 1952, p.38. — *Below right:* ibid. p.43. — *Far right:* ibid. p.45.

|20|21| See Lucas de Groot: *FF Thesis – TheSans, TheSerif, TheMix.* Type specimen with his interpolation theory from 1987 (leaflet), FontShop, Berlin 1994.

|24|25| In: Helmut Kraus: "Milliarden von Myriaden." In: *PAGE,* no.1. MACup Verlag, Hamburg 1996, p.64.

|31|32| In: Manfred Klein, Yvonne Schwemer-Scheddin and Erik Spiekermann: *Typen & Typografen.* Edition Stemmle, Schaffhausen 1991, pp.27, 31.

|33| www.typenetwork.com/brochure/decovar-a-decorative-variable-font-by-david-berlow [Nov 10, 2019].

6
Typeface combination | Criteria →149

|22| In: Hildegard Korger: *Schrift und Schreiben.* Fachbuchverlag, Leipzig 1991, p.34.

Postscript

My fascination with type and typography was one of the driving forces that led to this book. I take great pleasure in observing well-formed typefaces. Immersing oneself in beautiful typography can evoke a feeling that is close to sublime. Harmonious relationships between formats, columns, edges, and spaces in conjunction with appropriately proportioned typefaces, the correct type size, and the right spacing between letters, words, and lines – that is to say, the beauty of lettering achieved by a perfect interplay between macro-typography and micro-typography – can trigger a true sense of pleasure. Unfortunately, it is not often that I feel really satisfied in this regard. The goal seems so seldom achievable and is hardly ever actually achieved.

It is far too often the case that the typefaces and typesetting we encounter are of a poor quality. And yet the preconditions for achieving outstanding results are in place. Today we have access to an immense range of typefaces in a wide variety of forms, often organized into typeface families. Given a good knowledge of their functionality, modern technologies are capable of achieving an outstanding level of setting quality. Moreover, extremely high-quality paper is readily available. It must be added, however, that offset printing – as precise as it is – cannot compete with the centuries-old method of letterpress printing in terms of coloration. The watery colors typical of offset prints make them appear thin and flat, dark gray instead of black.

The necessary knowledge to remedy this situation is likewise available. We have access to both older and newer books that provide examples of good typesetting. In addition, a diverse range of specialist articles and teaching materials is available that explains the means of achieving high-quality typesetting. And the Internet offers an enormous resource in terms of knowledge and examples that can be easily accessed at any time.

Good typefaces and good typography are available. So why is it so seldom that we find truly impressive typographic work? This is probably because good typography is not something we can spot in the everyday world. It is overwhelmed by a sea of mediocrity. Because it often has a restrained, quiet character, it is not often noticed and therefore seldom serves as a standard. The type designer GÜNTER GERHARD LANGE* once remarked, "Typography is a demure beloved, but to those who are prepared to give their all, she will reveal all her beauty." Getting there is a long process. Many designers at the beginning of their career find it difficult to apply their interest in lettering and typography in a coherent manner. However, the initially demure beloved

---

* GÜNTER GERHARD LANGE
*April 12, 1921 in Frankfurt (Oder), Germany, †December 2, 2008 in Munich, Germany was a typographer and teacher, and was for many years Artistic Director for the type foundry H. Berthold AG in Berlin/Stuttgart/Munich. GGL was given to witty remarks, which were best delivered in his caustic lectures on a subject he cherished – rediscovered at: www.typolis.de [Jan 3, 2020].

becomes – at least for those who have fallen completely under her spell – a generous one. This does not necessarily mean that the relationship becomes simpler; it is an eternal struggle. So many dependencies between content and form have to be taken into account, so much understanding of form and aesthetic perception is required, so many rules need to be observed and understood correctly (especially when there is a desire to question or even break them), so many details play a decisive role, and so much precision is needed. Above all, the eye needs to be so well trained that it is capable of recognizing the full range of optical qualities. And yet even if all these conditions are satisfied, good quality is still not guaranteed.

It may be that gimmickry has for too long impaired the perception of quality in our Western culture. It may be that the immense number of products, limited time, and the loss of a sense for work of lasting value has resulted in a loss of quality. It may be that the preferences of consultants and customers, or financial conditions, have played a role. Nevertheless, we should not see ourselves only in the present but also as a model for future generations. We need to be aware that we have inherited and adopted a rich heritage that dates back millennia. This is a heritage that needs to be cultivated and, wherever possible, augmented in terms of quality. Evidence that this task is indeed being embraced lies in the many outstanding specialist publications on type, typography, and graphics, including and particularly those from Switzerland.

Author | Thanks

Philipp Stamm, *1966 in Schaffhausen, Switzerland. 1982–86: Typesetting apprenticeship at Meier+Cie AG, Schaffhauser Nachrichten, Schaffhausen. Vocational studies in Zurich. 1990–92: Further education in typography and type design at the School of Design in Basel. 1992–95: Postgraduate Studies in Visual Communication at The Basel School of Design, HFG Basel (diploma project: PhonogrammeF). Since 2000 lecturer, since 2011 Professor of type design, typography and corporate design at the HGK FHNW Academy of Art and Design in Basel.

My sincere thanks go to the mentors and teachers who taught me about type and typography, and indeed to all those whose instruction in design I was able to benefit from. They sharpened my perception, extended my knowledge, and steered my ways of seeing and thinking in directions I had previously not even been aware of. They challenged and fostered us students in equal measure. And they shaped our awareness of quality. In the process, they increased the pleasure in lettering and typography that I had first come to know in my family home – and they each did so in their own way. Despite or indeed because of the fact that they so clearly expressed their particular understanding of quality, I was always able to go my own way.

My special thanks to my parents; Romuald Bohle, instructor for apprentice typesetters at Meier+Cie in Schaffhausen; Jean-Pierre Graber, instructor in typography at the trade school in Zurich; Heinrich Fleischhacker, head of further training for typographic designers (originally established by

The typeface combinations in chapter 8 were drawn for the most part from my typography course. My sincere thanks to the following former students:
ss 2004:
Kathryn Cho, Julia Eyer, Kim Gussi, Simon Hauser, Dejan Jovanovic, Susanne Käser, Jonas Leuenberger, Matthias Rohrbach, Brigitte Rufer, Olivera Sakota, Manon Siebenhaar
ws 2004/05:
Jason Angelakos, Karin Borer, Dominik Brustmann, Laetitia Buntschu, Cornelia Descloux, Céline Dillier, Kaija Etter, Theres Guggenbühl, Nina Hug, Valérie Leu, Anja Lupberger, David Schwarz, Denise Spitz, Christian Stindl, Stefan Zahler
ws 2014/15:
Anja Birrer, Nicolas Brivio, Jeanne Bussmann, Nicole Ebneter, Melanie Jäger, Lorena La Spada, Aline Meier, Thi Minh Hoang Nguyen, Carla Petraschke, Paula Pfau, Eliane Simon, Sinja Steinhauser

For their work on this book,
my thanks to:
Anja Birrer, Kenan Brunner, Johanna Bühler, Jeanne Bussmann, Nicole Ebneter, Lucian Kunz, Aline Meier, Thi Minh Hoang Nguyen, Carla Petraschke, Eliane Simon, Kajetan Som, Maxim Staehelin, Sinja Steinhauser

For their services,
my thanks to:
Dr. Marina Bernasconi Reusser, Research Associate, e-codices, Université de Fribourg/Switzerland;
Miriam Brodbeck (and Team), Head of the Library of Design, School of Design SfG Basel/Switzerland;
Roland Früh, Sitterwerk, St. Gallen/Switzerland;
André Gürtler, Therwil/Switzerland;
Kantonsbibliothek Vadiana, St. Gallen/Switzerland
Remo Keller, Basel/Switzerland

For the provision of typefaces,
my thanks to:
Dalton Maag Ltd, London – www.daltonmaag.com
Dinamo GmbH, Basel – www.abcdinamo.com
Elsner+Flake, Hamburg – www.fonts4ever.com
Fabian Harb, Basel – http://fabianharb.ch
Jost Hochuli, St. Gallen – www.vgs-sg.ch
Lineto GmbH, Zurich – https://lineto.com
Monotype GmbH, Bad Homburg – www.linotype.com
Nouvelle Noire, Basel/Zurich – www.nouvellenoire.ch
Optimo, Genf – www.optimo.ch
Jonas Schudel, Zurich – www.effra.ch
Roland Stieger, St. Gallen – https://tgg.ch
Team 77, Basel – André Gürtler, Christian Mengelt and Erich Gschwind – http://mengelt-blauen.ch

Emil Ruder) at the Basel School of Design; and to my teachers at what was then called the Höhere Fachschule für Gestaltung Basel: Peter von Arx (audiovisual projects); André Gürtler † (type design – supervisor of my diploma project *PhonogrammeF*); Reinhart Morscher † and Gregory Vines (verbal communication and semiotics); Michael Renner (computer projects); and Wolfgang Weingart (typography).

Following a total of five years of study, I had the good fortune to meet someone who was instrumental in the development of my subsequent work. A very special thank you therefore goes to Erich Alb as the initiator of, and to Adrian Frutiger † as my interlocutor in, many highly instructive interviews; and to Heidrun Osterer as co-author of *Adrian Frutiger – Typefaces. The Complete Works* for her collaboration in, among other things, the conception, design, and realization of this publication.

The fact that the aforementioned book was also published by Birkhäuser Verlag in Basel conveniently leads me to the expression of my thanks to my publishers, and to Ulrich Schmidt and Katharina Kulke. Despite many delays on my part, they maintained their confidence in the project, and their communication with me was always pleasant and understanding.

I would also like to thank all my former and current students at the Academy of Art and Design in Basel who have contributed to the present publication. This debt of gratitude is primarily owed to those former students listed here. The numerous examples they provided in the context of my course on typeface combinations constitute a significant proportion of chapter 8. Particular thanks go to Nina Hug. As a former graduate, the issues she raised some time ago were fundamentally responsible for the fact that this project survived its long journey to the point it has now reached. A good part of the selection of word pairs came from Lucian Kunz.

For their support, I would also like to thank the Institute of Visual Communication at the Academy of Art and Design hgk fhnw, and my colleagues, especially, Marion Fink, Fabian Kempter, Dirk Koy, along with Jinsu Ahn, to whom I owe a debt of gratitude for his meticulous reading of the German-language manuscript and valuable corrections.

A very special thank you is due to Rainer Keller in New York for editing the technical vocabulary in the English translation.

Finally, I would like to thank my wonderful wife Jazaa. The value of her understanding and support for all my endeavors over the years is inestimable.

Credits

Book concept | Design | Layout | Typesetting
Philipp Stamm

Translation into English
Joe O'Donnell

Copyediting
John Sweet

Proofreading
Keonaona Peterson

Projectmanagement
Katharina Kulke

Production
Heike Strempel

Reproductions | Image editing
Fotolabor St. Gallen AG, St. Gallen
LVD Gesellschaft für Datenverarbeitung mbH, Berlin

Printing | Bookbinding
Kösel GmbH & Co. KG, Altusried-Krugzell

Paper
Fly weiß 05, 130 g/m², FSC®
f.Color 430 hellrot

Typefaces
Freya · Saku Heinänen | Today Sans Now ·
Volker Küster | Arsis · Gerry Powell | Freytag ·
Arne Freytag | Teknik · David Quay | Wilke ·
Martin Wilke | Zapf Dingbats · Hermann Zapf |
Abelina · Guille Vizzari, Yani Arabena
For all other typefaces see: Index of typefaces

© 2021 Birkhäuser Verlag GmbH, Basel
P.O. Box 44, CH-4009 Basel, Switzerland
Part of Walter de Gruyter GmbH,
Berlin / Boston

Printed in Germany

ISBN 978-3-0356-1114-4
e-ISBN (PDF) 978-3-0356-0905-9

9 8 7 6 5 4 3 2 1

www.birkhauser.com

Bibliographic information published by the German National Library – The German National Library lists this publication in the Deutsche Nationalbibliografie; detailed bibliographic data are available on the Internet at www.dnb.de

This work is subject to copyright.
All rights are reserved, whether the whole or part of the material is concerned, specifically the rights of translation, reprinting, re-use of illustrations, recitation, broadcasting, reproduction on microfilms or in other ways, and storage in databases. For any kind of use, permission of the copyright owner must be obtained.

As well published by the author
at Birkhäuser:
H. Osterer, P. Stamm: *Adrian Frutiger – Schriften. Das Gesamtwerk* (ISBN 978-3-03821-524-0)
H. Osterer, P. Stamm: *Adrian Frutiger – Typefaces. The Complete Works* (ISBN 978-3-0356-2362-8)
H. Osterer, P. Stamm: *Adrian Frutiger – Caractères. L'Œuvre complète* (ISBN 978-3-7643-8582-8)

German language edition:
Schrifttypen · Verstehen | Kombinieren
(ISBN 978-3-0356-1113-7)

The book was supported by:
University of Applied Sciences and Arts
Northwestern Switzerland FHNW
Academy of Art and Design
Institute of Visual Communication,
Münchenstein near Basel, Switzerland
www.fhnw.ch/hgk

n|w University of Applied Sciences and Arts Northwestern Switzerland
Academy of Art and Design